THE FACTS ON FILE HISTORY OF THE AMERICAN PEOPLE

JOHN ANTHONY SCOTT

THE FACTS ON FILE HISTORY OF THE AMERICAN PEOPLE

JOHN ANTHONY SCOTT

Facts On File
New York • Oxford • Sydney

The Facts On File History of the American People

Facts On File, Inc.   Facts On File Limited   Facts On File Pty Ltd
460 Park Avenue South   Collins Street   Talavera & Khartoum Rds
New York, New York 10016 Oxford OX4 1XJ   North Ryde NSW 2113
                                        United Kingdom   Austrailia

Scott, John A., 1916 -
    The Facts On File history of the American people / John A. Scott.
        p.   cm.
    Includes bibliographical references.
    Summary: A complete history of tghe United States, from the first settlers up to the period
  following the conflict in Vietnam, withspecial attentiongiven to the original sources.
    ISBN 0-8160-1739-5
    1. United States—History—Juivenile literature. {1. United States—History.} I. Facts On File, Inc.
II. Title.
E178.3.s34 1990
973—dc20

British and Australian CIP data available on request
Facts On File books are available at special
discounts when purchased in bulk quantities
for businesses, associations, institutions,
or sales promotion. Please contact the Special
Sales Department at 212/683- 2244.
(Dial 1-800-322-8755, except in NY, AK, HI)

Text Design by Ron Monteleone

Composition by Facts On File
Printed in the United States of America

10 9 8 7 6 5 4 3 2 1

This book is printed on acid-free paper.

For Barbara, Cynthia, and Donald

Acknowledgments

Over the years my work has brought me into contact with students and teachers in all parts of the country. This has enabled me to participate in many discussions about United States history that have provided inspiration and ideas for the writing of this book. I am very grateful to all these people for the numerous insights they have provided and the searching questions they have raised. Jamie Warren, director of Facts On File's young adult program, read the manuscript carefully, offered many suggestions for improving it, and guided it expertly through the press. Thanks are also due to Domenico Firmani for the helpful and efficient manner in which he tracked down needed illustrations.

John Anthony Scott
Spring 1989

CONTENTS

THE FACTS ON FILE
HISTORY OF THE AMERICAN
PEOPLE

JOHN ANTHONY SCOTT

1

WANDERERS AND SETTLERS
From Earliest Times to the
Coming of the Whites

People have been living on the planet Earth for a long time—two million years, maybe more. But human beings arrived in the Western Hemisphere only very recently. Though all the evidence is not yet in, it is likely that the first immigrants came here from eastern Asia not much more than 40,000 years ago. Small hunting bands crossed the Bering Strait one after another at a time when the level of the ocean was very much lower than now, and America was linked to Asia by dry land. With the passage of time these migrating hunters spread over the entire hemisphere from the shores of the Arctic Ocean to the tip of Patagonia.

These hunters who came here tens of thousands of years ago were nomads, or wanderers. They hunted wild animals, they caught fish and snared birds; they dug up roots and tubers, gathered wild fruits, vegetables, seeds, berries and nuts. They took from the wilderness, sometimes easily, sometimes with difficulty and danger, whatever the wilderness had to offer. Nomadic life was a hard, constant struggle for survival, for food, shelter, and clothing.

Nomads sometimes set up camps or villages where they might pass a portion of the year, but they did not lead what we would think of as a settled existence. Most of the time they needed to be on the move: following and trapping game, visiting the rivers to fish, roaming the forests in search of acorns or berries. Wanderers are also explorers, and these early Americans were the first explorers of this continent. America's splendor has found expression in the names that they gave to its mountains, forests, deserts and lakes—names like Yakima, Yuma, Mohegan, Winnepesaukee, Kansas, Merrimac and a thousand more.

Three or perhaps four thousand years ago, some of the nomads stopped wandering and began to settle down. Towns and villages were built, and people stayed in these all the year round; gardens began to be dug and crops produced. At about the same time as Old World peoples in China, India and the Near East, our native American peoples began to carry through the first great technological revolution in human history. Instead of roaming the forests in search of food, they learned to domesti-

1

Bering Land Bridge

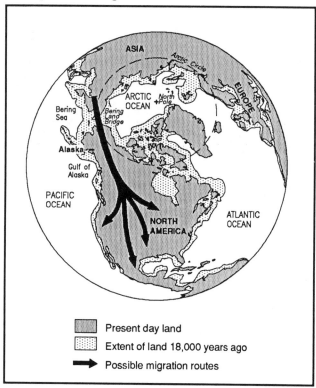

Present day land
Extent of land 18,000 years ago
→ Possible migration routes

cate the wild plants and roots: that is, to bring the seeds back home and to plant them in village garden plots until they sprouted and bloomed. They learned to take, and to sow, only the seeds of individual plants that bore most fruitfully and that gave the best crops. Native Americans tried out this domestication process with dozens of wild grasses, shrubs and roots. Much of this experimentation was done by women; they have been among the most gifted food producers that the world has known.

A complete list of native American contributions to the world's food crops would be a long one. It would include corn, white and sweet potatoes, tomatoes, pumpkins and squash, peanuts, avocados, and many types of beans. The fibers they domesticated include cotton and the dyes cochineal and indigo. Drugs would include tobacco and quinine.

This Native American agriculture had its beginnings in southern Mexico, Central America, and the highlands of Peru. From centers such as these, the new knowledge about how to raise crops, fibers,

drugs and dyes gradually spread northward into what is now the United States. Corn, more than any other single domesticated plant, made possible the new civilizations that began to flourish here three or four thousand years ago.

Corn is an extraordinary plant that gave enough food to support an ever-growing population. It gave people, too, much more free time than they enjoyed in the hunting-gathering way of life. Hunter-gatherers lived in underground caverns, in clefts in the rocks, in caves, tents and wickiups (grass-covered huts). Farmers had the time to build stone houses and even, as in the case of the Pueblo peoples of New Mexico, huge apartment complexes. Hunters clothed and warmed themselves with the skins of wild animals. Farmers clothed themselves with the finest of woven cotton fabrics; and, more than that, they found time to create luxuries of which most earlier peoples scarcely dreamed: baskets of woven fiber, cooking pots of fired clay, jewelry of beaten gold.

Among many peoples in what is now the United States who grew corn were the Hopis, Zunis and Pueblos of New Mexico and Arizona. These people, like most others, had their own special stories about how the world began, which they passed on by word of mouth from mother and father to daughter and son. These people thought of corn as a gift from God—indeed, the very greatest of all the gifts of life that they inherited when they were born.

According to the old Zuni tradition, the very first Zunis were born following the union of Sky, the father, and Earth, the mother. In this beautiful legend, Earth-mother speaks to her mate and tells him that soon she will bring forth life. "Soon," she tells Sky-father, "I shall bring forth children from my womb. They shall live in the hollow places of my lap with mountains circling each hollow. My warm breath will drift across the mountains; as it meets your cold sky-wind, the rain will fall in a fine mist. This falling water will give life to my children for ever."

ZUNI CREATION MYTHS

Human beings in every age have confronted the puzzle of existence. Where do we come from, and why are we here? Is there a reason to be living?

Different people have worked out different answers. They have constructed philosophies and religions to explain creation, to instruct their children about their chosen way of life and to give reasons why that way of life is good.

The creation stories of the Native American peoples are among the most beautiful in the world. We reproduce below one incident from the sacred epic of the Zunis. It tells how God (Awonawilona) created the universe, how Sky and Earth came into being, and how from the embrace of these two Earth, the mother, conceived life and gave birth to it.

The Zuni priests recited the epic at regular intervals to their people. This episode is given, with slight modifications, as reported by Frank Hamilton Cushing, a pioneer American anthropologist. Cushing lived for five years (1879–1884) with the Zunis of New Mexico; he became familiar with their language and made careful records. His *Outline of Zuni Creation Myths* was published in 1896.

* * * *

Before the world was made, the only being was the Great Spirit, Awonawilona, he who contains all and who has made all. There was nothing else throughout space, only darkness and desolation.

With her warm breath Earth-mother blew across the terraced bowl. White flecks of foam broke away and floated up over the water. As Earth-mother's breath fell upon the foam it condensed, falling down in mist and rain.

"White clouds, just like this," said Earth-mother to Sky-father, "shall rise up from the great waters that lie at the fringes of the world. They will cluster near the mountain terraces, rise upward, and become scattered. They will be condensed and broken up by your cold breath. They will fall down upon the earth as the spray of rain, moistening the hollow places in my lap. In places such as these our children—human beings and other living creatures—will cluster for warmth, for protection from your cold."

So indeed it is. The trees that grow on high mountains close to the clouds and Sky-father crouch low toward Earth-mother for warmth and for protection. Woman is warm, like Earth-mother, and man is cold, even as Sky-father.

"It shall be as you say," said Sky-father, "but you shall not nourish and sustain our children without my help. See!"

Sky-father spread out his hand. He set stars in the crevices between his fingers; they gleamed there like shining grains of corn. In the dark of the world's dawn the stars gleamed like sparks of fire, as Sky-father stretched forth his hand over the bowl. Moving in the depths of the sky the stars also sparkled in the waters below.

Sky-father pointed to the seven stars that his fingers held. "These," he said, "shall guide our children when they come to live at the center of space, and all the other regions of space lie out around them. Seed grains, like these but numberless, shall spring up from your bosom when my rain falls upon them; and they shall nourish the people."

This engraving was made from a painting by Jacques Le Moyne, who accompanied a French expedition to northern Florida in 1562 and remained there for three years. It shows members of a group of northern Florida people, called Timuacans, working together in the field. The labor is divided: Men break up and level the ground; the women drill holes for the seed with digging sticks and plant the corn. Timuacans were members of the southeastern Indian culture that covered much of the south as far west as the Mississippi Valley. Theirs was a mixed economy of hunting, farming and gathering.

Over the tens of thousands of years that passed after the first hunting bands arrived, human life on the North American continent unfolded with truly marvelous variety. When the first white men came here five hundred years ago, some native peoples were still following the hunting-gathering ways that they had been following from the first. This was true over vast areas of our country—among the peaceful fisherfolk and food gatherers of California's coasts an forests, among the warlike salmon-fishing peoples of the Pacific Northwest, among the buffalo hunters of the endless prairie that stretched eastward from the Rocky Mountains. Some—and this was true of peoples who lived upon the coastal strip running from Florida to Maine—were at the very beginning of the new

agricultural life. The women, who often owned the fields, did most of the work of preparing the soil, sowing seed and raising crops. They planted corn, squash and beans in the gardens around their homes and put away much of the harvest in pits or storage houses for winter use. Men and women alike fished in the streams, gathered oysters on the shores, and collected berries, roots and nuts in the forests. During the winter the men also spent time hunting elk, bear, and deer while the women carried supplies, set up tents and prepared food.

These eastern peoples, as we see, combined the old food-gathering ways with the new crop-raising ones. Other peoples had totally abandoned the old ways and had learned to depend almost entirely upon field and garden crops for their food. This was true of the peoples of the Southwest like the Zunis, Hopis, and Pueblos. It was also true of the so-called Mound Peoples who lived throughout the Mississippi valley from Wisconsin to the Gulf of Mexico.

Many of these peoples were skilled not only in cropraising but in the building of houses and the making of boats. None knew how to use metals like copper, iron or steel. They did indeed make fine tools and weapons but only out of bone, wood or stone.

* * * *

About one thousand years ago, at the dawn of modern times, a few Europeans began to probe the shadows that fringed the western edges of their world. Erik (called the "Red" no doubt on account of his flaming hair) and his son Leif were the pioneers in this new adventure. Erik was a Norwegian who quit Norway during troubled times and settled on the far-off island of Iceland, in the North Atlantic; there his son Leif was born. This move to Iceland was the first of three giant steps that would take father and son to the shores of North America.

Erik did not rest in Iceland. Late in the 10th century, moving always westward, he explored the western shore of a huge Arctic landmass that was almost completely covered with ice, which he named Greenland. Then he organized an Icelandic expedition to settle on this western shore. Erik's expedition to Greenland had over 30 ships; hundreds of men, women and children sailed with

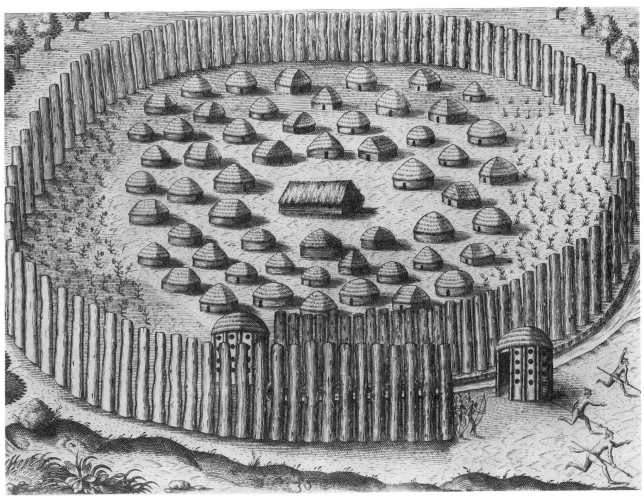

Timuacans spent the winter months hunting in the forest; during the rest of the year they lived a settled existence in villages that were clusters of round huts like those that Le Moyne shows here. The chief's hut stands in the center of the enclosure. Tall stout palings planted in a ditch give protection from enemy raids and wild animals.

Route of the Vikings from Scandinavia to Newfoundland

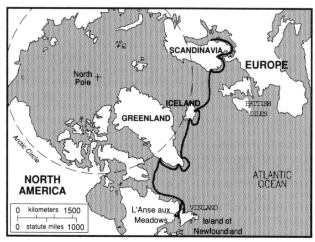

him. Erik called this colony Brattalid; it was separated from the American mainland by a stretch of water only a few hundred miles wide.

Soon Leif, Erik's son, was a grown man. In 1001 he and a few companions landed upon the North American shore; perhaps they were driven there by a storm, perhaps they were looking for settlements with which to trade. They came to a place where a stream of water flowed out of an inland lake and emptied into the sea. Here on a meadow by the stream they unloaded their sleeping bags and set up a house in which they spent the winter. Leif found it a beautiful spot and a fisherman's paradise. "There was," as he told the Brattalid people on his return to Greenland, "...no lack of salmon either in the river or the lake," and it was bigger salmon than they had ever seen. Nature was so generous here that it seemed to them no cattle would need any winter fodder, but could graze outdoors. There was no frost in winter; and the grass hardly withered..."

Other Greenlanders followed where Leif had led, to the place that he named Vinland. Thorfinn Karlsefne settled in Vinland with a whole colony: men, women and cattle. But these colonizing efforts came to nothing. For one thousand years Leif's voyage and his American discovery were almost forgotten. Leif's adventures, to be sure, were written down in the *sagas*, or records, of the Icelandic historians. But these sagas were viewed by most people as just quaint old tales. What proof was there anyhow, they asked, that any of this had really happened?

In the early 1960s Helge Ingstad, an archaeologist, once more studied the sagas and then made up his mind to go looking for the proofs that people wanted. He found what he was looking for in Épaves Bay, at the northeastern tip of Newfoundland: a grassy meadow by the sea, near a river that flowed down from an inland lake. He and Ann Stine, his wife, began to dig; there, with their spades, they uncovered the site of the old Viking settlement. Go check it out for yourselves: It is called L'Anse aux Meadows.

Were Leif and his companions the only Europeans to visit America before Columbus came here? Were they the first to settle, even briefly, upon American shores? It is more than possible that there were indeed other visitors, but we don't yet know for sure. As the Vinland story shows, history often has to be rewritten as new evidence is brought to light. What is just a guess today may become fact tomorrow.

Take the explorer Thor Heyerdahl, for example. In 1946 Heyerdahl sailed a balsa-wood raft, *Kon-Tiki*, all the way from Peru to the island of Raroia in the central Pacific; and in 1970 he sailed a reed boat, *Ra II*, such as the ancient Egyptians used, clear across the Atlantic Ocean from the west African coast to Barbados. Tides or currents of water, Heyerdahl says, move through the oceans like rivers. He believes that Europeans or Africans may have sailed across the Atlantic centuries ago, just as he did, using only the simplest of boats. Some of these people, he believes, may even have ended up, just as he did, in the central Pacific.

So it is quite possible that America has had from time to time close communication with the ancient Near Eastern and African worlds. But it

Le Moyne depicts young male Timuacans at the sports they like best: archery, throwing balls at a square target placed on a tall tree and competitive running. "They take great pleasure," Le Moyne also wrote, "in hunting and fishing." Americans, evidently, have loved sports and played ball for thousands of years.

will need more discoveries like Helge Ingstad's at Vinland before such possibilities can be accepted as fact.

* * * *

In 1492, nearly five hundred years after Leif had sailed to Vinland, Christopher Columbus, a tall, white-haired sea captain in the service of the king and queen of Spain, sailed westward from the port of Gomara in the Canary Islands. Columbus reached the Caribbean Sea 33 days later and landed upon a number of islands, including Cuba and Santo Domingo. He found these islands covered with trees and beautiful. The nightingales, he wrote, "were singing in countless numbers, and that in November, the month in which I arrived there." The peoples who lived in this tropical paradise were totally naked and totally peaceful.

When Columbus came to an island in the West Indies that he named San Salvador, he was especially delighted with the gentle Taino people who came down to the shore to say hello. "They are so free with all they have," wrote Columbus in his journal, "that no one could believe it who has not seen it; of everything that they possess, if it be asked of them, they never say 'no'; on the contrary, they invite you to share it."

But the Spaniards and other Europeans who soon followed them did not come in order to share; they came in order to take. These invaders were often simply pirates and robbers. Their expeditions were all-male affairs, boatloads of soldiers and bullies armed with swords, guns, and knives. Some were greedy to get their hands on silks and spices that would bring a fortune when carried home and sold

The first English expedition to the New World was sent out to the coast of Virginia in 1584 under Captains Amadas and Barlowe. In this drawing they are shown approaching Roanoke Island (modern North Carolina) in a ship's boat.

in Europe. Some dreamed of finding a sea route through or around America that would take them to the Far East and its fabled riches. Some dreamed of great estates and willing slaves. Almost all of them were eager to find the gold, silver, pearls and rubies that they believed were hidden in the New World in huge amounts. The hundred years that followed Columbus's first voyage in 1492 might with truth be called the first modern gold rush.

Columbus's explorations and those that followed opened up a world bigger and richer than anything that Europeans had ever dreamed existed. Spain, and following her France, Britain and Holland, began to claim, and to seize, huge territories in North America. These overseas possessions, or empires, that the Europeans now began to build, usually lay close to the shores of the oceans or were easy to reach by great American rivers like the Rio Grande, the Hudson and the Mississippi, upon which ocean-going vessels could sail. Since Europeans were becoming masters of boat building, seafaring, and the sea, the vast waters that once had separated the Old and New Worlds now began to link the two together. The sea captain was a commanding figure of this new age. Often he was explorer, soldier, merchant, pirate and ruler of empire, all rolled into one. These sea captains were hard, fearless men. They were driven not only by greed for gold but by a great curiosity to know more about the strange and beautiful world that was opening up around them.

The Spanish were the first to begin serious exploration of North America. What amazing travels they made! Typical of these was Francisco Coronado's expedition in 1540. The discoverer of the Grand Canyon, Coronado marched across the continent, over mountains, deserts and prairies, from California to Kansas. Hundreds of soldiers

8

and horses sickened in the summer heat and died. In two years of such wandering, Coronado learned much about America, but he found nothing that might make him rich. As the men who survived bitterly complained, "they had not found riches, nor had they discovered any settled country out of which estates could be made."

Where the Spanish led, others followed. John Cabot, an English sea captain and merchant, sailed across the northern Atlantic in 1497 to the land where Leif had once been, and named it Newfoundland. Jacques Cartier, a French sea-captain, made no less than three trips across the Atlantic between 1534 and 1541; he discovered the St. Lawrence River and sailed deep into the interior of the continent, as far as the Indian village of Hochelaga, now called Montreal. Martin Frobisher, a Welsh sailor, set off in 1577 in a northwesterly direction far along the Canadian shore, looking in vain for a "northwest passage" that would take him to China.

A little more than one hundred years after Columbus's first voyage, explorations such as these had begun to revolutionize European knowledge of the globe. The earth, to be sure, was shrouded for the most part in water; but it was much bigger than Europeans had ever thought. The New World began to take shape on 16th- and 17th-century maps as a landmass that straddled the world waters practically from pole to pole.

The Spanish, French, English, and Dutch began to make their first serious efforts to establish permanent settlements in North America toward the end of the 16th century. In 1598 Don Juan de Onate pushed up the broad valley of the Rio Grande with 400 colonists and settled at San Gabriel. In 1608 Samuel de Champlain, one of France's greatest soldiers and sea captains, founded the first French New World Settlement of Quebec.

Sir Walter Raleigh was the pioneer of English settlement in the New World. Raleigh was a soldier, a pirate and a great favorite of England's Queen Elizabeth. In the early 1580s he began to dream of

When the English arrived at Roanoke in 1584, the region was inhabited by a tribe called the Powhatans, who lived beyond the northern margin of the southeastern Indian culture. The Powhatans depended far more on hunting and fishing than upon agriculture for their food. In this respect there was a marked difference between them and the Timuacans to the far south. This engraving shows a Powhatan chief ready for the hunt. Dressed in the skins of wild animals he carries his bow in his hand; a quiver of arrows is slung across his back. The hair is dressed across the top of the head in a *coxcomb*; the rest of it flows down across his shoulder.

a settlement somewhere on the eastern coast of North America—a fine pirate's lair from which his ships might sail out to capture and to loot the Spanish galleons as they sailed homeward through the Caribbean, loaded with Peruvian silver and Mexican gold. In 1584 Raleigh sent out two captains, Philip Amadas and Arthur Barlowe, to explore the coast and find a likely spot. Amadas and

Barlowe put ashore on Roanoke Island, in Pamlico Sound, North Carolina. Giving thanks to God for their safe arrival, they took possession in the name of the queen, looked around, and then came back to England with glowing reports. Flocks of white cranes, they wrote, glided and wheeled and cried out in the still air; the rivers were filled with pearl-bearing oysters. The seashores were "sandy and low toward the water's edge, and so overgrown with grapes that the surging waves flowed over them."

As for the Roanoke natives, they planted corn for a living, fished and hunted in the forests. They were, said Amadas and Barlowe, "gentle, loving, faithful, lacking all guile and treachery."

The queen was impressed. She gave Sir Walter a charter, or permission, to explore these coasts and the "remote, heathen and barbarous lands" that lay beyond them. She was pleased to call this new American kingdom of hers Virginia.

The next year, 1585, Sir Walter sent a couple of hundred settlers to Virginia. This was an all-male expedition on the Spanish model. They hunted for gold and stole corn from the Indians, and they didn't survive for long. The Indians stopped being "gentle and loving" and fought back. War and starvation killed many of the whites. British ships had to rescue the survivors and bring them home.

Raleigh tried again in 1587. This time he sent out a group of 110 people, 17 of whom were women. These settlers, too, had a rough time of it, and their leader, John White, went back to England to get help. Then war broke out between England and Spain, and White could not return to Roanoke until 1590.

He found the settlement deserted. The fort that the settlers had built was overgrown with weeds; broken cannon were scattered about. White's precious sea chests had been broken open, his precious books and maps ruined. "My books," as he wrote, "were torn from their covers, the frames of my maps and pictures were rotten and broken by rain, and my armor was almost eaten through with rust."

As for the Roanoke settlers, they had vanished for good. Among them was John White's own daughter, Eleanor Dare, and Eleanor's child Virginia, who had been born in Roanoke in 1587—the first English child ever to be born on American soil.

In 1606 the English tried again, but this time Sir Walter Raleigh was not the leader, for he had lost all his influence at the royal court with the death of Elizabeth in 1603. Now it was a group of wealthy gentlemen who called themselves the London Company. These people put their money into a settlement project in the hope that gold might be found and that they would get a share of the profits. The London Company, just like Raleigh, had a charter from the king to occupy land in America, to recruit settlers in England, to transport them across the Atlantic and to run the settlements as they pleased once they had been set up. Organizations like the London Company were the first English governments in America. Their agents, or *governors*, passed laws in the name of the king and made all the colonists obey them.

The London Company sent out its first three ships late in 1606. They picked a spot on the sheltered waters of the James River and named it Jamestown, after the English king, James I. At the start the London Company's settlers at Jamestown didn't do much better than Sir Walter Raleigh's people at Roanoke. They looked for gold, stole from the Indians and starved by the hundreds. By 1609 only a handful of survivors remained, who were, in the words of their leader, the sea captain and explorer John Smith, "most miserable and poor creatures … preserved for the most part by roots, herbs, acorns, walnuts, berries, and now and then a little fish."

Proving incompetent to run the colony, the London Company was dissolved in 1624 and Virginia came directly under the rule of the Crown. Settlers continued to move in and to "plant" farms up and down the James River. John Rolfe was one of these planters. Most people remember him because in 1614 he fell in love with Pocahontas, a woman of

the Pamunkey tribe and the daugher of its chief. When the couple announced that they wished to get married, English settlers attacked Rolfe for daring to think of choosing for his bride a native person "whose education was rude, her manners barbarous, her generation accursed." Torn between love for Pocahontas and rejection by the white community, Rolfe prayed to God to release him from his suffering, from "the many passions…which I have daily, hourly, yes and in my sleep endured."

In the end John Rolfe married his Pamunkey bride, but their happiness was brief. Pocahontas died during a visit to England in 1617. As for Rolfe, he was killed when Pocahontas's people took the warpath a few years later and tried to drive the English invaders off their land and back into the sea.

John Rolfe is remembered not only for his love for Pocahontas but because he was the first white Virginian to plant tobacco. The Native American peoples had been growing and smoking this plant for centuries. For them the white calumet, or tobacco pipe, was a holy thing that stood for peace. To the English settlers, soon enough, it spelled only "money." There was a booming demand in Europe for the new American weed. Soon the James River was studded with farms where tobacco grew well on the wonderfully fertile soil. By 1630 the James River began to be crowded with English ships coming in to pick up the tobacco crop from the planters' docks and to carry it across the ocean to England. Englishmen began to flock to Virginia to make tobacco fortunes.

In 1609 another English sea captain, Henry Hudson, who was working for Dutch merchants, arrived off the American coast to the north of the Virginia colony and began to explore the lovely river that now bears his name. Hudson sailed 150 miles northwards in the hope, like Martin Frobisher before him, of finding a northwest passage to China. Hudson, of course, found no such thing, but he was amazed at what he did find: a beautiful valley filled with mountains, lakes and forests and with wildlife teeming in the wilderness. Wild pigeons, he wrote, flew in flocks so vast that "they shut out the sunshine." As for the Indian peoples of the valley, they were Mohicans and Wappingers who made tools of bone and stone, who raised crops of corn, who hunted and fished and who clothed themselves in the skins of fur-bearing animals—beaver, otter, fox, mink, wildcat and bear.

Soon merchants of the Dutch West India Company began organizing settlements in the Hudson Valley, like the London Company was doing on the James River. But for these people it was not tobacco that spelled wealth but the wonderful furs that the Indians took from the furry animals that they trapped and that brought fortunes when sold upon the European market. The Dutch soon built forts at Albany and at the tip of Manhattan Island to serve as centers for this fur trade.

Forts were also intended to help protect the settlers against Indian attack. Built first of wood and then of stone, these forts were strongholds in which guns and gunpowder could be stored and soldiers housed. Europeans built such forts in America wherever they went. Along with iron axes, iron ploughs, firearms and knives, forts were part of the white man's superior technology, which helped him move inland and successfully overcome Indian resistance.

The West India Company needed settlers to grow food for its trading centers in New York, which it called Fort Orange and Fort Amsterdam. In this respect the careful Dutch did a much better job than the London Company. Farmers and craftsmen were picked, who brought with them their families as well as seed, ploughs and tools. The company also saw that the settlers had all the animals that they needed for farm and breeding purposes. In 1625 two shiploads of stallions, mares, bulls, cows, hogs and sheep were sent across the Atlantic. Aboard ship each animal had its own stall, with a floor of sand three feet deep, and also, we are told, "its servant who attends to it. … All

This is one of many renderings of a famous scene. It illustrates the words of William Bradford: "In back of them lay the blue-gray wastes of the Atlantic Ocean… [T]he whole country, full of woods and thickets, represented a wild and savage hue."

suitable forage is there, hay and straw, and what else is useful."

In New England, still farther up the coast of "Virginia," the earliest settlements were not made by gold diggers, or soldiers, or farmers and traders who wanted to get rich quick with luxury crops like tobacco or furs, but by a band of one hundred people mostly from the ranks of English villagers—small farmers, farm workers, village craftsmen and fisherfolk. The leaders of this group were men used to holding responsible positions. William Brewster, for example, was a postmaster; William Bradford was a farmer, silk weaver, and merchant. None of them came to the New World to get rich but simply to cultivate the soil, to follow their trades and to be left alone to worship in their own way and to live in peace. When they wrote to their friends back home, these New England settlers said nothing about gold or silver or how to get to China; they talked about "ground to plant, seas and rivers to fish in, a pure air to breathe, good water to drink."

There were very few wealthy people among these pilgrims and only one professional soldier. As for women and children among the emigrants, there were more of them than of men. Elizabeth Hopkins was pregnant when she boarded the *Mayflower* with her husband, Stephen, and their three children, Giles, Constance and Damaris. The baby, who was christened Oceanus, was born as the ship crossed the Atlantic.

The pilgrims settled at the foot of Cape Cod in 1620 and built the village of Plymouth. The first years in the wilderness were a painful struggle with hunger, disease and death.

Plymouth remained a backwater in new England life. The first truly important New England settlement was launched in 1629 by the Massachusetts Bay Company, a group of well-to-do gentlemen; these, unlike the London Company people, did not stay home in England while others settled their colony, but all crossed the Atlantic themselves to share the hardships and the rewards of the enterprise. Soon tiny settlements dotted the estuary of the Charles River where it flows past Boston into Massachusetts Bay. In the years following 1630, the first trickle of emigrants to the Boston area would turn into a flood.

Many of the first colonists who came to New England in the 17th century were known as *Puritans.* Most Puritan settlers were farmers or fishermen who came from England's southwestern counties or northeastern shires; there were, to be sure, some people of rank, or "gentlefolk," among them.

Pomp or idle display had little place in these people's hard-working lives. They believed in simplicity: Their style of life, their homes, their clothes—all were simple, quiet and unadorned.

For the English Puritans the word of God was everything. They sought God's message not in the teaching of priests but in the Bible itself. Not for them bishops and clergy dressed in silken robes and adorned with glittering jewels. Not for them cathedrals of chiseled stone with windows blazing fire from glass of many colors. Not for them images of saints and martyrs, even of God himself, carved in wood and painted blue, red and god. They wished to purge, or *purify,* the English Church of what they felt were false beliefs, empty rituals, luxurious ornamentation.

For common people to be able to seek for themselves God's message in the Bible was, in the 17th century, something new. In Europe the ancient Chinese art of printing only began to be used late in the 15th century. Printed books were simply not available to ordinary people at that time. The Bible was the first book ever to be translated from Latin into the English language and printed so that thousands of common folk could read it for themselves.

Puritans considered that true believers must study the Bible and obey its laws. Obedience to God, they thought, was more important than obedience to priests and kings. The history of Plymouth, their first settlement in North America, tells of men and women who were prepared to sacrifice life itself for the sake of their faith.

Persecution, on account of both their religious ideas and also their politics, made 17th-century England unbearable for the English Puritans, among them William Bradford. The son of a Yorkshire farmer, Bradford was a leader of the group that settled Plymouth. He wrote the story of that colony in a justly famous work, *Of Plymouth Plantation.* William Bradford tells how he and his friends, who lived near Scrooby, Yorkshire, in the north of England, "were hunted and persecuted on every side." The king's agents arrested them, threw them into jail for no reason, watched them day and night, and drove them from their homes.

Bradford and his friends decided to leave their native land. First they fled to the Netherlands, where they went to live in the town of Leyden; there Bradford took up the weaver's trade. But after a few years in Leyden, some of the exiles realized that it was no longer possible for them to go on living there. Life was hard. Worst of all, the young people were turning away from the faith of their mothers and fathers. "That which was most lamentable," wrote Bradford, was that "many of the children were drawn away by evil examples into extravagant and dangerous courses." This, said Bradford, was "to the great grief of their parents and the dishonour of God."

To keep their families together and to protect their way of life, the exiles decided to leave the Netherlands and find a home someplace else. Their thoughts turned, wrote Bradford, to "those vast and unpeopled countries of America which are fruitful and fit for habitation."

Then and there, a debate broke out among the Leyden Puritans. Some liked the idea of going to America; others felt that they ought to stay where they were. The more cautious pointed out that the long sea voyage was dangerous—hard for men to endure, harder for women. For if they survived the trip, what would they find on that distant shore? They would be exposed to famine, to nakedness and want. "The change of air, diet, and the drinking of water," they said, "would infect their bodies with sore sicknesses and grievous diseases." As if this were not enough, they would also have to face the native peoples of that country, who thought of it as their own: These were "cruel, barbarous, and treacherous, being most furious in their rage and merciless when they overcome."

William Bradford answered simply that "all great actions are accompanied by great difficulties and must be both undertaken and overcome with answerable courage."

In the end some of the Puritans decided to stay in the Netherlands, some to leave. Those who decided to leave embarked with their families on the tiny ship *Mayflower*. Their friends gathered at the dock to say good-bye. "Truly doleful," wrote Bradford, "was the sight of that sad parting, to see what sighs and sobs and prayers did sound amongst them, what tears did gush from every eye."

Nine weeks later the emigrants, numbering in all about one hundred, arrived in the New World and settled on the shores of Cape Cod. They named this settlement Plymouth, after the lovely Devonshire harbor in the west of England from which some of their number had come.

It was November in the year 1620. A hard winter lay ahead. "They that know the winters of that country," wrote Bradford, "know them to be sharp and violent and subject to cruel and fierce storms." Behind them lay the blue-gray wastes of the Atlantic Ocean. On the landward side the forests were clothed in red and gold. "Summer being done," wrote Bradford, "all things [stood] upon them with a weatherbeaten face, and the whole country, full of woods and thickets, represented a wild and savage hue."

In the years that followed more settlers arrived and made their homes upon the shores of Massachusetts Bay. They spread throughout New

Spread of Colonial Settlement

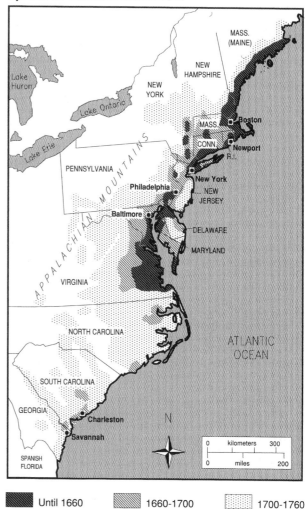

Until 1660   1660-1700   1700-1760

England, founding a Puritan society that in the course of time contributed much to the building of American civilization. New England's communities were formed for the most part of farming people who lived in townships carved out amidst the forests. Settlers dreamed of living much as they had in the Old World—close to the soil and in intimate daily contact with family and friends.

Land provided the basis for a comfortable existence in New England. When a man died, he passed his land on to his sons; his sons married the daughters of neighbors. The population multiplied because land was plentiful and because people were free, for many years, of serious infectious disease. As numbers grew, new settlements split off from the old and claimed the right to divide up hitherto uncultivated land. The more venturesome members of the younger generation moved on to the west or north to found new communities of their own.

The Bible provided these New England people with a meaning for man's life on earth and a vision of the American future. Men and women were to live together as brothers and sisters and in obedience to God's commands. The village meetinghouse was a symbol of this life and this faith. Here the people met to transact their business, to pass laws and to resolve the conflicts that threatened to divide them. Here on Sundays and sometimes on weekdays, the Puritan minister stood before the community with the Bible open in front of him. He expounded the word of God for the guidance of his listeners.

The Puritan minister was a leader of his flock; most communities chose the man they wanted from a number of candidates. The purpose of early New England colleges, like John Harvard's at Cambridge, was to train ministers so that they might better serve the people they were called upon to lead.

New England meetinghouses, unlike the stone churches of the Old World upon which to some extent they were modeled, were built of wood sawn from New England pine. These simple structures with their tall spires soon came to dominate the New England landscape. In the course of time, as communities prospered, the Puritans painted their meetinghouses white and installed large windows with clear glass so that the light of day might flood the interior space.

Each family had its allotted pew in the building, just as it had its allotted place in the community. "Servants," or farm workers newly arrived and without land, worshiped alongside the family whom they served. Black slaves, of whom a few were to be found in most townships, had to sit at the back or in the gallery.

2

WILDERNESS COLONIES

Frontier, Farm and City in British America, 1630-1763

When the British colonists first came to settle America's Atlantic seaboard, it was for the most part forest. Lakes and rivers teemed with fish in numbers, as one colonist remarked, "almost beyond believing." Wild strawberries grew so thick in the water meadows that "one can lie down and eat them." Birds flew overhead in flocks so dense that the earth became dark with their passage. The wild white cranes that flocked together on the Virginia coast made the air ring with their cries, "as if an army had shouted all together." This land, too, was the haunt of fierce creatures—bears, leopards, wolves and wildcats, which preyed upon the deer that roamed the woods in endless droves. Some writers warned people to stay clear of the dangerous snakes that were to be found everywhere; people, they said, should take care especially for "serpents called rattlesnakes that have rattles in their tails, that will not fly from a man as others will, but will ... sting him so mortally that he will die within a quarter of an hour after." And nobody forgot to mention the "long-tailed gnats," which bred in marshes and swamps and made life during the hot summers miserable for the settlers.

English settlements grew and spread more rapidly than the Spanish ones in New Mexico and Florida or the French on the St. Lawrence waterway and in the Mississippi Valley. These settlers now put aside dreams of quick wealth from the discovery of gold and silver and set themselves to clearing land, building houses and raising crops. In southern New England, small farms began to spread across the countryside. In the Hudson Valley and eastern Pennsylvania, spacious landed estates and large well-equipped farms began to appear. Tidewater Virginia became a land of tobacco plantations where, by the end of the 17th century, black slaves in rapidly growing numbers were seen. Growers of rice began to stake out their domains on the huge watery tracts of the South Carolina lowlands, and they built elegant homes for themselves in Charleston. Charleston itself was one of several fine harbors that were to be found upon the Atlantic shore; others were Boston, Newport, Manhattan and Philadelphia. Merchants settled in

17

This print shows New Amsterdam in the middle of the 17th century. The tiny settlement clusters around a fort at the tip of Manhattan Island.

these seaports and began to grow rich by carrying fish, lumber, tobacco and wheat to Europe and the West Indies, bringing back wine, molasses, clothing, guns and axes for sale to the colonists.

So rapidly did these British settlements grow that by 1750 there were 13 separate colonies strung out along the Atlantic seaboard. Except for a wilderness section in North Carolina, the settlements stretched in an unbroken band all the way from the swampy shores of Georgia to the rocky coasts of Maine. Each of these colonies was ruled by a governor appointed by the king of England, with the help of an assembly, which voted taxes and passed laws that the people were supposed to obey.

For 150 years—from the very first settlements, that is, until the Revolution broke out in 1775—new immigrants from Europe arrived in increasing numbers. Most of these people were very poor—so poor, indeed, that they had no money to pay the cost of their transatlantic trip. This meant that instead of paying with money, they paid with their labor. They hired themselves out for a number of years to well-to-do people in the colonies—farmers, planters and merchants—who paid the fare for them. For four, five, six, seven or more years they did whatever these employers wanted done: For the most part they cut down forests, cleared the land and cultivated the crops. Then, as soon as they were free, most moved on into the back country, carrying their few wordly goods upon their backs, to carve out clearings for themselves.

Up and down the frontier, from Georgia to Maine, the settlers faced a hard struggle for survival against winter cold, summer heat, loneliness and disease. Charles Woodmason, a British clergyman, visited the backwoods people of North and South Carolina during the 1760s and wrote of what he saw. "Their cabins," he wrote, "are quite open and exposed. Little or no bedding, or anyting to cover them. Not a drop of anything, save cold water, to drink. And all their clothing, a shirt and trousers, shift and petticoat … No shoes or stockings—children run half naked. The Indians are better clothed and lodged."

Many people who lived on the frontier—and this was especially true of those who were far from overland trails or navigable rivers—either had to raise food and make clothes for themselves or go without. Large families were a necessity: There was so much work to be done that a family could not survive without the help of many hands, and even small children had to work. There were no hospitals or doctors in the countryside in those days. If you became sick, the cure was simple: "There you must lie," as Woodmason put it, "til nature gets the better of the disease, or death relieves you."

Parents worked side by side in the endless task of making a home; the woman's job was certainly as hard as the man's. She had to spin thread, weave cloth and stitch the clothes together, stitch by stitch, and every stitch by hand. She had to dig and weed the garden, raise the vegetables, store and dry them for winter use. She had to watch the hens and collect the eggs; she had to draw water from the well, haul it to the cabin, heat it for washing clothes and cooking. To make fire she had to strike flint with steel and let the sparks fall on tinder. Matches, of course, had yet to be invented.

The woman, too, had to make soap in order to wash the clothes, and she had to make candles if she wanted light during the long winter evenings. In addition, she had to bear children and serve as midwife and give comfort to other women of the neighborhood when their time came ("It will ease your pain, honey, if you lay on your side and holler.").

Much of the suffering of childbirth went for nothing. Many infants died before they were a year old, and the graveyards were filled with the remains of children who did not make it through the first five years of life.

As for education on the frontier, it was little enough. Children were needed for the daily work of the farm; they grew wise in the ways of the forest and in doing well the tasks to which they were set. Little girls spun wool and did knitting; boys minded the cattle and the sheep. John and David Brainerd, raised on a Connecticut farm in the 1720s, told how it was. A boy, they wrote, "must rise early and make himself useful … His whole time out of school must be filled with some service, such as bringing in fuel for the day, cutting potatoes for the sheep, feeding the swine, watering the horses, picking the berries, gathering the vegetables, spooling the yarn."

A child's labor, then, was part of his life, so much so that mothers even sang about it in the lullabies with which they cradled their little ones. "On the westward hill," sang Irish mothers, "the sheep will stray … My child will watch them from break of day … Berry picking shall be his play … Sleep now, my darling, 'til break of day."

As more and more people arrived to clear the thickets, to kill the animals, and to push back the forest, new problems arose. The native peoples, whose land this was, watched with angry eyes and despairing hearts as the whites moved in with their axes, guns and ploughs. Some of the Indians fled farther west; others, to save their homes, took the only remedy open to them: They went on the warpath.

The sorrows of frontier warfare fell upon women and children as well as men when the war whoop was heard at the edge of the clearing; when native people armed with tomahawk, bow and arrow, or gun swooped down to kill the European intruders or to drive them away. So it was in 1675, when the Indians went on the warpath along the whole frontier, both in the North and the South.

In New England war broke out between Philip, chief of the Narragansetts of Rhode Island, together with other tribes who were his allies, and the New England settlers. On February 10, 1676, a band of Nipmuck Indians attacked Lancaster, Massachusetts, killed 50 whites, and carried off Mary Rowlandson, the minister's wife. Mrs. Rowlandson spent three months as a Nipmuck prisoner before she was freed, and she later wrote down what had happened to her. Her story tells us what frontier women and children had to expect, and it reveals the courage a woman had to show if she wished to survive. "Now," she wrote of the Indian attack,

is the dreadful hour come, that I have often heard of, but now mine eyes see it. Some in our house were fighting for their lives, others wallowing in their blood, the house on fire over our heads. I took my children to go forth and leave the house, but as soon as we came to the door ... the Indians shot so thick that the bullets rattled against the house, so that we must go back.

Mary was taken prisoner with her six-year-old daughter, who had been wounded. Off they went with the Nipmuck band over the frozen, snow-covered ground, into the forest. One of the Indians placed the child upon a horse, and, as Mary wrote, "it went moaning along, *'I shall die! I shall die!'* I went on foot after it with a sorrow that cannot be expressed."

The first night Mary and her little girl passed in the open, upon the ground. The child was delirious with fever and kept calling pitifully for water. "My sweet babe," she wrote one week later, "like a lamb departed this life on February 18, 1676, it being six years and five months old, nine days in this miserable condition without any refreshing of one nature or another, except a little water."

The Nipmucks moved onward through the cold, empty forest, with New England militiamen in pursuit. They traveled slowly, because there were old people in the party, as well as many women and children. There were indeed, as Mrs. Rowlandson tells it, hundreds in the group, "old and young, some sick, some lame, many had papooses on their backs, the greatest number at this time with us were squaws, and they traveled with all they had, bag and baggage." Rivers had to be crossed, and this took a lot of time. Everybody had to wait while rafts were made and while the rafts shuttled back and forth, ferrying people across.

In warfare against the Indians, the whites sought out and destroyed the growing corn whenever possible, hoping that starvation would force their enemies to surrender. This was seen in the war against King Philip. The Nipmucks in this case had two enemies to fight at the same time: the New England soldiers and starvation. So these hungry people, as they fled through the forest, ate anything that they could find. Their food, as Mrs. Rowlandson tells it, was "groundnuts, acorns, artichokes, lily roots ... old bones ... horse's guts, all sorts of wild birds that they would catch; also bear, beaver, tortoise, frogs, squirrels, dogs, skunks, rattlesnakes, yea the very bark off the trees."

The Nipmucks, like other native peoples of New England, were forced to give way before the whites. Outnumbered, they died bravely in battle or were rounded up, taken captive and enslaved. By the middle of the 18th century much of the land between the Atlantic Ocean and the Appalachian Mountains had been cleared of its Indian inhabitants and was being cultivated by the whites.

By this time, too, America's five fine harbors at Boston, Newport, Manhattan, Philadelphia and Charleston had become great seaport towns, each with more than 10,000 inhabitants. In all, more than 55,000 people lived in these coastal cities, roughly 4% of all the people in the country. Today we would think of such towns as tiny places, but in 1750 their importance was great. They were the gateways through which tens of thousands of immigrants passed on their way inland. They were centers of communication with Europe, American windows to the outside world; and they were, too, the homes of wealthy and powerful leaders. From these towns information and ideas were spread by means of books and newspapers. Here skilled craftsmen followed their trades as printers, shipbuilders, papermakers, sail makers, carriage makers, bricklayers, rope makers and many more.

Philadelphia is a good example of the way that these towns grew. In 1680 Philadelphia didn't exist; by 1750 it had risen from nothing to become America's biggest city and Pennsylvania's capital.

Philadelphia's founder was an English nobleman named William Penn, who belonged to a religious group in England known as the Society of Friends. Many of the Friends were poor, and all of them received rough treatment on account of their beliefs. The Friends, for example, thought that

20

This painting, made in 1817 from an earlier sketch, illustrates the growth of the city in one century. The huddled dwellings and cramped lanes of the first settlement have given way to broad streets lined with spacious houses. The big building in the middle of the picture is a meetinghouse—Wesley's Chapel, the first Methodist church erected in America.

all people were equal in God's eyes, so they refused to "uncover," or take off their hats, when the king was driven by in his coach. This type of behavior was considered a terrible insult to His Majesty, and the Friends were often punished for it. Members of the Society spent a good deal of time in the pillory, where people threw rotten eggs or tomatoes at them. Since, too, the Friends were determined to hold church services in their own way and not in accordance with the rules of the Church of England, they had to pay heavy fines; their tools were smashed, their sheep and cattle driven away, and they themselves were put in jail.

William Penn dreamed of starting an American colony in which the Friends could live and worship in peace. In 1680 he visited the court of His Majesty Charles II and asked if the king would give him some American land in payment of a debt owed by Charles to the Penn family. The king agreed, and so it was arranged. Charles wrote a charter giving Penn a tract of land lying between the latitudes 40° and 43° N and bounded on the east by the Delaware River. This fine piece of real estate was named *Pennsylvania*, which is Latin for the "woodlands that belong to Penn."

Penn made plans to build a town on the elbow of land formed at the place where the Delaware and Schuylkill rivers flow together. In spite of swamps and marshes, it was a fine location. To the west lay fertile and level lands, which would support prosperous farmers and provide food for the city's inhabitants. The city would also make a great port. Seagoing vessels could sail right up the Delaware to the town docks. Philadelphia was also so far inland that it was well protected from Atlantic storms and breakers.

Penn named his city Philadelphia, or "brotherly love." Before long the place was growing fast. The produce of the hinterland, the rich farmlands surrounding the town, was sent abroad in return for ironware, guns, clothes and luxuries; oceangoing vessels were built in Philadelphia shipyards to make this possible.

Late in the year 1750, a ship named the *Osgood* sailed up the Delaware River and docked at Philadelphia. The *Osgood* carried immigrants from Germany, among them a minister named Gottlieb Mittelberger. When Mittelberger went ashore and strolled around the town, he was amazed by its wealth. Broad streets were lined with elegant houses built of brick or stone. Women wore "fine aprons, on their shoes generally large silver buckles, around their throats fine strings of beads, in their ears costly rings with fine stones, and on their heads fine white bonnets embroidered with flowers and trimmed with lace and streamers." On Sundays, when they rode on horseback to church, Mittelberger saw women wearing "blue or scarlet cloaks reaching down to the waist."

As for the town's docks, how many precious things were being loaded and unloaded there! These included, Mittelberger tells us, "fruit, flour, corn, tobacco, honey, hides, furs, wines, spices, sugar, tea, coffee, rice, rum, fine china vessels, Dutch and English cloth, leather, and silks."

With Mittelberger on the *Osgood* arrived hundreds of very poor people who would never live to have silver buckles on their shoes or ride to

The Guinea Coast showing Centers of the Slave Trade

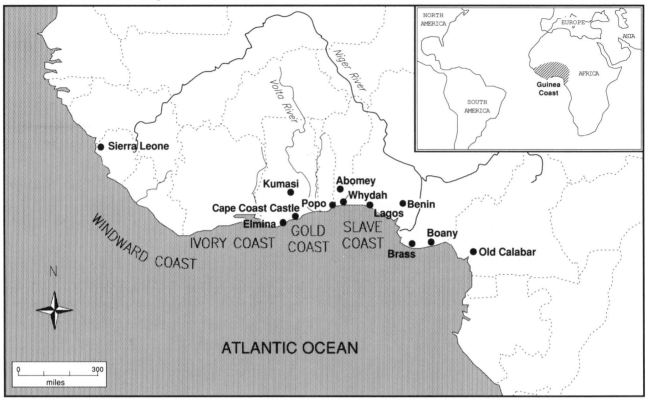

* Dotted lines represent current political boundaries

church in a scarlet cloak. They had come to America to escape the poverty and misery of the Old World and to do hard work: to clear land for the well-to-do Pennsylvania farmers, to labor in the fields and on the docks. These people faced the dangers of the Atlantic because they had dreams of a better life in the New World for themselves and for their children. But the Atlantic crossing was more horrible than they could have imagined; many who set sail from the Dutch port of Rotterdam never lived to see the new country. They fell ill, died at sea, and were thrown overboard. The water they were forced to drink during the long weeks of the crossing was "often very black, thick with dirt, and full of worms." Even, Mittelberger added, "when one is very thirsty, one is almost unable to drink it without loathing." As for the food provided, it was little enough. "We had to eat the ship's biscuit," he wrote, "full of red worms and spider's nests. True, great hunger and thirst teach one to eat

and drink everything; but many forfeit their lives in the process."

Most of these immigrants were destitute; when they reached America they had no money left to pay for their passage, and so found themselves

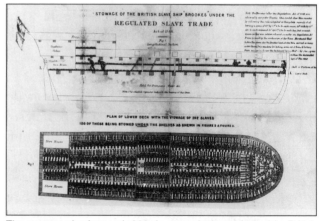

The stowage plan for nearly 300 slaves on the lower deck of the British slave ship *Brookes* toward the end of the 18th century. A space of 6 feet by 16 inches was allotted to each man and 5 feet by 16 inches to each woman. As the longitudinal section of the plan indicates, the people were able to sit up or crawl but not to stand erect. Here in darkness, except for brief spells on deck, if the weather was fine, they were doomed to lie for the four to six weeks of the transatlantic trip.

This engraving illustrates the thriving slave trade being conducted during the early 18th century. It shows a French fort (Fort des Maures) on Moyella Island, off the coast of West Africa in the Senegal River region. The ship's captain and an African trader (or chief) exchange *manifests*, or lists of goods. Their bodyguards stand behind them. In the background trade goods are being unloaded.

completely in the power of the *Osgood*'s captain. He sold them just like slaves to any farmer who would come to the ship and pay the debt owed to him. In order to pay the debt that the immigrant now owed to the farmer, he would have to work for that farmer for several years. Thus many of these poor immigrants became for a time the servants of Pennsylvania farmers; no matter how young they were, or how old, they were to work all day and do whatever they were told. "Our Europeans who have been purchased," Mittelberger wrote, "must work hard all the time. For new fields are constantly being laid out; oak tree stumps are just as hard in America as they are in Germany."

White immigrants did their service for the wealthy farmers and planters and then moved on. William Penn valued these people because they were, as he put it, "the hands and feet of the rich." But there were never enough of them; they were here today, gone tomorrow. So it was that after the middle of the 17th century, especially in the South, employers began to tap another source of labor, the peoples of Africa.

At the mouth of the Gambia River, the western coastline of Africa makes a wide sweep toward the east and continues in this direction for almost 2,000 miles before turning south once more beyond the delta of the Niger. The area lying along this coast—steamy, tropical and palm fringed—is known as Equatorial Africa; American and European slave traders called it the Coast of Guinea. For three centuries they found there an inexhaustible supply of African people whom they could seize, transport and sell for use upon the New World's plantations.

The African slave trade began in the 16th century, almost as soon as the New World was discovered. Spanish, French and English traders and sea captains kidnaped Africans and dragged them across the ocean to toil upon large sugar plantations in the Caribbean. American merchants, too—mostly from Newport, Boston and New York—fell over themselves in their haste to cash in on this trade, to mint profits from the sale of human beings. By the middle of the 17th century, black slaves were being brought directly to the American mainland; and by 1700 announcements like the following were becoming common in the newspapers: "TO BE SOLD, A PARCEL OF NEGROES, JUST ARRIVED—MEN, WOMEN, BOYS AND GIRLS."

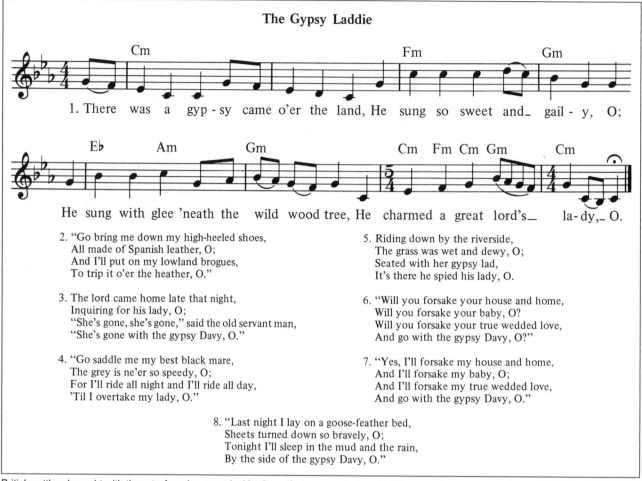

The Gypsy Laddie

1. There was a gyp-sy came o'er the land, He sung so sweet and_ gail-y, O;
He sung with glee 'neath the wild wood tree, He charmed a great lord's_ la-dy,_ O.

2. "Go bring me down my high-heeled shoes,
   All made of Spanish leather, O;
   And I'll put on my lowland brogues,
   To trip it o'er the heather, O."

3. The lord came home late that night,
   Inquiring for his lady, O;
   "She's gone, she's gone," said the old servant man,
   "She's gone with the gypsy Davy, O."

4. "Go saddle me my best black mare,
   The grey is ne'er so speedy, O;
   For I'll ride all night and I'll ride all day,
   'Til I overtake my lady, O."

5. Riding down by the riverside,
   The grass was wet and dewy, O;
   Seated with her gypsy lad,
   It's there he spied his lady, O.

6. "Will you forsake your house and home,
   Will you forsake your baby, O?
   Will you forsake your true wedded love,
   And go with the gypsy Davy, O?"

7. "Yes, I'll forsake my house and home,
   And I'll forsake my baby, O;
   And I'll forsake my true wedded love,
   And go with the gypsy Davy, O."

8. "Last night I lay on a goose-feather bed,
   Sheets turned down so bravely, O;
   Tonight I'll sleep in the mud and the rain,
   By the side of the gypsy Davy, O."

British settlers brought with them to America a musical heritage that was centuries old. Wherever they went, music would be one of the bonds to unite them. "The Raggle Taggle Gypsies" is an example of the stirring ballads that they loved so well.

These "parcels" were sometimes taken off the boats, as one observer noted, "entirely naked, having only corals of different colors around their necks and arms."

Like the white servants, many Africans did not make it across the Atlantic. They died during the crossing from disease, despair or the battering that they suffered while crammed like sardines in the stinking holds of the slaving ships. Some broke their chains, attacked the ship crews and died fighting. Others, once they had revolted, refused to be captured alive. As one ship's mate wrote, they "leaped overboard and drowned themselves in the ocean with much resolution, showing no manner of concern for their life."

By 1750 there were more than 250,000 African slaves in British America, doomed to toil until they died for the white people who were their masters and mistresses. Most of these slaves, but by no means all of them, labored on the big tobacco, rice and indigo plantations of the South. Slavery was, by this time, a condition that a person inherited. That is, a child was a slave from birth if its mother was a slave. Black mothers brought their babies into the world knowing that their children would face the same lifetime of toil and torment that they themselves were going through.

Whether free or slave, most Americans in 1750 lived in the countryside, scattered over a huge area. Getting from one colony to another was a slow and difficult business. There were in those days no roads with hard surfaces and no bridges spanning the broad rivers. Sailing along the coast was the easiest way to travel; if you went by land you had to go on foot, or on horseback or in a horse-drawn carriage. When you came to a stream you either had to ride your horse across, wade and swim, or be carried over on a boat. At best this took a lot of time; at worst, when the weather was cold or the waters were in flood, it was a hard and dangerous experience.

In 1670 the first mail system was set up, and this was a very important step in developing communication among the colonies. The first mails were carried by horseback riders on the trails that wound along the rivers and over the hills and through the forests. These mailmen were called postriders; the first mails were carried by postriders from New York to Boston in 1673 along a track that soon came to be known as the Old Boston Post Road. It took the early postriders two weeks to cover the two hundred miles separating Boston from New York; a modern automobile covers the same ground in about four hours.

The postriders got to know their roads well, but for travelers who were not familiar with the path the experience was a rough one. Sarah Kemble Knight, Boston schoolteacher and shopkeeper, went by horse on the Old Post Road from Boston to New York in 1704 and kept a journal, which gives us a pretty vivid picture of what traveling was like in those days. For part of the trip, Sarah rode along with the postriders, who guided her on the hard-to-follow tracks through forests and over hills and who helped her to cross streams and rivers, either riding over on her horse or being ferried by boat. "We came to a river," she says,

which the Post generally rode through. But I dare not venture; so the Post got a lad and Canoe to carry me to the other side, and he rode through and led my horse. The Canoe was very small and shallow … she seemed ready to take in water, which greatly terrified me and caused me to be very careful, sitting with my hands fast on each side, my eyes steady, not daring so much as to

lodge my tongue a hair's breadth more to one side of my mouth than t' other.

Sarah had to sit upon her horse many hours each day, becoming stiff and saddlesore. One day when the sun went down, there was no inn in sight, and darkness multiplied the terrors of the road. "The only glimmering we now had," she wrote, "was from the spangled skies … Each lifeless Trunk, with its shattered limbs, appeared an armed Enemy; and every little stump like a ravenous devourer. Nor could I so much as see my guide, when at any distance, which added to the terror."

What a relief Sarah felt when the moon rose and she could see where she was going! "The raptures," she said, "which the sight of that fair planet produced in me, caused me, for the moment, to forget my present weariness."

Though the roads were bad, it would be wrong to think that the colonists lived in isolation from each other and had nothing in common. Exactly the opposite was the case: By the middle of the 18th century it was becoming clear that British Americans shared a great deal. They spoke the same English language, they sang the same songs, and they lived under the same law. This was so because most of them came from England and shared a common memory of their English homeland, its life-style and its past. The colonists, too, were all shaped by the hard, common struggle to clear the wilderness and to make a new life in a new country. They had a common vision of the New World as a Promised Land, where their children and their children's children would multiply until their numbers were like the stars in the sky, countless. Whites with few exceptions were Christians, and the black slaves were becoming rapidly converted to Christianity too. This was a Christian people who shared much the same beliefs about the meaning of life on earth, the God who was in the heavens, the reality of a life to come.

THE GREAT AWAKENING

One fine day in October 1740, Nathan Cole, a Connecticut farmer, heard the news that George Whitefield was to preach that morning in Middletown, twelve miles off. He saddled his horse, mounted up with his wife and trotted away. Coming to the road, which was dusty and unpaved, the Coles joined a stream of riders hastening toward Middletown. There was "scarcely a horse more than his length behind another," as Cole remembered, "all of a lather with foam and sweat, their breath rolling out of their nostrils."

When they reached Middletown, the Coles found a throng of people gathered around the meeting-house—three or four thousand of them, as Nathan estimated.

Middletown lies upon the Connecticut River. Ferry boats were "running swift backward and forward bringing over loads of people, and the oars rowed nimble and quick." On both sides of the water, "the land and banks over the river looked black with people and horses." As for the countryside all around, it appeared empty. "No man," as Nathan said, "was at work in his field, but all seemed to be gone."

George Whitefield spoke to his huge audience from a platform in front of Middletown meeting-house. He was a very young man, 25 years old, but already an almost legendary figure. Arriving in America from England only two years before, in 1738, he had traveled the length and breadth of the country, preaching the gospel and calling upon people to repent.

Cole described Whitefield, as he stood upon the platform that October day, as

a slender youth, before some thousands of people with a bold undaunted countenance ...

[I]t put me into a trembling fear before he began to preach; for he looked as if he was clothed with authority from the great God, and a sweet solemnity sat upon his brow.

By the middle of the 18th century, there were close to two and a half million people living in colonial America, both free and slave. The great majority of these people were Protestants. As Christians they were united in their fundamental religious beliefs about the world and the hereafter; but they were also divided into a large number of sects and denominations: Lutheran, Baptist, Quaker, Congregational, Anglican, Mennonite, Presbyterian, and so on. Americans, as George Woodmason put it, were "a mixed people—of different countries, dialects, and denominations."

In colonial America the Protestant churches did not always keep pace with the growth of population and of the country. Older communities grew larger and new ones came into being faster than the churches could keep pace. Thus religious fervor slackened, and church attendance dropped off. On the frontier, many found themselves living in areas where churches had as yet hardly penetrated at all.

In this situation the country was gripped from time to time with "awakenings." These were periods of passionate revival of interest in the religious life; people flocked to church, confessed their sins, became inspired with the joy of faith and burst into song.

Awakenings were linked to an inner loneliness of spirit that was a part of the colonial experience for many ordinary people. Life was hard and dangerous. Medical skill was primitive and scarce. Many mothers died in childbirth, and infant mortality was high. Disease took its toll. Death lurked

European visitors during the 18th century frequently remarked upon the profusion of churches and meetinghouses to be found in America. Old Bruton Parish Church, built in 1715 at Williamsburg, Virginia, is a grandiose structure testifying to the wealth and prosperity that made such church building possible. Elegantly dressed planters and their wives, with well-groomed horses and fancy coaches, throng the roadway.

everywhere in snakes' fangs, tempests, icy winters, falling trees, galloping horses, flooded rivers and Native American raids.

An awakening of religion might be triggered by any incident that brought home to people the nearness of death, that reminded them how unprepared they were to face their Creator. The outbreak of an epidemic might trigger an awakening; or the arrival of a traveling minister like Whitefield might set the process in motion. The contagion, again, might simply spread like a chain reaction from one community to another.

The Great Awakening was the greatest of these movements in colonial days, and it swept the country during the 1730s and 1740s. Many notable ministers took part in it. They belonged indeed to different denominations, but they brought the same message to the people of the cities, the farms and the frontier.

Poor sinners, said they, have you given thought to the salvation of your eternal souls? Are you destined for everlasting hell? Or are you ready to cast yourself upon the mercy and forgiveness of Christ and beg Him to guide you to eternal life? Take action today, before it is too late. *For who knows, when he leaves home in the morning, whether he will return at night?*

Nobody said it better than Jonathan Edwards, the pastor of the Presbyterian church in Northampton, Massachusetts. "O sinner!" he said in a famous sermon delivered in 1741,

consider the fearful danger that you are in: it is a great furnace of wrath, a wide and bottomless pit, full of the fire of wrath, that you are held over in the hand of that God, whose wrath is provoked as much against you as against any of the damned in hell: you hang by a slender thread, with the flames of divine wrath flashing about it, and ready every moment to burn it asunder; and you have nothing to lay hold of to save yourself, nothing to keep off the flames of wrath ... nothing that you can do, to induce God to spare you one moment.

Sermons such as these might be delivered at night, in a meetinghouse lit dimly by flickering candles. They often produced an explosion of fear, sorrow and joy among the listeners, who began to cry out, fall to the ground and beg the Lord for forgiveness and mercy for their sins. Critics of the awakening denounced such scenes of "enthusiasm." But there were practical results, as new congregations were formed, meetinghouses built, schools established.

The Great Awakening was important for the life of the colonists because it was *ecumenical*. That is, it brought a message to all Christians, not just to the members of a given sect. It affected all sorts of people, Edwards noted, "sober and vicious, high and low, rich and poor, wise and unwise ... old men and little children." Thus Americans became bound more closely together in the shared beliefs of a religion that revealed the meaning of life, the destiny of man and the road to salvation.

The Awakening made no distinction between black and white, free and slave. Jonathan Edwards noted the presence of slaves in the crowds that attended his revival meetings during the 1730s. Francis Asbury, a Methodist bishop, noted that his meetings later in the century were attended by "hundreds of negroes ... with the tears streaming down their faces."

3

'TIS TIME TO PART
The Struggle For Independence, 1763–1783

The Road to War, 1763–1774

The fortress of Quebec was built by the French to guard the approaches to Montreal and their great North American empire. Quebec was perched upon high cliffs on the western bank of the St. Lawrence River. On September 13, 1759, just before dawn, British soldiers landed at the foot of the cliffs and wound their way up a steep path to the top. They found themselves on a plateau outside the town walls, called the Plains of Abraham. Their leader, a pale, red-haired young general named James Wolfe, drew them up in battle formation. Quebec's defender, the Marquis de Montcalm, marched his men out through the town gates and gave the order to attack. The British fired their muskets and charged. The French fled. James Wolfe was killed by a bullet, the Marquis de Montcalm by an exploding shell.

This clash on the Plains of Abraham was the last and decisive battle in a struggle between British and French that had been going on for 70 years. The

prize for which the two sides battled was nothing less than North America itself. France now had to admit defeat. By the Treaty of Paris signed in 1763, the French king, Louis XVI, was forced to give up all the lands that he claimed in America except two tiny islands. He gave up the St. Lawrence Valley and the vast spaces of Canada that lay beyond; and he gave up two-thirds of what is now the United States—the lands reaching all the way from the Appalachians to the Rockies that the French had named Louisiana, in honor of Louis XVI's grandfather, who had been king before him.

The American colonists were very happy at James Wolfe's victory. They had taken part in all the wars against the French and had often been victims of French attacks. They were afraid, too, that so long as the French remained in America they might one day drive the colonists right off the eastern shore and into the Atlantic. James Wolfe, as a matter of fact, became quite a hero in America. A song called "The Death of General Wolfe" was popular in the early 1760s. It tells how Wolfe came to America to save the country from the French and how he died at the moment of victory. "The drums did loudly beat," it went,

> colors were flying,
> The purple gore did stream, and men lay dying,
> When shot off from his horse fell this brave hero,
> And we lament his loss in weeds of sorrow.

The government in London was as pleased by this success as the colonists were. It took steps at once to tighten its grip upon the new empire that it had won. In October 1763, the king, named George III, handed out a royal proclamation telling the colonists that they were not to cross the Appalachians and settle in Louisiana. As George himself put it in the fancy language that he liked to use, "We do hereby strictly forbid all our loving subjects from taking possession of any of these lands." Americans had no trouble understanding what he meant. The French had valued North America mostly for the furs that it supplied; French merchants bought these furs cheaply from the Indian trappers and then sold them for a fat profit on the European market. But if American pioneers crossed into Louisiana with their axes and rifles, they would kill the Indians, cut down the trees and drive away the fur-bearing animals. The British, who wanted to take over the fur trade, weren't about to let this happen.

At the same time that this royal proclamation appeared, George announced that he was going to keep an army of 10,000 men at all times in the New World for what he called "imperial defense." Events that had taken place in the spring of 1763 were still very much on the royal mind. At that time Pontiac, chief of the Ottawas, had united a dozen midwestern tribes in revolt against British rule, seized several forts, and set the whole frontier from New York to Virginia ablaze with warfare.

This news was not welcome to the colonists. They believed, along with most English people, that soldiers should take off their uniforms at the end of a war and go home. Peacetime or "standing"

armies, as they were then called, cost a lot of money. All armies did in time of peace was march up and down and fire off their guns for practice. They didn't work in the fields or contribute in any way to their keep. They had to be clothed and fed; and, of course, they needed pocket money.

When 10,000 men eat three meals a day, somebody has to pick up the tab. George III decided that the Americans must pay the bill. Were they not, after all, the ones who would get the most protection out of this imperial defense? In order to make this possible, the British Parliament passed the Stamp Act in 1765. All colonists, said the act, must as of November 1, 1765, pay a tax to Great Britain whenever they bought a newspaper, a pack of playing cards, or a pair of dice. The money raised by these and many other such taxes would be paid into His Majesty's treasury and then used to pay the army's bills.

How would this work? Suppose you are publishing a newspaper called the *Pennsylvania Gazette*, which you sell once a week for three pennies (3p.). Under the terms of the Stamp Act, before you may sell a single copy of the *Gazette*, you will have to go to a royal agent and buy a sheet of one-penny (1p.) stamps; then you will have to stick one stamp upon each copy of the newspaper. People who want to buy the *Gazette* will now have to pay not 3p. but 4p. for it. Assuming that 1,000 people buy the *Gazette* each week, the king will be richer at the end of each week by 1,000p., or £10.0 (under Britain's modern currency system), which is the same thing.

In passing the Stamp Act, Parliament broke a rule that the colonists thought of as the very foundation of the British constitution: Only assemblies elected by the colonists themselves had the right to decide how much money should be raised by taxation, how it should be raised, and upon what it should be spent. Long experience had shown that if kings took money from people as they pleased, without asking permission, they often used it for wicked purposes or wasted it in all kinds of stupid or selfish ways—like starting unnecessary wars or building luxurious palaces. The imperial government, of course, actually did need money for "imperial defense"; but the Parliament in London had given it permission to lay taxes, or duties, on goods that were carried by ship between England, the colonies, and the outside world. Americans, indeed, were already paying taxation in the form of duties on furs, wheat, tobacco and other items that they shipped out of the country.

News of the passage of the Stamp Act arrived in America in May of 1765. The Virginia Assembly—or House of Burgesses, as it was called—was meeting in Williamsburg at the time. This little town had been the colony's capital for nearly 70 years. Its 300 houses were clustered between the York and James rivers in a land of broad tobacco plantations, stately mansions and slave cabins. Williamsburg had a single street. The town, as one visitor said at the time, "is very disagreeable to walk in.... There is no shade or shelter to walk under unless you carry an umbrella."

Spring had come and was almost gone. The burgesses, or representatives, were itching to leave their stuffy meeting hall and to head home. George Washington was among them. A planter's son, Washington had fought in the Seven Years War against the French—the same war during which James Wolfe was killed at Quebec—and left the military service in 1759. That year he married a wealthy lady, Martha Custis, and soon settled down on the family estate at Mount Vernon, on the Potomac. By 1765, Washington was a respected leader of Virginia society and the master of 135 black slaves. He and other senior members of the House must have been a little surprised when a young lawyer stood up on May 29 and made a bold attack on the British government.

This young man was from Louisa County and his name was Patrick Henry. He had a number of proposals, or resolutions, which he hoped the members of the assembly would agree to. One of these proposals stated that nobody had the right to lay taxes upon Virginians except the Virginia Assembly itself. Henry told the burgesses bluntly that if the king were allowed to tax Americans as and when he pleased, they would no longer have any control over what he—or his American governors—did. It would mean the end of British freedom in America.

An angry debate followed. None of it was written down, but the memory lingers. "Tarquin and Caesar," thundered Henry, "each had his Brutus, Charles I his Cromwell, and George III may profit from their example." Some of the listeners must have turned pale when they heard these words. Tarquin and Caesar were rulers of ancient Rome; one lost his throne, the other his life on account of his evil deeds. As for Charles I of England, the memory of his misdeeds was still fresh in American minds when Henry spoke. Charles was king of England from 1625 until 1649, at the very time that the first settlements were being made along the Atlantic coast. During the 1630s he had forced English people to pay taxes that Parliament had not discussed or consented to. If they refused to pay these taxes, Charles put them in prison and kept them there as long as he pleased, sometimes until they died. Oliver Cromwell was one of the leaders of the revolutionary movement that made war against the king, caught him, and in the end executed him.

As news of the debate spread through town, a young lawyer quit his office and hurried over to the House of Burgesses to listen. Thomas Jefferson was at the time 22 years old. The son of a rich tobacco grower, he had come to Williamsburg in 1760 to go to school at the College of William and Mary; two years later he had begun work in a law office in town. In 1768 he would be chosen a member of that same House where he now heard Patrick Henry speak.

When the debate was finished, the House of Burgesses passed Henry's resolutions, and these appeared in print in many newspapers. Soon the country was alive with protest against the Stamp Act. Committees that called themselves the Sons of

Liberty organized street parades and demonstrations. Burning houses, bonfires, dummies dangling from trees—sent a clear message to the agents whom the king had appointed to sell the stamps: *Resign your jobs, or get out of town.*

Early in 1766 the British Government gave in and repealed, or withdrew, the Stamp Act. The colonists, of course, were very happy about this, and they held all sorts of parties and celebrations. But it wasn't long before a new British finance minister was appointed, named Charles Townshend, who returned to the attack. In 1767 Townshend persuaded Parliament to pass a law that required Americans to pay taxes—or, as he called them, *duties*—on a number of items that they imported from England, like glass, tea, paper and lead. These new taxes were labeled the Townshend Duties.

The Townshend Duties sparked the same kind of resistance as before; but this time it was Boston, in Massachusetts, not Virginia, that led the fight. By 1767 Boston had grown, like Philadelphia, into a prosperous seaport that provided a living for 16,000 people. Boston was also the capital of the colony of Massachusetts. When George III sent over a flock of tax officers in 1767 to collect the new duties, His Majesty's custom house on King Street in Boston became the headquarters of this fresh effort to make the Americans contribute to the cost of imperial defense.

Again the people came out into the streets, led this time by Boston sailors and dockworkers who were soon throwing stones at the British officials and breaking the windows of their houses. These Boston workers had their own scores to settle with the British. Some of them had in the past been kidnaped and dragged off to serve against their wills on British men-of-war. Others risked the loss of their jobs if American ships were seized and sold because they had tried to smuggle goods in without paying the duties.

Now the government in England decided that there must be no more demonstrations, no more challenges to its authority; the colonists must be made to obey the law. In October 1768, a fleet of warships dropped anchor in Boston harbor, with the muzzles of their cannon trained upon the town. Two regiments of soldiers landed, with drums rolling and flags flying, and pitched their tents on Boston Common.

This show of force didn't scare the Sons of Liberty; they asked the townspeople to sign a paper promising that they would not buy any British goods at all until the Townshend Duties had been withdrawn. The Daughters of Liberty joined them in this "Don't Buy British" movement. These were women of all ages who learned to spin and weave so that they might clothe their families with American-made cloth. A charming song appealed to women to make sacrifices for the American cause:

> *Young ladies in town, and those that live round,*
> *Wear none but your own country linen;*
> *Of economy boast, let your pride be the most,*
> *To show clothes of your own make and spinning.*
> *What if homespun they say, be not quite so gay*
> *As brocades, be not in a passion;*
> *For once it is known, 'tis much worn in town,*
> *One and all will cry out, 'tis the fashion!*

The British troops remained in Boston for 18 months. The Bostonians hated them for their bad manners, their brutality, their drunken behavior and their thieving ways. Soldiers and civilians traded jeers and sometimes blows. As for Boston women, they did not escape insult, attack and even rape.

In the evening of March 5, 1770, the pent-up fury of the Bostonians boiled over in an incident that led to violence and death. The streets were lit by a new moon and covered by a light mantle of snow. As so often before, soldiers fought with townspeople, insults were hurled, blows exchanged. Then the crowd flocked to the custom house on King Street, where a lone soldier stood on guard. *Kill him!* the crowd howled. *Knock him down!* Terrified, the man yelled for help; seven more soldiers and their captain marched out of the nearby guardhouse and took positions in front of the custom house. As Andrew, a slave, later told it, "A stout man with a long cordwood stick threw himself in and made a blow at the officer ... *Kill the dogs,* he cried, *knock them over!*" Then a soldier yelled *Fire!* and seven shots rang out. Five men were killed and three were wounded. Among the dead was the "stout man" who had led the attack. He was a black dockworker named Crispus Attucks, who had probably once been a slave.

Such was the Boston Massacre. The British soldiers had only been defending themselves against the fury of the mob; but Americans saw them as symbols and instruments of British tyranny, greed and illegal taxation. So great was the anger aroused by the Boston Massacre that the British government was once more obliged to bow its head before the storm. The Townshend Duties were withdrawn—all except for a tax on tea—and the troops sailed away.

People were happy with this victory, but Samuel Adams, who was the leader of the Boston resistance movement, looked ahead to fresh struggles. In 1770 Sam Adams—tax collector, politician, an able organizer and writer—was 48 years of age. In 1767 he took the lead in the movement against the Townshend Duties. In 1772 he persuaded the townspeople to set up a group and to "enter into correspondence" with other towns in Massachusetts. This Committee of Correspondence was a very important step. What Sam was actually doing was setting up a "shadow government" that could organize resistance to the British throughout Massachusetts whenever the time came. So successful was Adams in this that soon the Boston committee was in touch with hundreds of other committees in Massachusetts alone. Networks of the same type came into being as people in the other colonies followed this example.

In 1773 the British tried once more to tax the Americans. The scheme was to bring a huge amount of tea over from India and sell it to the Americans, tax included, at a price so low that people would not be able to resist buying it. The American reaction was just the same as before. When the tea ships began to arrive in the American ports—New York, Philadelphia, Charleston and Boston—the people would not let the sailors unload it or the merchants sell it. It had to be shipped back to England, or else it just rotted on the docks. As for the Bostonians, they took violent action when it became clear that the royal governor of Massachusetts, Thomas Hutchinson, was going to unload the tea under the protection of British troops. On December 16, 1773, men in disguise boarded three tea ships in the harbor, seized 340 tea chests, broke them open and tossed the contents into the sea. Such was the Boston Tea Party.

Britain swiftly answered this act of defiance. On May 17, 1774, the British fleet sailed back into Boston harbor and prepared to set up a blockade of the port, cutting off its seaborne trade. Pay for the spoiled tea, the king told the Bostonians, "make proper submission," or starve. All summer long British troops poured back into town. By August 14,000 soldiers were there, crammed into whatever barns or warehouses could be found to shelter them. This time, evidently, the imperial government was not going to back down.

On May 24, the Virginia House of Burgesses met and decreed that June 1, when the blockade of Boston was to begin, should be set aside as a day of prayer, when the burgesses would ask God "to give us one heart and mind firmly to oppose ... every injury to American rights."

The Coming of the Revolutionary War

The Virginians also called upon patriots everywhere to elect delegates to a Continental Congress, to meet and to decide what was to be done in this new crisis. In September of 1774, 54 men assembled in Philadelphia for the first meeting of this new, all-American group that would direct the struggle against Great Britain until the end of the

Revolutionary War. One of those who came to Philadelphia was John Adams, a cousin of Sam Adams and an ambitious young Boston lawyer. From New York came Philip Livingston, a wealthy merchant; from Virginia, George Washington and Patrick Henry. South Carolina sent Henry Middleton, one of its wealthiest planters and the owner of 800 slaves.

John Adams boarded the coach for the trip to Philadelphia on August 10; his wife, Abigail, watched him with a heavy heart. America and Britain, clearly enough, were moving towards war. On her shoulders alone would fall the burden of running the Adams farm and caring for their five children. "The great distance between us," she wrote to her husband, "makes the time appear very long to me … The great anxiety I feel for my country, for you and for our family renders the day tedious and the night unpleasant … Did any kingdom or state regain its liberty when once it was invaded, without bloodshed? I cannot think of it without horror."

As for John and the rest of the Massachusetts delegation, they drove along the Post Road west to Springfield, then down the beautiful Connecticut River, with people waving and cheering as the coach rolled by. "As we came into New Haven," he wrote in his diary, "all the bells in the town were set to ringing, and the people—men, women and children—were crowding at the doors and windows as if it was a coronation." Hot, dusty and tired, the party arrived in Philadelphia on August 29, after being on the road for nearly three weeks. They had traveled as fast as they could—about 12 miles a day—for they were on urgent business.

Congress held its first meeting on September 5; and it decided to send a letter to the king, urging him to lift the Boston blockade. "We will never," Congress told His Majesty, "submit to be hewers of wood or drawers of water for any nation in the world." Soon militiamen were marching up and down on village greens, and towns began gathering supplies of ammunition. Americans were preparing

to fight a government that they no longer trusted, that they were beginning to view as an enemy.

When the British navy arrived in Boston in 1774, it had brought with it a new commander-in-chief of His Majesty's forces in America, General Sir Thomas Gage. On the night of April 18, 1775, a year after his arrival, Gage sent troops to seize rebel supplies at Concord and to arrest rebel leaders there. This marked the beginning of the Revolutionary War. How Dr. Joseph Warren gave warning of the British troop movement and how Paul Revere the silversmith carried the warning through the countryside is a well-known, often-told story. When dawn broke, the Lexington militia were drawn up on the village green, waiting for the British to pass through. As John Robbins, a Lexington militiaman, later recalled, "There suddenly appeared a number of the King's troops, about a thousand, as I thought, at the distance of about sixty or seventy yards from us, with three officers in their front on horseback and on a full gallop towards us, the foremost of whom cried, *Throw down your arms, ye villains, ye rebels.*" Then came the British command: *Fire, by God, fire.* Eight militiamen fell dead.

Elizabeth Clarke, daughter of Lexington's minister, the Reverend Jonas Clarke, was 12 years old at the time. She was present at the funeral of the eight men who were the first to die in the revolutionary struggle. Years later, when she was an old woman of 78, she told about it in a letter to her niece.

"In the afternoon," she wrote, "Father, Mother with me and the Baby went to the Meeting House, there was the eight men that was killed … all in Boxes made of four large Boards Nailed up." After a brief ceremony, the coffins were placed upon two carts and drawn by horses to the graveyard. "There," Elizabeth went on, "we followed the bodies of those first slain … There I stood and there I saw them let down into the ground."

Elizabeth and her family waited there in a light rain until the trench dug to receive the bodies had been filled with earth. "And then," she added, "for fear the British should find them, my Father thought that some of the men had best cut some pine or oak boughs and spread them on their place of burial so that it looked like a heap of brush."

The British moved on to Concord, found the guns and powder they were after, and destroyed them. At three o'clock in the afternoon, they began the long march back to Boston. It was a tormenting experience. Armed colonists hid behind walls and trees, waited for the British to appear, and picked them off as they passed by. These New Englanders were, as one British officer noted, "good marksmen, and many of them used long guns made for duck shooting." They killed 20 British soldiers this way and wounded 200 more. Long after night had fallen, Gage's troops were still limping wearily back to town. A thousand campfires burning in the surrounding fields told the British that they themselves were now under siege.

When Congress heard about the events at Lexington and Concord, it decided to raise an army of 20,000 men. These men were called Continental soldiers because they promised to fight for a full year anywhere on the continent that the commander-in-chief might send them. Continental troops often fought alongside of militiamen; soldiers in the militia, however, were troops raised and paid not by the Continental Congress but by the separate colonies or states. In the colonial tradition all able-bodied men, from boys of 16 to men in their sixties, were obliged to fight in militia companies if the colony in which they lived was invaded, say, by the French or by Indians. But militiamen fought only on their own home ground; nobody had the power to make them fight outside of the colony in which they lived.

Congress also appointed George Washington commander-in-chief of the American military forces. The general hastened off to join the Massachusetts militia that was besieging Boston. He made his headquarters in the little village of Cambridge, at a college named in honor of a Puritan minister, John Harvard. Upon his death in 1638, Harvard had left the college his library of 300 books.

Abigail Adams's dismay when she saw her husband leave home and the country inching daily towards war was shared by many other people throughout the colonies. There was everywhere, as one newspaper, the *Constitutional Gazette*, reported, "a prejudice of the mind against the doctrine of independence;" there was still, in spite of the blood shed at Lexington and Concord, a deep hope that somehow reconciliation with Great Britain might be achieved. Britain was the world's greatest empire, with the wealth to put great armies in the field and keep them there; she had well-trained generals, factories in which cannon could be cast, and a navy that commanded the seven seas. The Americans, by contrast, were a poor and scattered people who in 1775 numbered at most 2,500,000, with no navy and no money to raise and supply a large army. Five hundred thousand of her people were black slaves; many of these would not be permitted to fight. Surely, people thought to themselves, reconciliation under these circumstances made much more sense than war.

In January 1776, while the British were still bottled up in Boston, a pamphlet called *Common Sense* appeared. The writer of this essay was Tom Paine, a poor English immigrant who had arrived in Philadelphia in 1774. Paine boldly defended the idea of independence. "Everything," he cried, "that is right and natural pleads for separation. The blood of the slain, the weeping voice of nature cries, '*Tis time to part*." Americans, he told his readers, must not only *decide* to be free of England, they must *tell the world* that freedom was what they were fighting for. If, he argued, Congress proclaimed independence, Americans would not just be rebels against the British government but a new people with a new government all their own. Congress could then send agents to Europe to win help for the American cause in men, money, ships and guns. As for the American cause, he wrote, it was a righteous one, and one worth dying for. "The sun," he said,

never shined on a cause of greater worth. 'Tis not the affair of a city, a county, a province, or a kingdom, but of a continent—at least one eighth part of the habitable globe. 'Tis not the concern of a day, a year, or an age; posterity are virtually involved in the contest, and will be more or less affected, even to the end of time, by the proceedings now.

Common Sense was a sensation; copies were passed from hand to hand and read until they became tattered. "That's exactly right," people told each other. "That's exactly what I've been thinking, but I couldn't say it half as well!"

Soon Congress itself was swept away in this new enthusiasm to be rid of Great Britain, and in June of 1776 it set up a committee to prepare a Declaration of Independence. Thomas Jefferson, a member of the committee, wrote the first draft, which the committee gave to Congress at the end of June. Congress then examined what he had written, made some important changes and adopted the revised Declaration on July 4.

In the Declaration Jefferson explained that Americans, like all people in the world, had a right to a decent government to help them lead lives that were both happy and free; but the British government had shown itself to be evil. To prove this charge he listed many of the grievances that Americans had against the British government, such as keeping a standing army in the colonies, which it used to bully the people and to take their freedom away. He ended by saying that for these reasons the Americans had decided to free themselves of the British government and to set up a new one of their very own that could do a better job of protecting their rights. The American colonies, Jefferson told the world, had now become free and independent states, with full power "to make war,

conclude peace ... and do all other acts and things which independent states may of right do."

In the Declaration of Independence the 13 states told the world that they were free and independent, and also that they were united. The 13 states joined together in 1776 for just one reason: to make war against England and to pool manpower, leadership and wealth so that this war might be waged as effectively as possible. The "United States" had no power, no money and no men except what the 13 independent states gave to it of their own free will. The "United States" at that time was also called "the Confederation," which is another word for "alliance of states."

Messengers soon rode out of Philadelphia, taking copies of the Declaration of Independence to all 13 states. Everywhere people assembled on the town commons and in the public squares to listen and to cheer as the ringing phrases of the Declaration were read to them. Soldiers marched, batteries of guns were fired, bonfires were lit and fireworks were set off. In some places, as in Newport, Rhode Island, 13 guns were fired, one for each of the states that were now proclaiming independence.

Not everybody greeted the Declaration of Independence with such enthusiasm. There were still many people who opposed independence and longed for reconciliation with the Crown. There's no way to tell exactly how many such *Loyalists* there were, but their numbers certainly ran to many thousands. Loyalists were to be found in all classes of society—in the towns, in the countryside and on the frontier. Slaves and indentured servants were also to be found among them, especially after the governor of Virginia, Earl Dunmore, promised freedom to such people if they joined the British forces. "I do ... declare," said he, in his emancipation proclamation of November 7, 1775, "all indentured servants, Negroes, or others, [belonging] to rebels, FREE, that are willing and able to bear arms, they joining his Majesty's troops, as soon as may be."

This engraving shows the fire that engulfed New York on September 21, 1776, and consumed the eastern side of the city, "the wind blowing very fresh from the south," as the *New York Gazette* reported, "and the weather exceeding dry ... Several women and children perished in the fire. Their shrieks, joined to the roaring of the flames, the crash of falling houses, and the widespread ruin that everywhere appeared, formed a scene of horror beyond description." The fire raged for ten hours before burning itself out.

Loyalists made a valuable contribution to the British cause during the Revolutionary War as soldiers, sailors, writers and spies. On many battlefields Americans confronted not only British soldiers but other Americans as well. This gave the struggle the character of a civil war.

That same month of July 1776, the British launched an attack to end the rebellion. Their plan was first to take New York City, then occupy the Hudson Valley and the Lake Champlain waterway with ships and troops. Success in this operation would seal off the New England states from all the others. The Crown could then move ahead at its own pace to reconquer New England and, after that, the rest of the country.

At first all went well for the British. Their commander-in-chief was now Sir William Howe, a fine soldier who was fond of the Americans and who had taken part with James Wolfe in the storming of

Quebec in 1759. Howe's troopships and men-of-war streamed into New York harbor all through July. "So vast a fleet," as one observer wrote, "was never before seen in the port of New York ... the multitude of masts carries the appearance of a wood." Howe landed his forces on Staten Island. On August 22 he struck, falling first upon the American encampment at Brooklyn village, then upon Manhattan. Washington's army fled in panic northward to White Plains, westward across the Hudson, southward through New Jersey to the Delaware River. The British took hundreds of prisoners, many of them teenage boys, as well as a young Connecticut schoolteacher named Nathan Hale. Caught behind the British lines, Hale was hanged in Manhattan as a spy on September 21. He made a short speech from the gallows. "The British," he said, "are shedding the blood of the innocent. If I had ten thousand lives I would lay them all down in defense of this injured, bleeding country."

As winter closed in, the American army melted away. Many of Washington's soldiers had been taken prisoner by the British during the campaign. Many more were lacking the warm clothes and camp equipment that they needed in order to face winter in the field; many had farms and families that needed them. By December 20, Washington had not much more than 1,000 men under his command. "The game is nearly up," he wrote. "Ten more days will put an end to the existence of our army."

But the commander-in-chief still refused to admit defeat. On Christmas Day he attacked Trenton from across the Delaware in the face of a freezing storm. Trenton was occupied by Hessian troops, men whom the English king had recruited in Germany and paid so that they would fight for him. Such soldiers are called *mercenaries*— people, that is, who fight and kill because it's their job and because they get paid for it. Washington took the Hessian mercenaries by surprise as they were trimming up their Christmas trees; they soon surrendered.

The people of New Jersey were so inspired by this success that they began to wage their own war against the British—hiding behind stone walls and picking off the enemy troops wherever they found them. So fiercely did these people fight that Howe was forced to pull back his forces into Manhattan. By the spring of 1777, all of New Jersey was free of British and German troops.

That year the British continued to carry out their plan of action. Taking Manhattan had been the first step. Next, one army was supposed to move down from Canada, occupying the Lake Champlain water route, and another was to move up the Hudson Valley from New York. The two forces were supposed to meet at Albany, thus splitting the rebellious colonies into two parts.

The army heading south from Canada was under the command of General Sir John Burgoyne.

"Gentleman Johnny," as he was called, liked making war, and he liked doing it in style, carrying wine, women and silken clothing with him in his baggage train. Burgoyne did his share by sailing his army all the way down Lake Champlain in June and early July. But Sir William Howe, instead of taking his army *up* the valley from New York, sailed his men down the Atlantic coast in the opposite direction.

Nobody since has ever really been able to explain very well why Howe did this; it was a decision that sealed Burgoyne's fate and brought the Americans one step closer to final victory over the British. Early in July, Burgoyne seized Fort Ticonderoga at the head of Lake George and then marched his army overland to the Hudson River, reaching Fort Edward at the end of the month. There he became bogged down, with an army under General Horatio Gates in front of him and swarms of militiamen in his rear, cutting off his vital supply lines to Canada. Early in September, Burgoyne crossed to the west side of the Hudson, hoping to move southward to Albany. To halt this advance, General Gates fortified Bemis Heights, a thickly wooded plateau that dominated the narrow path between the hills and the river. Here Burgoyne fought two bloody and costly battles in a futile effort to break through the American lines.

The first of these battles, known as the Battle of Freeman's Farm, took place on September 19. Benedict Arnold, a dashing soldier from Connecticut, commanded the left wing of the American forces. When the second engagement took place on October 7, General Gates and Arnold had quarreled, and Gates had taken away Arnold's command. But this did not stop him from galloping into the thick of battle and leading furious and heroic attacks that finally put the British to flight. Arnold's horse was killed under him, and he himself had his leg shattered by a bullet.

Ten days later Burgoyne's army surrendered at Saratoga, a few miles north of Bemis Heights. It was the greatest of American military triumphs. As for Arnold, he was now known and loved as America's bravest soldier.

While all this was going on, Howe had landed his troops at the tip of Chesapeake Bay and then marched northward to occupy Philadelphia early in September. George Washington offered some resistance but then fell back; he took his army in December 1777 into winter quarters at Valley Forge, on the wooded slopes of the Schuylkill River, some 18 miles from Philadelphia. There the patriot army kept watch on Sir William through the long winter months. There they froze and starved in the silence and the snow. Without shirts, boots, or blankets, the barefoot army, as one soldier wrote, "might be tracked by their blood upon the rough, frozen ground."

In May 1778, good news arrived from France: Louis XVI, impressed with American fighting abilities as shown in the 1777 campaigns, had signed an alliance with the United States. The two countries would fight together against their common enemy; just as Tom Paine had foreseen, the Revolution would now get help from France in men, money, arms and ships. There was a big parade at Valley Forge in celebration of the alliance with France; men marched, cannon boomed, fifes squealed. The officers had a party with wine and cheese, and toasts were drunk: "To the King of France! To the American states!"

The British received the news with gloom. What had begun as a mere colonial rebellion had suddenly blossomed into a world war; the British empire was on one side and France, along with her ally, Spain, on the other. Sir William Howe gave up his position as commander-in-chief of His Majesty's American forces; he was replaced by Sir Henry Clinton, a skinny, sour-faced and humorless man who had arrived with Howe at Boston in 1775.

Clinton decided to abandon Philadelphia and to return to New York City; he had no wish to find his forces blockaded in Philadelphia by a hostile French fleet. On May 18 he threw a farewell party for the army's Loyalist friends. People dressed up

This engraving of Arnold is from a painting by John Trumbull (1756–1843), a famous artist some of whose historical pictures hang in the rotunda of the Capitol, in Washington, D.C. The son of a governor of Connecticut, Trumbull became an aide of General Washington's in 1775, then went to London to study art. Trumbull painted many pictures showing famous events and people of the Revolutionary War era.

in fancy dress as medieval knights, squires and pages. Loyalist women came in gold, blue and scarlet gowns. There were fireworks when it got dark and, late at night, a grand supper for the officers and their ladies.

When it was all over, the British left. Early in June 1778 they made the long, slow march back to New York across the Jersey meadowlands. More than three years had passed since the first shots of the war were fired at Lexington; the British had nothing at all to show for the money they had spent and the blood they had shed except two islands off the North American coast—Manhattan in New York, and Newport in Narragansett Bay, Rhode Island.

American hopes had been raised high by the conclusion of the alliance with France in the spring of 1778; but these hopes were not fulfilled. The French navy arrived and left again. The bright promises of spring faded. The colonists' cause faced its darkest hour. The years 1778 and 1789,

Ballad of Major André

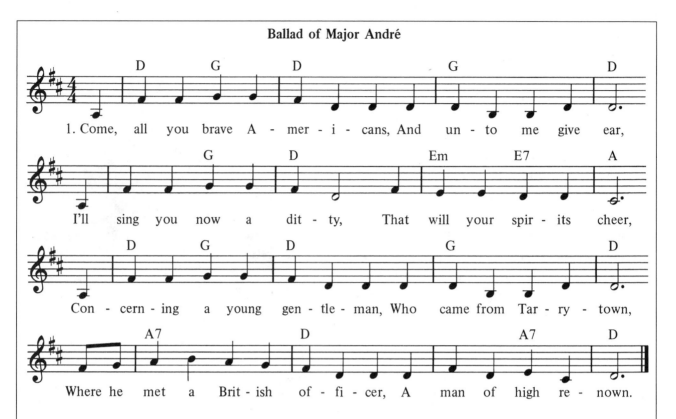

1. Come, all you brave A - mer - i - cans, And un - to me give ear,
I'll sing you now a dit - ty, That will your spir - its cheer,
Con - cern - ing a young gen - tle - man, Who came from Tar - ry - town,
Where he met a Brit - ish of - fi - cer, A man of high re - nown.

2. Then up spoke this young hero,
Young Paulding was his name;
"O tell us where you're going, sir,
And also whence you came."
"I bear the British flag, sir,"
Up answered bold André,
"I have a pass that takes me through,
I have no time to stay."

3. Then others came around him,
And bade him to dismount:
"Come tell us where you're going,
Give us a strict account;"
Young Paulding said, "We are resolved
That you shall ne'er pass by;"
And so the evidence did prove
The prisoner a spy.

4. He begged for his liberty,
He pled for his discharge,
And oftentimes he told them,
If they'd set him at large,
"Of all the gold and silver
I have laid up in store,
But when I reach the city
I will send you ten times more."

5. "We scorn this gold and silver
You have laid up in store,"
Van Vert and Paulding both did cry,
"You need not send us more."
He saw that his conspiracy
Would soon be brought to light,
He begged for pen and paper
And he asked for to write.

6. The story came to Arnold
Commanding at the Fort:
He called for the Vulture
And sailed for New York;
Now Arnold to New York has gone,
A-fighting for his King,
And left poor Major André
On the gallows for to swing.

7. André was executed,
He looked both meek and mild,
His face was fair and handsome,
And pleasantly he smiled.
It moved each eye with pity,
And every heart there bled,
And everyone wished him released
And Arnold in his stead.

8. He was a man of honor!
In Britain he was born,
To die upon the gallows
Most highly he did scorn.
And now his life has reached its end
So young and blooming still—
In Tappan's quiet countryside
He sleeps upon the hill.

This ballad telling the story of Major André was part of the singing tradition of the Hudson Valley until the early 20th century.

An American battery at the siege of Yorktown.

when Benedict Arnold was military commander of Philadelphia, were a time of stalemate in the struggle against the British. The patriots had little in the way of money, weapons, ships, or well-equipped soldiers; there was no way for them to dislodge the British from their New York and Rhode Island bases.

The British, on their side, did not have the power to move inland and conquer the Americans throughout their spacious country. They launched, instead, cruel raids upon coastal towns and frontier settlements, burning, robbing and killing. This, they considered, might be the easiest way of breaking the American will to resist, of bringing the rebels, as they put it, "to a sense of their duty."

The winters of the late 1770s were unusually cold, and the winter of 1779–1780 was the coldest of them all. Roads were impassable, supplies were cut off, soldiers starved. "I did not put a single morsel in my mouth for four days," wrote one

soldier, Joseph Martin, "except a little bit of birch bark I gnawed off a stick of wood."

Civilians, too, suffered bitterly. The snow lay so thick upon the ground in New England that wood to warm people's houses could not be brought in with wagons and ox teams. Men hauled in the logs upon hand sleds, along narrow icy paths that they beat through the woods. In places where teams could go out, men and beasts froze in their tracks. No water flowed in the icebound streams; mills could grind no grain, and many went hungry. As for horses, cattle and sheep, they starved to death.

In the spring of 1780, Sir Henry Clinton took the offensive with an invasion of the South. In April the British army and navy laid siege to Charleston, South Carolina, and seized the town on May 12. They had won a key port and several thousand prisoners. Sir Henry then sailed back to New York, leaving to Lord Charles Cornwallis the job of "pacifying" the South.

41

Lord Cornwallis, followed by his troops, passes between the French and American ranks at the surrender ceremony, October 19, 1781. The painting, by John Trumbull, hangs in the Capitol.

To carry out this pacification, Cornwallis had to seek out and destroy the Continental army and whatever militia forces were in the field. In August 1780 he made a good start in this direction by meeting the forces of General Horatio Gates at Camden, South Carolina, and putting them to rout.

Cornwallis now planned to move into North Carolina, with his army marching in three columns—up the coast, in the center, and in the hilly country to the west. The last of these columns was composed of loyalist troops under Major Patrick Ferguson. But Ferguson, whom the patriots hated for his brutality, became separated from the other British forces. He and his men camped on King's Mountain, a rocky height just south of the North Carolina border. "I hold a position," he boasted to Cornwallis, "that all the rebels out of hell cannot drive me from!"

On October 7, 1780, the patriots stormed King's Mountain and overran it. The whole loyalist force, 1100 men, was killed, wounded, or taken prisoner. James Collins, a 16-year-old with the patriot militia, described the scene: "The wives and children of the poor Tories [loyalists] came in," he wrote, "in great numbers. Their husbands, fathers, and brothers lay dead in heaps, while others lay wounded or dying."

This defeat discouraged loyalists from rallying to Cornwallis, and it was a severe blow to his prospects for victory. With the South in arms against him, he decided to move northward to Virginia. It was a wealthy state and could provide food and forage for his men and horses. Other British generals, too, like Benedict Arnold, were operating there.

After a long overland march Cornwallis arrived in Virginia in April 1781; he settled down in Yorktown, at the tip of the York River peninsula on Chesapeake Bay, and made it the base of his operations. Actually Cornwallis was walking into a trap, which Washington now hastened to close.

By August a huge French force, under Admiral de Grasse, with 34 men-of-war and 3,000 troops, had arrived off Chesapeake Bay and was ready for action. Early in September, de Grasse beat off a British fleet that was coming to Cornwallis's assistance; by the end of the month Washington's army was laying siege to Yorktown by land. On October 19 Cornwallis's army, starving and out of supplies, marched out of Yorktown and laid down its arms. It was a dramatic scene. French and American forces, according to an American army doctor, James Thatcher, "were drawn up in two lines extending more than a mile in length. The Americans were drawn up in a line on the right side of the road, and the French occupied the left."

The British troops came out of Yorktown "in a slow and solemn step, with shouldered arms, colors cased and drums beating a British march." This was a colossal disaster for the British: It marked, in effect, the end of the War of American Independence.

* * * *

England and the United States signed the Treaty of Paris in 1783. Britain recognized the United States as an independent country and surrendered all the land lying between the Appalachians and the Mississippi, land she had herself won from France by the Treaty of Paris in 1763.

Treaty of Paris, 1783

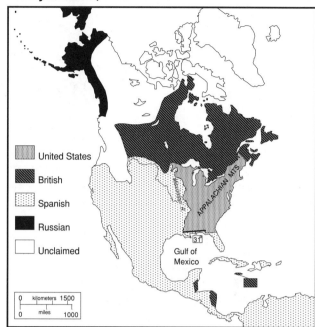

Americans won a great deal from the Revolutionary War—independence, an empire of land, the right to develop a country with flourishing industry and worldwide trade. The Revolution was a big success, but it remained incomplete. The ideals expressed by the Declaration of Independence, promising freedom and equality for all, were only partially fulfilled. Millions of black people and women would, in the years to come, embark upon fresh struggles for freedom, for equality with white men, for their own place in the sun.

BENEDICT ARNOLD, JOHN ANDRE, AND PEGGY SHIPPEN

The master of ceremonies at the British farewell party on May 18, 1778 in Philadelphia was John André, a young English captain who had marched into the city with Howe in the fall of 1777. He had enjoyed his winter's stay in Philadelphia, having passed time in the company of a pretty 17-year-old, Margaret Shippen. Peggy's father, Edward, was a well-known judge. The Shippens were a respected family with Loyalist convictions.

As soon as the British had gone, George Washington marched back into his capital; he made General Benedict Arnold the commander of the city. Arnold was at the height of his fame as America's bravest soldier. Late in 1775 he had led a group of men across the wilds of Maine in a freezing blizzard to make a bold but fruitless attack upon the fortress of Quebec. By his stand at Valcour Island he had held back the British when they advanced down Lake Champlain in October 1776. The following year his leadership had contributed much to Burgoyne's defeat at Saratoga, and he suffered a broken leg in that action.

Soon after reaching Philadelphia, Arnold met Peggy Shippen and fell in love with her. The two were wed early in 1779. Arnold found his wife fascinating. She spared neither time nor effort to shake his Patriot convictions and to convince him that the Loyalist cause was right. By this time John André was Clinton's chief assistant. From then on, Arnold and André were regularly in touch with each other.

The following year, after long negotiations, Arnold offered to bring about the surrender of West Point and its garrison to the British for £20,000.

At the outbreak of the war in 1775, West Point was a village on the west bank of the Hudson River, some fifty miles north of New York City. It is a spot

John André was hanged at the American military headquarters, Tappan, New Jersey, on October 2, 1780, clothed in full dress uniform. This engraving was made in 1783.

where the waters flow in a narrow channel between steep banks and mountain ridges. After the victory at Saratoga in 1777, Washington began to realize how important West Point was, and he built a fort there. If West Point were in American hands, no British warship could sail through the channel. But if the British controlled the pass, they could take their fleet clear up to Albany, which would give them control of a 150-mile stretch of the Hudson Valley. It would then be easy for them to occupy all of the Lake Champlain waterway and to succeed in doing what Burgoyne had failed to do—seal off communications between New England and the central states.

Following Saratoga the British, too, understood that West Point held the key to success in the struggle for America.

Early in 1780, Benedict Arnold asked Washington to give him the command of West Point; in August Washington, though surprised that a field soldier would want to idle away his time at a defensive post, granted the request. On the evening of September 21, the new commandant stood alone in a forest of firs on the bank of the Hudson south of Haverstraw, some 30 miles below West Point. Soon Major John André joined him; he had been rowed ashore from the British sloop *Vulture* by an accomplice of Arnold's, Joshua Hett Smith.

Arnold and André spent several hours discussing the planned British attack upon the fort and how it was to be surrendered. Having received fire from an American gun battery, the *Vulture* had dropped back downstream; André was therefore obliged to find his way back to New York City by land. Arnold gave him a pass through the American lines, and Smith provided civilian clothes and a horse.

On the evening of September 22 André was ferried back to the eastern bank of the Hudson River. Early the next day he began to make his way south through Orange County; he carried the plans of West Point in his boot. When he reached Tarrytown American militiamen stopped and searched him, and found his papers. The militia commander at once sent a message off to Arnold, warning that he had caught a spy and that an attack upon West Point might be imminent.

This dispatch reached Arnold on September 25th. After saying goodbye to Peggy he mounted his horse, galloped to the river, and had himself rowed downstream to the *Vulture*. Washington, who was on an inspection tour, arrived at Arnold's headquarters just a few minutes after Arnold himself had fled. Hours later a messenger brought a letter addressed to Washington and written by André the previous day. "The person in your possession," it said, "is Major John André, Adjutant General to the British Army."

Taken to Washington's headquarters in Tappan, André was tried, found guilty of espionage, and sentenced to death.

One week later, on Monday October 2, a crowd of soldiers and civilians gathered around a gallows set up on Tappan Hill. A cart with a black coffin in it stood beneath the dangling rope. John André mounted the cart. As one witness recalled, the

Route of Major Andre from Interview with Arnold to his Arrest near Tarrytown

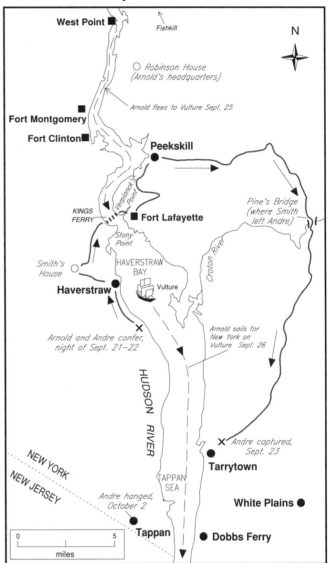

young British major was dressed in full uniform, "coat of the brightest scarlet, faced or trimmed with the most beautiful green … He had a long and beautiful head of hair, which, agreeably to the fashion, was wound with a black ribbon and hung down his back."

André took the rope in his hand, put the noose over his head and adjusted the knot. The wagon was pulled away, the body fell and swung. He remained hanging, as the witness wrote, "more than thirty minutes, and during that time the chambers of death were never stiller than the multitude by which he was surrounded." He was buried on Tappan Hill, and the marker over his grave reads: "His death … moved even his enemies to pity, and both armies mourned the fate of one so young and brave."

* * * *

Arnold's treason cut him off from his native land and earned him the contempt of the British as well. He died in London 20 years later, a lonely and unhappy man. Peggy died in 1803. She bore Arnold four sons, all of whom became officers in the British army, and one daughter, Sophie, who herself became the mother of five children.

4

THE EARLY YEARS OF THE REPUBLIC, 1783–1815

In 1783 the long war was over. Roads were thronged with ragged soldiers heading home; some limped on crutches, some wore coats with a dangling sleeve. These men were leaving the army with empty pockets. George Washington, writing that same year, described them as people who had

shed their blood or lost their limbs in the service of their country, without shelter, without a friend, and without the means of obtaining any of the necessaries or comforts of life, compelled to beg their daily bread from door to door.

Congress had not paid the soldiers the wages that were their due because the federal government had no money. In 1781 the states had agreed upon a constitution for the United States. This constitution was called *The Articles of Confederation*, because it contained 13 separate *articles*, or clauses. Article 8 of this constitution said that Congress should have a Treasury from which it would pay the wages of the soldiers, as well as other expenses of govern-

ment. This sounded fine, but in actual practice the Treasury was nearly always empty. Congress was supposed to set quotas, or amounts of money, which each state was to pay into the Treasury every year. Many states fell behind and failed to pay into the Treasury what they owed. Under the Articles of Confederation, there was nothing at all that Congress could do about this. It couldn't pay its soldiers, and it couldn't do anything else.

In May 1787, four years after the end of the war, 55 men arrived in Philadelphia. Selected by the different states as their delegates, they had come to take part in a meeting to discuss ways to provide the federal government with more power. Among these men who arrived in Philadelphia on horseback, by coach and by ship were some of the most talented leaders in the country.

Alexander Hamilton came from New York. Hamilton was born on the island of St. Christopher, in the West Indies, in 1757, and was left without mother or father at the age of 11. The boy was clearly brilliant; in 1773 friends packed him off to

This picture of a Philadelphia street scene was made in 1800.

King's College, in New York City, to get an education. Like Tom Paine and Thomas Jefferson, Hamilton was soon caught up in the Revolution; in 1776 he was given command of a New York artillery company, and he won Washington's admiration for his coolness under fire and the skill with which he handled both men and guns. The following year the commander-in-chief placed Hamilton on his personal staff, and there he remained until the end of the war. Hamilton then went back to New York to practice law. He soon became known as a champion of the Federalist viewpoint—the opinion that the federal government must be made stronger and more effective.

Benjamin Franklin, now 81 years of age, came to Philadelphia as a Pennsylvania delegate. In 1787 he was perhaps the most famous of all American Revolutionary leaders. Franklin began life as a master printer and made a name for himself in the years 1730 to 1765 as the editor of a Philadelphia newspaper, the *Pennsylvania Gazette*. In 1753 George II made Franklin one of two American postmasters general; he held this position for 20 years and won a reputation for the fine way in which he organized the colonial mail services. For a number of years before the outbreak of the Revolution, Franklin represented Pennsylvania and other colonies as a spokesperson, or agent, in London. He became known not just in America but in

Europe as well for his writings and his scientific experiments. In 1776 the Continental Congress sent Franklin to France as its commissioner, or ambassador. Much of the credit for the French-American alliance that was signed in February 1778 must go to Franklin's skill as a negotiator.

George Washington came to Philadelphia as a delegate from Virginia; he brought with him two of his neighbors, James Madison and George Mason, both of them planters and slaveholders. Madison, who became the fourth president of the United States in 1809, was the only person to keep a really careful record of the discussions that took place at the Philadelphia meeting throughout the summer. Mason was already famous as a constitution maker: He had written the Declaration of Rights that became part of the constitution of Virginia in 1776, and that served as a model for people writing constitutions in the other states.

Next to Washington, Madison, and Mason, the most influential Southerner at the Philadelphia meeting was Pierce Butler, of South Carolina. Butler was a British soldier who came to the colonies before the Revolution, married Polly Middleton, a plantation heiress, and settled down to grow cotton and rice, first in South Carolina and later in Georgia. With many hundreds of slaves, Butler was one of the South's biggest slaveowners.

In 1787 Philadelphia was, by modern standards, quite a small city. The streets were named after trees and shrubs that had grown in the wilderness when the town was first built—like Vine, Walnut and Chestnut. Philadelphia was a market town; twice a week it filled up with noisy country folk crying their wares and selling their produce. But in between market days the place was sleepy enough. "By ten o'clock in the evening," as one visitor wrote, "all is quiet in the streets; the profound silence … is only interrupted by the voices of the watchmen."

The delegates to the Philadelphia meeting—or convention, as they called it—assembled in Carpenter's Hall. All agreed that "nothing spoken in this House be pritned or otherwise published … without leave." The delegates, in other words, were going to meet in secret. There were 10 newspapers being published in Philadelphia in 1787, but not a single one was allowed to send a reporter to cover the discussions. Guards were placed at the doors of Carpenter's Hall; the windows were closed.

Week after week the delegates sat there and debated in the stuffy hall, in the awful summer heat. By early September their job was done. Rather than "improve" or "revise" the Articles of Confederation, they had in fact produced an entirely new body of laws for the United States; and now they were anxious to place their draft before the American people for their approval. Pierce Butler, like the other delegates, was quite worn out by the long summer's effort. But, as he wrote to a friend, if the people liked the new constitution, and it became the law of the land, he would feel well rewarded "for my share of the trouble, and a summer's confinement which injured my health much."

Congress, said the Constitution in its first article, "shall have the power to lay and collect taxes." In these nine words was the essence of the change that the Philadelphia delegates were proposing. For the first time the federal government was granted a power that the American people had denied to the British government itself. This power to extract money from people is the lifeblood of government, and it is called "the power of the purse." Money, as we know, is power. With the power to tax, the federal government could now raise an army, build a navy, hire public servants, set up courts and jails to make sure that its decisions were obeyed.

Clearly enough, the people would not give the federal government this power of the purse unless they had the right to elect their own government officials, unless they had a voice in deciding how much money was to be raised by taxes and what it was to be spent upon. The Constitution, accordingly, set up a House of Representatives to be elected by popular vote; each state was to be given representatives in this House in proportion to its popula-

Here the Constitution was framed during the long hot summer of 1787.

tion: States with more people in them would have more representatives in the House, and therefore more votes, than states with fewer citizens.

This principle, which we call *proportional representation*, was acceptable to the Philadelphia delegates, but they had a rough time working out the details. Were representatives in the House, some asked, to be allotted to a state in proportion to its *total* population, or in proportion to its total *nonslave* population? If representatives were allotted in proportion to total population, then states like Virginia or South Carolina, with many slaves, would have more votes in the House than was fair. Slaves, obviously enough, would not be allowed to vote, nor would they be allowed to have any say in choosing representatives.

There was heated discussion about this at Carpenter's Hall. In the end an agreement was worked out. It was decided that three-fifths of the slaves were to be counted in figuring not only the number of representatives that a state would be allowed but the taxation that it must pay. Later this agreement would be called "the three-fifths compromise."

Some of the people at Carpenter's Hall accepted the idea of a House of Representatives, but they were not happy about it. In their view, popular assemblies, elected by ordinary people, were too "enthusiastic"—liable to be carried away by all sorts of carzy ideas. They looked for a way to put a brake upon such enthusiasm. For this purpose they set up a second lawmaking group called the Senate; and they said that no proposal could become law until it had been passed, not only by the House of Representatives, but by the Senate as well. Each state, whether large or small, would be given two senators. The Senate, as William Morris, a Pennsylvania delegate, put it, "ought to be composed of men of great and established property—an aristocracy … Such an artistocratic body will keep down the turbulency of democracy."

The Constitution gave Congress the power to raise and maintain armies and navies, to deal with "Indian affairs," to operate a mail service and to control trading activities among the different states, as well as between the United States and foreign countries. These were the functions that, during the colonial period had been carried on by the imperial government in London, acting through its colonial governors.

One important clause in the Constitution also gave Congress the right "to provide for calling forth the militia to execute the laws of the Union, suppress insurrections and repel invasions." From now on, if there were an uprising or slave revolt in a given state, the federal government could bring in militiamen from the farthest corner of the Union and send them to the scene of the disturbance to take part in putting it down.

Under the Constitution, Congress would make the laws; a president, holding office for four years,

would carry them out. He would also be commander-in-chief of the armed forces, and he would make treaties with Native American peoples and with foreign countries. He would appoint people to help him do his work—officials like judges, ambassadors and members of his cabinet.

Laws become real when people who refuse to obey them are caught and punished. Here the Constitution did something quite new. It set up a system of federal courts to settle disputes in which the federal government and citizens might become involved, and to punish people who broke a federal law. This meant that the new federal government, unlike the old, could build jails, hire guards, imprison people and even inflict the sentence of death. Under the Articles of Confederation, Congress had possessed none of these powers, not in the slightest degree.

Article VII of the Constitution said that it would become the law of the land if and when the people of nine out of the 13 states voted for it. So from December of 1787 to July of 1788, special assemblies were called together, state by state, to examine the Constitution, to debate its provisions and to approve it. These meetings were called constitutional conventions; the delegates were elected by the voters. This entire process of securing the adoption of the Constitution by the American people was called *ratification.*

During these months the three leading Federalists—Alexander Hamilton, James Madison, and John Jay—put down their ideas about the Constitution in a series of essays known as *The Federalist Papers.* Here they set forth the main reasons why, in their view, the people ought to ratify the document that the Federalists had drafted.

Before the ratification process had even begun, the Federalists realized that they faced an uphill battle in winning popular approval for the Constitution they had created. All the people who for one reason or another disagreed with their proposal for a new government came to be called An-

George Mason, celebrated as the father of the Bill of Rights, is shown at his writing desk at Gunston Hall, his plantation residence in Virginia. A household slave places logs in the fireplace.

tifederalists; it is likely indeed that a majority of Americans shared Antifederalist sympathies in 1788.

Few Americans at that time had much enthusiasm for a strong national government. They knew well enough from their own experience with the British how dangerous strong governments could be, how much harm they could inflict upon innocent people, how seriously they could threaten popular liberties. Strong governments took money out of your pocket without your permission. If you resisted, strong governments sent troops against you to punish you. Strong governments had no scruples against shedding blood in order to suppress resistance. Had Americans, the Antifederalists asked themselves, overthrown British rule at so high a cost in blood and money only to allow yet another strong government to be set up in their very midst? Would not such a government abuse the power entrusted to it and become once more a tool to rob the people of their liberties?

Yet many Antifederalists found themselves in a dilemma: They knew well enough how dangerous it was to have a weak and powerless government; continued weakness would invite further interference from foreign powers like the British or the French. They realized, too, that the 13 separate states might start quarreling amongst themselves and come to blows. Then nothing would save the American people from civil war, from the condition of poverty and suffering that accompanies enless armed struggle.

During the Philadelphia meeting itself, it is true, some delegates had pointed out that there was a common-sense solution to this dilemma of a choice between freedom and order. Virginia delegate George Mason was Federalist and Antifederalist at the same time. He participated energetically in the discussions that led to the drafting of the Constitution, but he refused to sign his name to the document when it was finished.

Mason told his fellow delegates that he would only approve the Constitution on one condition: a Bill of Rights must be added to it. Governments, according to his philosophy, must respect the rights of the people. These rights, he believed, must be written down. If the people knew their rights, and were always on guard to protect them, they would remain free.

This practice of writing constitutions that contained a declaration (or bill) of rights had been followed when British rule was overthrown after 1775. New states were formed, and constitutions were drawn up and submitted to the people for their approval. In many cases, these documents included some declaration of individual rights that the new governments were supposed to observe and to protect.

Virginia was the first American state to produce a declaration of rights. This Virginia declaration, adopted by the state legislature early in 1776, provided a model for the other states to follow. George Mason was its author.

Mason began the Virginia Declaration of Rights by saying that all men "have certain inalienable rights … the enjoyment of life and liberty, with the means of acquiring and possessing property, and pursuing … happiness and safety." He went on to spell out what these rights were, ending with the statement that "the freedom of the press is one of the greatest bulwarks of liberty, and ought not to be restrained"; and he added that "all men are entitled to the free exercise of religion."

When Mason arrived at the Philadelphia convention 11 years later, he believed, along with the other delegates, that setting up a strong national government ought to be a top priority; and he participated in the long summer's deliberations with as much enthusiasm as anybody else. But as the summer wore on, the awesome nature of the power that the constitution makers were setting up dawned upon him. He knew well that power is a two-edged sword and may be used for bad purposes as well as good ones. It was as important, in his view, to have a declaration of rights in the new national constitution as it was to have such declarations in the state constitutions.

Mason raised his concern with other delegates; they brushed his objections aside. So he wrote them down in the form of notes labeled "Objections to the new Constitution of Government." What he said was to be of key importance in the coming struggle for the Bill of Rights. "There is no Declaration of Rights," he wrote, "and the laws of the central government being paramount to the laws and constitution of the several States, the Declarations of Rights in the separate States are no security."

Mason then recorded his opposition publicly by refusing to sign the finished Constitution. He was one of three delegates who took this course; the others were Elbridge Gerry, of Massachusetts, and Edmund Randolph, also of Virginia.

George Mason returned to Gunston Hall, his plantation on the Potomac, in mid-September 1787. Near Baltimore he suffered painful injuries to his head and neck when his coach overturned on the road. As soon as he felt well enough, he made a copy of his "Objections" and sent them off to George Washington. He enclosed a note with the document, saying that "I got very much hurt in my Neck and Head, by the unlucky accident on the road; it is now wearing off. I take the liberty to enclose you my Objections to the new Constitution of Government; which a little Moderation … in the latter end of the Convention, might have removed."

George Washington replied the same day. "I am sorry to hear you met with an accident on your return," he wrote. "I hope you experience no ill effect from it. The family here join me in compliments and good wishes to you, Mrs. Mason and family." As for Mason's objections to the Constitution, Washington did not mention them. He was, in fact, extremely upset. Mason's action, he feared, might make it much more difficult to win public approval for the new Constitution. In letters to friends, Washington referred to Mason's behavior as "obnoxious," saying "he is no longer any friend of mine."

The Federalists launched a campaign late in 1787 to secure the ratification and adoption of the document that they had drafted in Philadelphia.

State by state, special assemblies were summoned to meet in order to examine and discuss the Contitution and, the Federalists hoped, to ratify it. The delegates to these assemblies—or constitutional conventions, as they were called—were elected by the voters.

The first states that called together conventions to debate and ratify the Constitution were Pennsylvania, New Jersey, Delaware, Connecticut and Georgia. In all five states, conventions voted for the Constitution either unanimously or with resounding majorities. The Federalists were elated. Washington's fears that Mason's opposition might create difficulties appeared to be groundless. By early January 1788, the Constitution bandwagon was rolling.

This situation changed when the Massachusetts ratifying convention met in Boston on January 9, 1788. As the debate unfolded, the Federalists listened with a growing sense of alarm. Much time was taken up with talk about a declaration of rights and the absence in the draft of any guarantees for the inalienable rights of man. Probably a majority of the representatives elected by Massachusetts townships—and these included some on the coast of what is today Maine—were Antifederalists.

Now George Mason began to come into his own; the debates in Boston revealed how farsighted his stand in Philadelphia had been. Massachusetts was not "just another state," like Delaware or Georgia. It was one of the three most populous and powerful states in the Union, and in the other two—New York and Virginia—there was also deep-seated Antifederalist feeling. If Massachusetts failed to ratify the draft, there would be no hope at all of winning ratification in either New York or Virginia. Without Massachusetts, New York and Virginia, there would be no Union under the new Constitution, no matter how many other states ratified it.

By the end of January 1788, the Federalists realized that any hope of winning ratification of the Philadelphia draft of the Constitution would vanish if they did not change their tactics. From now on they would have to reckon seriously with the Antifederalist opposition.

Faced with this situation, the Federalists in Boston decided that they *themselves* would propose amendments to the Constitution. They would ask the delegates to vote for the Constitution as it had been drafted, in return for a promise that a Bill of Rights would be added later on, when the new government met.

And so it turned out. In the resolution by which it ratified the Constitution, the Boston assembly said that "certain alterations and amendments in the said Constitution would remove the fear of the good people of this Commonwealth and … guard against an undue administration of the federal Government." The resolution made a beginning by suggesting a couple of important rights—like the right to indictment by a grand jury—that ought to be written into the Constitution. This was the first forging of an historic compromise between the Federalists on the one side and moderate elements in the Antifederalist opposition on the other. For the first time a sovereign state, Massachusetts, had *itself* gone on record for the adoption of amendments as a part of the ratification process.

Respect for human rights, the convention said, would guard against an "undue administration of the federal government." The words were a masterpiece of delicate phrasing. What they meant was that a Bill of Rights in the Constitution would be an obstacle to the practice of governmental tyranny.

Ratification in Massachusetts squeaked by with a bare plurality of 19 votes. In New York and Virginia, the ratifying conventions assembled a few months later. There the Federalists adopted the same tactics as in Massachusetts and with the same successful results. Again, the vote was close. In Virginia, where George Mason was a delegate and spoke eloquently, ratification carried by 10 votes; in New York State it carried by only three.

In 1789, when the first Congress elected under the new Constitution assembled, James Madison set about the work of drafting a national Bill of Rights and securing its adoption. Congress then debated and adopted the proposal, and it was submitted to the states for their approval. In 1791, when 10 states had ratified the Bill of Rights, it became part of the American Constitution.

In the fall of 1788, the first national elections were held under the new Constitution; George Washington was elected president, and a Federalist majority was installed in Congress. At noon on April 30, 1789, the new president was driven to Federal Hall in New York City, which was to be the country's capital for the time being. Washington took the oath to defend the Constitution; a huge crowd outside the hall cried "Long live George Washington, president of the United States!"

For a little while in 1790, the new Congress turned its attention to the western lands won from Great Britain at the end of the Revolutionary War. These lands were split roughly in half by the Ohio River as it flowed from the Pennsylvania hills to join the Mississippi at Cairo. Jefferson described the northern half, called the Northwestern Territory, in his *Notes on Virginia*, published in 1781. This land, he said, bloomed with scarlet strawberries, black raspberries, red flowering apple, yellow jasmine, white and yellow pine and Cherokee plum. Deer, otter, mink, badger, fox and wolf swarmed in its forests. Birds of a thousand kinds hovered and wheeled in the pure air—the bald eagle, misty blue heron, gold-winged woodpecker, wild pigeon, purple finch.

In 1784 Jefferson drew up a plan for the government of this territory, which Congress agreed to in 1787 and then confirmed for second time in 1790. This law was called the Northwest Ordinance; it was important because it set the pattern by which new states from then on would be admitted to the Union from the western territories.

While the Northwest Territory was still thinly settled, said the Ordinance, it would be run by a governor appointed by Congress, working with an assembly elected by the "free male inhabitants" of each district. When the number of people in a given area reached 60,000, those people were then entitled to knock at the Union's door and ask for admission to the republic as a state. All they had to do was to draw up a written constitution and submit this to Congress for approval. Five states would in the course of time be carved from this territory and admitted to the Union: Ohio, Indiana, Illinois, Michigan and Wisconsin.

The Northwest Ordinance also had an antislavery clause. "There shall be," it said, "[no] slavery … in the said territory." Jefferson believed that in those western lands men and women must live free forever from the curse of slavery. But south of the Ohio, in the Southwest Territory, Congress did not ban slavery. While free settlers moved into the Northwest, planters and farmers with their slaves moved into the Southwest. Four states would in the course of time be carved out of the Southwest Territory and admitted to the Union with slavery: Kentucky, Tennessee, Alabama and Mississippi.

In 1791 the Federalist party was at the height of its popularity. With men like George Washington, John Adams and Alexander Hamilton at its head, it had led the American nation in a successful struggle against England. It had created the Constitution of 1787, had persuaded the people to adopt it and then had organized the first government to wield power under the Constitution. But in spite of these achievements, the Federalists soon lost much of their public support when they began to carry out programs that made people angry at them.

Federalist Rule, 1790–1800

A good example of this is the Whiskey Rebellion. In 1791 Alexander Hamilton, as secretary for the Treasury, thought up a scheme to pay the federal war debt by putting a tax on whiskey. This tax fell hardest upon the backwoods people of Pennsylvania, Virginia and North Carolina. Whiskey, for such people, was their main *cash crop*—a crop, that is, that when taken to market and sold, brought in enough money to buy things that the settlers could not make for themselves, like guns, bullets, axes and cooking pots.

How did this work? Whiskey was distilled from grain in backwoods stills, packed in big bottles onto saddlebags and then sent over the mountain trails on horseback to Philadelphia. Rye condensed into whiskey was a light but valuable crop that could be transported fairly easily when there were no good roads and no canals or railroads to haul goods to market.

When Congress passed the new tax law, frontier farmers were furious. What was this, they asked themselves, but the Stamp Tax all over again? Many people had bitter memories of liquor taxes in the Old World, where their daddies and granddaddies had carried on bloody struggles with the king's tax collectors. So meetings were held, petitions signed and statements nailed up, warning the tax collectors to stay away. Groups of "Whiskey Boys" seized the collectors, tarred and feathered them and drove them out of town.

This went on until 1794, when Hamilton decided that it was time to enforce the law and put down the protests. The antitax movement, said Hamilton, was an "insurrection" against the federal government. He pointed to the first article of the Constitution, which gave Congress power to "call forth the militia to suppress insurrections." In August 1794, the government gathered together 16,000 militiamen in Philadelphia, which had by now become the country's capital, and marched them off toward the western hills. The president of the United States and the secretary of the Treasury led the parade.

The troops marched from Philadelphia to the frontier town of Pittsburgh and all the way back again. From start to finish, the trip took nearly four months, from early September until mid-December 1794. It rained hard as the men crossed the Allegheny Mountain trails. The soldiers became soaked; part of the time they had to sleep out in the fields all night without any shelter. Hundreds of frontier people were arrested, and 22 were brought back to Philadelphia and put on trial. Only two of these were convicted, and even they were pardoned later on. Putting down the "rebellion" cost the taxpayers thousands of dollars. It cost the Federalists, too, in other ways, because their behavior earned them the undying hatred of ordinary people.

As the years went by, this antagonism between the Federalists and their critics deepened. In July 1789, only a few weeks after Washington had been inaugurated as president in New York City, revolution broke out in France. In 1792 the revolutionaries thrust the French king Louis XVI from the throne and set up a republic.

Many Americans, and Antifederalists in particular, hailed the event with delight; the French were right, they thought, to overthrow their tyrannical monarch. They were right, too, to take up arms and to defend themselves against Britain and the other European powers that made war upon France in order to put down the revolution and restore Louis XVI to his throne. The Antifederalists—who now called themselves "Jeffersonians," "Republicans," or even "Jeffersonian Republicans"—began to organize pro-France clubs, to sing French songs and to sport the French colors in their hats.

In 1793 Edmond Genet, the French republic's first envoy to America, arrived in Charleston, South Carolina. It was an occasion for rejoicing. Big crowds lined the route that he traveled to Philadelphia. The guns boomed, the people cheered, Citizen Genet made speeches.

The Federalists watched these celebrations with misgivings. They were afraid that the United States might get sucked into the European war on the French side. The danger was a real one. American hatred of Great Britain was kept alive by many grievances. One of these was the practice of *impressment*, by which the British seized American sailors on the high seas and compelled them to serve like slaves, perhaps for years, on British men-of-war. Anti-British feelings continued to mount; by the end of 1793 it seemed as though war with England was very close.

Such a conflict was something that the Federalists were anxious to avoid, at almost any cost. Their sympathies lay far more with the conservative British than with the revolutionary French. They sent John Jay to England with instructions to seek a settlement of all outstanding issues between the two countries.

Jay signed a treaty with the British at the end of 1794; but the British conceded nothing at all with respect to key issues such as the impressment of American seamen, violation of neutral rights, and compensation for American ships that had been seized. Jay was condemned for having signed a document that seemed to spell unconditional surrender. The treaty was ratified by the Senate in June 1795. Federalist prestige hit an all-time low.

When George Washington's second term as president came to an end in 1796, he was not unhappy to step down. When he first became president, he had hoped to rule as a man above parties, with the support of a united people. This dream evaporated amidst the political factionalism of the 1790s. The fame that Washington had won during the war years seemed tarnished. People were toasting each other with words like "a speedy death to General Washington."

George Washington was now 65 years old, worn out by a lifetime of service to his people; he walked with a stoop. Before stepping down from the presidency he composed, with the help of Alexander Hamilton, a Farewell Address to the American people. Live in peace with the whole world—this was his advice to Americans; steer clear of entangling alliances with foreign countries that might draw the country into overseas war. Learn to live as friends of England as well as of France, he said, for "the nation which indulges toward another an habitual hatred or an habitual fondness is in some degree a slave." War, he

stressed, is an evil to be avoided; it squanders resources that can be far better used at home to develop the American economy and to build a firm foundation for future prosperity.

Washington waited in Philadelphia long enough to see John Adams take the oath of office as president on March 4, 1797. Then he mounted his coach and drove away to Mount Vernon. Nearly three years later, on December 13, 1799, the father of his country died at his Virginia home.

John Adams, a devoted Federalist, was elected to the presidency over rival candidate Thomas Jefferson by a mere three votes. When he took up his office in 1797, popular anger against the French was rising. France as well as England was now seizing American ships on the high seas; hundreds of them were rotting in French ports. American fury rose to a new height in 1798, when news came that French officials would not discuss the fate of these vessels unless the Americans first paid them an enormous bribe.

In this situation, the Federalists might well have heeded Washington's advice—kept their cool and followed a neutral course. Instead, they resolved to exploit the people's anger for their own purposes, to break off relations with France and to declare war. But in order to carry out this plan it was necessary to take steps to paralyze the political opposition and to silence the critics. The Federalists did this by enacting a series of repressive laws, the most important of which was the Sedition Act. This act became law when John Adams signed it on July 14, 1798; it authorized the federal government to punish seditious libel.

Seditious libel, in the English legal tradition, was simply the "crime" of saying anything that the king did not wish to hear. Sedition laws were tools that English kings had used for centuries to punish people for speaking their minds.

Prosecution for seditious libel was a practice imported into America during colonial times. Peter Zenger, for example, a New York City publisher, was placed on trial in 1734 because his paper attacked the British governor, William Cosby. In 1775, after the battles of Lexington and Concord, the British government used this weapon to stifle opposition at home to its colonial policy. An English minister named John Horne was placed on trial for a "seditious utterance." Horne's only crime had been to place an ad in the newspapers urging the English people to give money to relieve the want of the widows and orphans of American patriots "inhumanly murdered by the King's troops at or near Lexington and Concord."

In 1798 the American Federalists, following British practice, passed their own Sedition Act to silence Antifederalists who dared to write or speak out against war with France. The act provided that "if any person shall write, print, utter or publish ... false, scandalous and malicious writings against the government of the United States ... such person ... shall be punished by a fine not exceeding $2,000, and by imprisonment not exceeding two years." The act was to remain in effect until the end of the Adams administration, in March 1801. The new president, Thomas Jefferson, allowed it to lapse at that time, and it was never renewed.

One of the first people whom the Federalists prosecuted under this Sedition Act was a Congressman from Vermont, Matthew Lyon. Lyon was placed on trial for a letter that he wrote in 1798; he had condemned John Adams for sacrificing the public good to "a continual grasp of power, an unbounded thirst for ridiculous pomp ... and selfish avarice."

Matthew Lyon defended his right to say what he had said on the grounds that the Sedition Act denied his First Amendment rights of free speech and free press and was, therefore, unconstitutional. The judge who tried the case overruled Lyon's plea and ordered the jury to ignore it. Lyon was convicted and sent to a lockup where, as he reported, he was confined in an unheated room "sixteen feet long by twelve wide, with a toilet in one corner which affords a stench about equal to the Philadelphia docks in the month of August." The Congressman

added that "I have to walk smartly with my great-coat on to keep comfortably warm some mornings."

In 1799 war was imminent, but the French drew back at the brink. They informed John Adams that they would welcome the restoration of normal relations with the United States. To the consternation and the fury of the Federalist party, John Adams at once responded by nominating a new American minister to France and sending him off to Paris. Adams's action assured peace; the war fever in America collapsed like a pricked balloon.

Adams knew well enough that what he had done would mark the end of Federalist power, but he was proud of his decision. "I desire no other inscription over my gravestone," he wrote, "than 'Here lies John Adams, who took upon himself the responsibility of the peace with France in the year 1800.'"

The year 1800 was also a presidential election year. Jefferson was by this time the leader of the Antifederalist opposition. He was described as "a tall man with a very red freckled face, and gray, neglected hair." Farmers, craftsmen, shopkeepers and frontier folk loved him because they thought that he stood for the poor rather than the rich, for the rights of common people rather than the power of government. His supporters prepared for the election with enthusiasm. The time had come to sweep out the hated Federalist administration and to elect Jefferson in the place of Adams.

Jefferson, therefore, was the Antifederalist candidate for president; the second person on the Antifederalist ticket was Aaron Burr, who practiced law in Albany, New York, and who had sat in the U.S. Senate since 1791. During the election campaign people celebrated the approaching end of Federalist rule with a new Republican song set to the tune of an old Irish jig. "The gloomy night before us flies," they sang, "the reign of terror now is over; / Its gags, inquisitors and spies, / Its herds of harpies are no more." Each verse was followed by a rousing chorus:

Rejoice, Columbia's sons, rejoice,
To tyrants never bend the knee;
But join with heart and soul and voice,
For Jefferson and Liberty.

When the returns were in it was found that the electors in the electoral college had given Jefferson and Burr an equal number of votes—73 for each of them, against 65 for the Federalist candidate, John Adams. What was to be done? People turned to the Constitution to read what it had to say about disputed elections. In Article II they found a clause that said that if two candidates for the presidency received an equal number of votes, "then the House of Representatives shall immediately choose by ballot one of them for President." Since the Antifederalists in the House of Representatives were pretty evenly split between supporters of Jefferson and supporters of Burr, the deciding votes were cast by the Federalists, now in a minority. Hamilton, as leader of the Federalists, persuaded his friends to vote for Jefferson. Hamilton didn't like either candidate, but he believed that Jefferson, at least, was an honest man, while he considered Burr to be a scoundrel.

Three years later, Hamilton once again used his influence to get Burr defeated in a New York election. Burr took revenge for these humiliations by challenging Hamilton to a duel. In those days gentlemen felt that if anybody insulted them by what they wrote or said, they must be made to give "satisfaction." This meant that you challenged your enemy to a duel and fought it out on the "field of honor" with pistols or knives or whatever weapon was agreed upon.

The two men met at Weehawken, New Jersey, in a forest near the west bank of the Hudson River. It was early morning of a bright June day; bird songs filled the air. An aide gave the signal; Aaron Burr fired first, and Hamilton fell. His friends rowed the wounded man across the river to Greenwich, a village that lay amidst green fields on Manhattan Island. Here he lingered in pain for a few days, then died, leaving a wife and seven children to weep for him. Since New Jersey had a law forbidding duels, Aaron Burr fled in order to escape being tried for murder. He found shelter at Pierce Butler's fine new mansion on St. Simons Island in Georgia.

Hamilton was one of the Federalist party's most brilliant leaders. His death marked the eclipse of the proud alliance of merchants, planters, lawyers and clergymen that had ruled the United States since 1789.

John Adams was the last Federalist president. In 1800, during his final year in office, the nation's capital was shifted from Philadelphia to a special federal district, called the District of Columbia, on the Potomac River in Virginia. There the government began to build a brand new town and named it in memory of George Washington.

In 1800, when John and Abigail Adams went to live there, everything in Washington, D.C. was still unfinished, including the president's new home. Abigail described the White House as it was in November of that year. "The house," she wrote, "is upon a grand and superb scale, requiring about thirty servants to attend and keep the apartments in proper order, and perform the ordinary business of the house and stables ... We have not the least fence, yard, or other convenience, without, and the great unfinished audience-room I make a drying-room of, to hang the clothes in."

In March 1801, Thomas Jefferson took up his residence in the White House. Immediately he found that he faced a crisis: There was new danger of a war with France.

The Louisiana Purchase and the War of 1812

In 1681 Robert LaSalle explored the Mississippi River from its source to its mouth. He claimed the huge territory drained by the river and its tributaries as the property of his king, Louis XIV of France; and he named it Louisiana, or the land belonging to King Louis. Louisiana stretched from the Appalachian Mountains to the Rockies, from the Great Lakes to the Gulf of Mexico.

LaSalle knew that this American empire would be of value to France for the gold and silver that it might contain, as well as for the trade in fur and timber that it might produce. Louisiana, he wrote, might yield each year "skins to the amount of 2,000 crowns, and abundance of lead and timber for ships." He dreamed of building a port near the mouth of the Mississippi that would receive the wealth of the great inland valley and send it abroad in exchange for goods from France and the West Indies.

LaSalle died in 1687, but his vision soon became a reality. Early in the 18th century the seaport of New Orleans was built on the eastern side of the Mississippi, one hundred miles north of the place where its waters pour out into the Gulf of Mexico. Sugar plantations and elegant mansions began to appear on the flat, well-watered lands around the town.

In 1763 France met defeat at the hands of Great Britain in the Seven Years War; she gave up Louisiana along with the rest of her New World possessions. England took eastern Louisiana, or all the lands east of the Mississippi, and Spain received western Louisiana, or the lands on the western side of the river. Along with this Spain also received the port of New Orleans.

The French people living in New Orleans grumbled at being put under Spanish rule, but they had to make the best of it. A *cabildo*, or council, now ran the city, and *alcaldes*, or magistrates, walked the streets with wands of office carried in front of them. They held trials in the jails, had people flogged for saying bad things about the Spanish king and hanged thieves who stole golden goblets from the churches.

The port of New Orleans meant a good deal to Americans after the Revolution was over. Westerners were getting their produce to market in a new way, loading it onto flatboats and floating it down the Ohio and the Mississippi rivers to New Orleans. The flatboats carried bulky stuff like cotton, corn, tobacco, hogs and cattle, as well as light but valuable crops like whiskey and the herbal root ginseng. The rivermen unloaded their crops at New Orleans, sold them and made their way home on foot.

When this trade began to develop during the 1790s, the Spanish were not very happy about letting the Americans use their port. But in 1795 Thomas Pinckney, the U.S. ambassador to Spain, signed a treaty with the Spanish government that allowed U.S. citizens to unload their produce at New Orleans and transfer it to oceangoing ships for transportation to east coast ports, or to Europe, or China. This was called the *right of deposit*.

In 1800 a French general, Napoleon Bonaparte, made himself master of France. He took back western Louisiana from Spain and in 1802 cancelled the American right of deposit at New Orleans. Napoleon, who later styled himself emperor of the French, dreamed of reviving the great French empire in the New World, which had been lost only 40 years before. Jefferson realized with a shock that Americans in the lands beyond the Appalachians were threatened by a European power headed by a brilliant soldier with many ships and many men to back him up.

The president at once sent James Monroe to France to work with Robert Livingston, the American ambassador in Paris. His instructions to the two men were that they should offer to buy back New Orleans from First Consul Bonaparte. In case Napoleon refused to sell the port, Livingston and Monroe were told to press hard for renewal of the right of deposit.

But in April 1803, much to Livingston and Monroe's astonishment, Napoleon offered to sell all of western Louisiana, New Orleans included, to the Americans for $15,000,000 in gold. What, they asked themselves, lay in back of this switch? Having taken Louisiana from Spain in

1800, why was Napoleon now so anxious to get rid of it?

The answer was to be found on the French island of Haiti in the Caribbean, where a half million black slaves toiled on sugar plantations for French and Spanish masters. In 1793 the slaves rose up in revolt under their leader, Toussaint l'Ouverture; they killed their European overlords or threw them out. Napoleon badly needed Haiti as a base if his armies were to operate in the New World, but his efforts to reconquer the island in 1802 failed; his troops were wiped out by black resistance and yellow fever. So much for Napoleon's dream of reviving the French empire in the New World!

Quickly the first consul decided that he would sell Louisiana to the Americans. The sale would bring him cash for his continuing war with England. Better, he thought, that Louisiana should fall into the hands of a weak power like the United States rather than a strong one like Britain. More than that: The two countries might come to blows over Louisiana, and this would bring the Americans into the war on the French side. As we shall see, this is exactly what happened; but it happened too late to do Napoleon himself any good.

One day in April of 1803, the first consul was soaking in his bathtub and talking at the same time with two of his brothers, Lucien and Joseph. Casually, as he was soaping himself, Napoleon mentioned that he had decided to sell Louisiana to the Americans. Lucien and Joseph were furious, and there was a scene. Joseph said that he would not accept the decision, that he would defy the first consul by speaking against it in public. Napoleon, now very angry, rose suddenly from the tub. A wave of warm soapy water hit Joseph and drenched him from head to toe. "This plan is mine," Napoleon yelled, "and I alone will carry it out. Do you understand?" His fury spent, the first consul sank beneath the bathwater again, like a hippopotamus, up to the nostrils.

This was too much for the bathroom attendant, who fell to the floor in a faint. When Jefferson got news of the agreement in June 1803, he almost fainted too: He was being asked to sign a treaty that would double the size of the United States by a single stroke of the pen.

Exactly how big was western Louisiana? Nobody knew for sure; but Thomas Jefferson could now realize a dream that he had long had about exploring the far West. He gave orders for an army expedition to be organized. At its head he placed a young Virginia officer, Meriwether Lewis, and his friend William Clark. The two received instructions to explore the Louisiana territory and, if possible, to find a route across the Rockies to the Pacific.

Lewis and Clark left St. Louis in the spring of 1804. Thirty-eight men went with them, mostly soldiers, and one Shoshone woman named Sacagewea, wife of the interpreter Chouteau. The explorers sailed up the broad Missouri to its source in Montana; crossed the Rocky Mountains at Lolo Pass on Indian horses amid bitter cold; then built canoes and followed the Columbia River to the Pacific Ocean. They came back the way that they had gone out, reaching St. Louis in September 1806, after being away from home for two years and four months. They brought with them much information about the peoples whom they had met and about the wild life that flourished in the great new West that the United States had won.

When Lewis and Clark returned to St. Louis in 1806 France and England, age-old rivals for world empire, were once more at war with each other. The United States took no side in the struggle and remained at peace; her merchant ships sailed with their cargoes to English and other European ports.

Soon the British and French navies were seizing hundreds of American vessels. The British wanted to cut off supplies from France, and the French wanted to stop supplies from reaching England. But Americans were angrier at the British than at the French: The British not only seized ships and cargoes but the sailors who manned them as well.

Some of these they dragged away for service in the British navy.

Many sailors deserted the British navy, preferring to work on American ships. This was not surprising. British sailors were usually conscripts; they were considered little better than slaves and were treated with barbarity. Men who got only slightly out of line were flogged. Heaven help the man who did something really bad, like striking an officer. He was tied down in one of the ship's boats and given 50 lashes with the cat-o'-nine-tails. Then the boat was rowed around to each ship in the fleet in turn; at each stop the boatswain's mate came down and laid on more lashes. At the end of such a trip the victim might have suffered 500 lashes or more. Men who survived this treatment, wrote Joshua Davis, an American who served in the British navy 11 years, "looked like a piece of raw beef from neck to waist."

In 1806 the American navy was still very small, and there was no way that it could protect merchant ships at sea from British search and seizure. Jefferson's solution to the problem was to forbid American ships from sailing to foreign ports: Obviously enough, if American ships didn't sail the seas, the British and French could not capture them, humiliate the captains and seize the crews. But the effect of this was disastrous. By 1808 American ports were crammed with idle ships and idle men; the country's foreign trade was at a standstill.

That same year Jefferson's second term as president ended, and James Madison replaced him. Madison's young and talented wife, Dolley, livened up the White House's social life. She held the first inauguration ball ever. The First Lady wore a dress of pale buff, with a pearl necklace and earrings to match.

Madison shared Jefferson's wish to keep out of war with England, but soon the feeling in the country became too strong for him. In 1810 a group of Congressmen called the War Hawks began to demand a confrontation with England. Their leaders were Henry Clay, of Kentucky, and John Caldwell Calhoun, of South Carolina. Both men demanded that the government start to build a big navy and that it declare war against England. Their speeches were received with enthusiasm throughout the West and South.

Why were the Hawks so keen on war? Was impressment, or the seizure of American sailors, the only issue that bothered them? To find an answer, we must follow the story of the Indian leader Tecumseh.

Born in 1768, Tecumseh was a brave of the Shawnee people who lived along the banks of the Ohio River; he took part in many of his people's struggles against the white settlers and the white soldiers who robbed them of their lands and pushed them always westward. By 1800 Tecumseh was famous as a warrior and leader. He and his brother, Laulewasika, began to travel far and wide throughout the Indian lands that lay on both sides of the Ohio River. The message was always the same: Indian peoples, unite and resist. Offer war to the whites not as separate tribes but as a single people. Teach them to respect you by dealing with them with mercy and humanity; but do not give up your land, which is the mother of us all. *Do not squabble amongst yourselves; organize an all-Indian resistance.* Otherwise the white invaders will wipe you out. "Where today," the great orator asked his listeners,

are the Pequot? Where the Narragansett, the Mohican ... and many other once powerful tribes of our people? They have vanished before the oppression and avarice of the white man as snow before a summer sun.

Tecumseh knew that if it came to war with the Americans the Indian peoples might form an alliance with the English and receive guns, ammunition and supplies. This was logical enough. Had not the Americans themselves made an alliance with the French in 1778 in order to carry on their war against the British? And should the native peoples

The famous sea duel between the British man-of-war the *Guerrière* and the American frigate *Constitution* took place early in August 1812. The *Guerrière*, dismasted by broadsides from the American guns delivered at point-blank range, drifts helplessly in mid-Atlantic and is obliged to surrender.

turn up their noses at foreign help if it was offered them?

The mere thought of this made the War Hawks furious. Their dream was to drive the British from the New World entirely; this would surely break the back of Indian resistance. As Felix Grundy, the Tennessee Hawk, told the House of Representatives in 1811, "We shall drive the British from our continent … [T]hey will no longer have an opportunity of … setting the ruthless savage on to tomahawk our women and children."

In the spring of 1812, James Madison gave in to the pressure; he sent the British his final word: Stop the search of American ships and the seizure of American sailors or face war. The British needed to avoid this war or, at the very least, to delay its outbreak. They were already caught up in a life-

and-death struggle with France in Europe. But they did not try hard enough, and their reply came too late. Congress declared war against Great Britain on June 12. Politicians said that American war aims were to vindicate the nation's honor on the high seas, to break native American resistance in the Midwest, to drive Britain out of Canada even as she had driven the French out in 1763.

The War of 1812 went on for two years in a series of battles that gave no clear-cut victory to either side. British and American men-of-war fought cannon duels on the Atlantic Ocean, on Lake Champlain, and on Lake Erie. Soldiers, many of them militiamen, became locked in a seesaw struggle along the northern frontier all the way from New York state to Lake Superior. The war was carried to Washington, D.C. itself in August 1814, when the British navy sailed into the Chesapeake Bay, landed troops on the Patuxent River and occupied the capital. Soon many government buildings, including the White House, went up in flames.

In this struggle some of the native peoples of the Midwest sided with the British, some with the Americans. Tecumseh and many of his warriors took the warpath alongside British troops and gave great help to the British cause. The end came when Canadian soldiers and Indian braves were defeated at the Battle of the Thames, north of Lake Erie, on October 4, 1813. Tecumseh and hundreds of his men were killed. Armed Indian opposition to the American advance in the old Northwest Territory was over.

In the southwest, Tecumseh's appeals for war against the Americans had been well received by a group of the Creek people who lived on the Alabama River. They were called Red Sticks. By 1812 both Kentucky and Tennessee had been admitted to the Union as slave states; the rest of the southwest was then known as the Mississippi Territory. At the time of the War of 1812, American pioneers were beginning to settle along the Alabama and Tombigbee rivers in the southern part of this territory. Much of its was Indian country, inhabited in the western portion by the Choctaws and Chickasaws, and in the eastern portion by the Creeks.

By July 1813, many white settlers were afraid that they would be attacked by the Creeks. These settlers became even more worried when a party of Red Sticks visited Pensacola, in Spanish Florida, and were provided with ammunition brought into the port by the British fleet. On their way back home, the Creeks were attacked by a party of militiamen at Burnt Corn Creek. This was the opening blow of the Creek War. Many settlers on the lower Alabama and Tombigbee rivers now fled to the stockades that they had built for protection against Indian attack. Fort Mims, on the Alabama River, was one of these stockades. Here in August 1813, 500 men, women and children assembled.

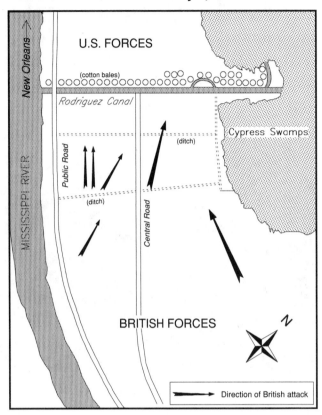

Battle of New Orleans January 8, 1815

The fort was in charge of Major Daniel Beasley, a militiaman.

Major Beasley did not share the settlers' fears. While the Creeks prepared for their assault, the soldiers drank or slept. The stockade gate hung open; indeed, it could not be closed because it was blocked by drifting sand; little children ran in and out. A black slave told his master that he had seen warriors in battle paint lurking near the stockade; he was tied to a post and lashed for spreading false rumors.

On August 30 at noon, the drums beat, the soldiers sat down to their midday meal, and the Creek warriors attacked. Many of the whites—young and old, men, women and children—fought with desperate courage, but the Creeks showed no mercy. Almost all were killed; the bodies, mutilated by knife and tomahawk and charred by fire, were left to rot or to be devoured by dogs and scavengers.

The Fort Mims massacre triggered an all-out war of extermination against the Creeks. A Tennessee

The decisive battle of the War of 1812 was fought under the leadership of General Andrew Jackson on January 8, 1815. This picture shows Kentucky militiamen lined up behind a barricade and firing their rifles. The British army is seen launching a frontal attack along the corridor of land stretching between the Mississippi River (to the right) and the swamps (to the left).

militiaman, General Andrew Jackson, assumed command. He was at the time 47 years old and a veteran of the Revolutionary War. A New Orleans woman who saw him in 1814 wrote the following description. "His dress," she wrote,

was simple and nearly threadbare. A well-worn leather cap protected his head, and a short Spanish coat of old blue cloth his body. His high boots, whose vast tops swayed uneasily around his bony knees, were long innocent of any polish. His complexion was sallow and unhealthy, his long hair iron gray, and his body thik and emaciated ... A fierce glare shone in his bright and hawk-like eyes.

From November 1813 until March 1814, Andrew Jackson with his Tennessee militia fought nine separate battles against the Creek braves; Indian towns were burned to the ground, hundreds of

Creeks were killed. The end came at the Battle of Horseshoe Bend, on the Tallapoosa River, March 27, 1814. Here the Creek warriors under their leader, Menawa, asked no mercy, and gave none. One thousand Creeks, men, women and children, lost their lives on a single day. The power of the native peoples to hold up the American advance into the Mississippi Valley was finally broken.

At the same time, in the spring of 1814, Britain's long struggle against Napoleon in Europe came to an end with the Battle of Leipzig and the total collapse of France. This meant that Britain could now turn her attention to unfinished business in the New World, reviving the British dream of empire in the Midwest and challenging the American claim to Louisiana.

In December 1814, the British navy sailed into Gulf waters and landed an army on the shores of Lake Borgne, due east of New Orleans. It was a formidable striking force of 10,000 men, stiffened

The Hunters of Kentucky

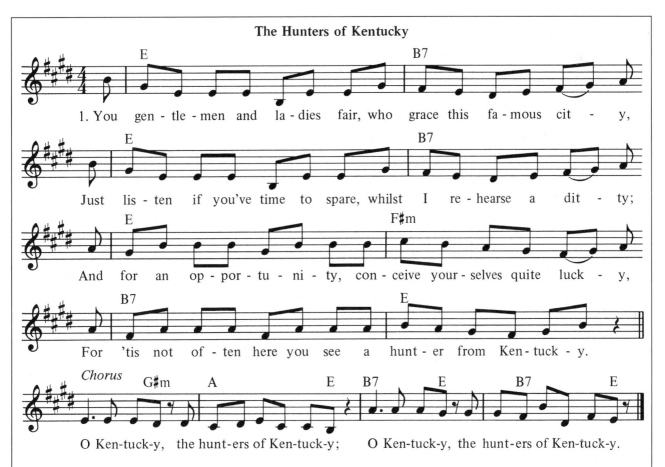

1. You gen-tle-men and la-dies fair, who grace this fa-mous cit-y,
Just lis-ten if you've time to spare, whilst I re-hearse a dit-ty;
And for an op-por-tu-ni-ty, con-ceive your-selves quite luck-y,
For 'tis not of-ten here you see a hunt-er from Ken-tuck-y.

Chorus
O Ken-tuck-y, the hunt-ers of Ken-tuck-y; O Ken-tuck-y, the hunt-ers of Ken-tuck-y.

2. We are a hardy freeborn race,
   each man to fear a stranger,
Whate'er the game we join the chase,
   despising toil and danger;
And if a daring foe annoys,
   whatever his strength and forces,
We'll show him that Kentucky boys
   are "alligator horses."
Chorus

3. I suppose you've read it in the prints,
   how Pakenham attempted
To make old Hickory Jackson wince,
   but soon his schemes repented,
For we with rifles ready cocked,
   thought such occasion lucky,
And soon around the hero flocked
   the hunters of Kentucky.
Chorus

4. You've heard I suppose how New Orleans
   is famed for wealth and beauty.
There's girls of every hue it seems,
   from snowy white to sooty,
So Pakenham he made his brag,
   if he in fight was lucky,
He'd have their girls and cotton bags
   in spite of old Kentucky.
Chorus

5. But Jackson he was wide awake,
   and wasn't scared at trifles,
For well he knew what aim we'd take
   with our Kentucky rifles;
So he led us down to Cypress swamp,
   the ground was low and mucky,
There stood John Bull in martial pomp,
   and here was old Kentucky.
Chorus

6. A bank was raised to hide our breast,
   not that we thought of dying,
But that we always like to rest,
   unless the game is flying:
Behind it stood our little force:
   none wished it to be greater,
For every man was half a horse,
   and half an alligator.
Chorus

7. They did not let our patience tire
   before they showed their faces—
We did not choose to waste our fire,
   but snugly kept our places;
And when so near to see them wink,
   we thought 'twas time to stop 'em;
And 'twould have done you good, I think,
   to see Kentuckians drop 'em.
Chorus

8. They found at last 'twas vain to fight
   when lead was all their booty,
And so they wisely took to flight,
   and left us all our beauty,
And now if danger e'er annoys,
   remember what our trade is,
Just send for us Kentucky boys,
   and we'll protect you, ladies.
Chorus

Written shortly after the conclusion of the war, "The Hunters of Kentucky" tells the story of how Andrew Jackson and his men defeated the hard-bitten British regulars at the Battle of New Orleans. "The Hunters of Kentucky" served as a campaign song during Jackson's first effort to win the presidency in 1824, and it became very popular during the years that he held that office (1829–1837).

by hardened veterans from the Napoleonic Wars. James Madison placed Andrew Jackson, fresh from his victories over the Creeks, in charge of the defense.

The Americans, mostly Kentucky and Tennessee militiamen, threw up mud walls six miles below New Orleans in the narrow passage of land between the Mississippi River on the one side and a wilderness of cypress swamps on the other. Here on January 8, 1815, American gunners and riflemen waited as the British marched to the attack, their scarlet-clad ranks half-hidden in the morning mist. American fire cut them down like grass under a scythe. The British lost 2,000 wounded and dead; the American casualties were only 80. "The field," a Kentucky soldier wrote, "looked at first glance like a sea of blood."

Thus ended one of the most decisive battles ever fought on the North American continent. By this defeat Britain lost her bid for control of the gateway to the West, the base from which she planned to move into the interior and to win the lands west of the Mississippi that once were claimed by France. American victory at New Orleans meant that from now on the Americans, not the British, would rule the huge western territory that stretched all the way to the Rocky Mountains.

The following month, the draft of a peace treaty drawn up by British and American representatives in the Belgian town of Ghent arrived in Washington. The treaty simply said, let's stop fighting. Western lands, impressment of sailors, search and seizure of American ships—none of this was mentioned. Both sides learned something from the long and futile struggle: the British, that they could no longer hope to win back what they had lost in America; the Americans, that they would have to learn to live next door to the British in Canada.

New York City put on a big celebration when the news arrived. Thousands came out onto the streets with candles in their hands, weeping and crying "A Peace! A Peace!" American ships could sail the seas and carry on a thriving trade with the whole world; the way was open to the West, all the way to the Mississippi Valley. A new era was about to begin.

5

THE AGE OF ANDREW JACKSON

Building a Continental Kingdom, 1815–1848

Between the War of 1812 and the Mexican War of 1846–1848, there is a timespan of roughly 35 years packed with dramatic and tumultuous events. This era is sometimes called "The Age of Andrew Jackson." It is, indeed, identical with the years when Jackson was a leading figure on the national stage. He became a popular hero with his victory over the British in 1815, was elected president of the United States in 1828 and died in 1845.

Andrew Jackson was born on the South Carolina frontier in 1767, the son of poor immigrant parents. His father died before Andrew was born, his mother before he was 14. In 1784, after the conclusion of the Revolutionary War, Jackson went to work in a North Carolina law office. Three years later, he packed his few belongings and moved out west. Settling in Nashville, he was appointed public prosecutor and began to practice law. He married Rachel Donelson, member of a leading Tennessee family, and began to speculate in land and to buy slaves. Soon he was a leading Tennessee politician: first as Tennessee representative to Congress, then as a United States senator and a major general of the Tennessee militia. Jackson finally emerged as a national figure in the War of 1812 with his victory over the British at New Orleans in 1815.

When, therefore, Jackson became president of the United States he was already wealthy and famous. People revered him as a man who had won success both on the battlefield and in his personal life. His was the story, so it seemed, of a person rising through his own efforts from anonymous poverty to honor and affluence. Westerners worshiped a bold, hard-drinking, hard-fighting frontiersman. Southerners made newly rich rich by land speculation, the purchase of slaves and booming cotton production saw in Andrew Jackson one of their own.

As far as the East was concerned, Andrew Jackson was not popular among the merchant aristocrats of Boston and New York, nor even among

Andrew Jackson, from a painting by Thomas Sully, made probably soon after the War of 1812. Sully (1783–1872) was an English immigrant who won fame as a portrait painter; he lived in Philadelphia from 1809 to the time of his death.

the slaveholder of Virginia. These wealthy families with their old aristocratic traditions had no special liking for men like Jackson, whom they regarded as vulgar, violent and newly rich upstarts. But with many city dwellers it was different. By the early 1830s tens of thousands of working people and immigrants were pouring into the factory towns mushrooming along the eastern seaboard. Jackson went out of his way to cultivate these "common men" and to win their votes.

Until the election of Andrew Jackson, the office of the presidency had been a monopoly in the hands of Virginia planters—people like George Washington, Thomas Jefferson, James Monroe and James Madison—or of well-to-do Bostonians like John Adams and his son John Quincy. These were educated men who had enjoyed the luxury of private tutors when they were children and had finished their education at elegant colleges like the one at Princeton, New Jersey, or William and Mary, in Virginia, or John Harvard's, at Cambridge, Mas-

sachusetts. Most of them could read Latin (or Anglo-Saxon English), had the time to write long and polished letters to their friends and were as much at home in London, Paris, or Moscow as they were in Virginia or Massachusetts.

Andrew Jackson, as his promoters took pains to point out, was no pampered member of this eastern elite, many of whom lived upon inherited wealth. He was the son of poor Scots-Irish immigrants, a boy without the benefit of school learning or special privileges. He had risen to the top thanks to his own courage and will. He was, in short, "a common man."

As president, Jackson continued to hammer away at this theme. He poured scorn upon men of wealth. He believed, he said, in equal opportunities for all, special favors for none.

Jackson's identification of himself with the common man was a sound political instinct. The first 70 years of the 19th century witnessed the unfolding in the United States of a movement in which this country led the world: the growth of political democracy based upon universal manhood suffrage. This was a concept that upheld the right of all male citizens to share, both through the casting of their vote and their own candidacy for office, in the direction of their country's affairs. Andrew Jackson became the symbol of this movement. It will be dealt with in more detail in what follows.

Jackson believed that businessmen and industrialists ought to be left alone to develop their undertakings with little or no direct help from government, with little or no government interference. He did not want the federal government, for example, spending the taxpayers' money to build roads or dig canals or promote, as it was called, internal improvements. Private capitalists, he considered, ought to be left to carry out this work on their own. As president he inherited, to be sure, a tariff system that Congress had enacted in previous years to give American industry protection from foreign competition; but he was not in favor of special favors of this sort that might benefit one group of people at the expense of others. Under his administration these tariff barriers began to be lowered after 1832.

Jackson, then, did not think that the federal government should interfere in the direction of the country's economic life. It does not follow, however, that he believed the federal role in the nation's affairs should be a small one. The opposite was true. He felt that a strong central government was of great importance for the nation; a strong central government alone, he believed, could raise the money, equip the military forces and conduct the national defense. In this he included the elimination, where necessary by force, of the unwanted Native American presence.

In 1832 John C. Calhoun, Jackson's vice-president and leader of the Democratic party in South Carolina, threatened to take that state out of the Union rather than submit to a tariff law passed that year by Congress. Jackson at once intervened. In a "Proclamation to the People of the United States," made public in December 1832, he warned Calhoun and his South Carolina supporters of the consequences that would follow if Calhoun carried out his threat. As commander-in-chief, he said, he would use all the force at his disposal in order to prevent this from happening. "The dictates of a high duty," he warned, "oblige me solemnly to announce that you cannot succeed [in an effort to quit the Union]. The laws of the United States must be executed ... Disunion by armed force is *treason* ... On your unhappy State will inevitably fall all the evils of the conflict you force upon the Government of your country. It [the federal government] cannot accede to the mad project of disunion ... Its First magistrate cannot, if he would, avoid the performance of his duty."

Jackson's firm position resolved the crisis and paved the way for a negotiated settlement between the federal government and South Carolina early in 1833. He is remembered as a forceful executive who contributed much towards broadening the powers and the prestige of the presidency.

Jacksonian America with its inventive people, its enormous vitality, its experiment in democracy on a breathtaking scale, was a place of wonder for visitors from abroad. But, as many Americans were only too well aware, there was much to criticize in this society and much to find fault with.

The very speed with which the country was growing presented its citizens with fresh and difficult problems. Slavery still existed throughout the South, inflicting great wrongs upon African-American people who had not yet won liberty in a land where everybody else was free. American women, too, were chafing against the age-old condition of inferiority to which males had consigned them. In the country of the common man they too sought a place in the sun. The frontier was a place where pioneers not only cleared away trees; they demanded that the federal government help them clear away the native peoples as well and eliminate them entirely. In the Northeast, industrial towns, springing into existence overnight, brought with them a flock of miseries: the harsh exploitation of human beings alongside poverty, disease, drunkenness, prostitution and crime.

People in the Jacksonian Age did not confine themselves to talking or writing about these problems; they also took action. A passion to change the world and make it better possessed them, along with a zeal to improve the human condition. Reform-minded Americans created a dozen or more separate reform movements. What sustained and inspired these people was a belief born of the revolutionary years: Most men and women, they felt, were not creatures tainted with inevitable sin, doomed to damnation, as previous generations had been taught, from the day they were born. On the contrary: Human beings possessed the capacity to grow better and live better. This was a new creative faith in human nature. A century later Anne Frank, the Dutch teenager who died in a German concentration camp, would summarize it in six words. "I believe," she wrote in her diary shortly before the Nazis destroyed her, "that people are good."

The reform impulse of Jacksonian America was too rich and varied in its expression to catalogue here, but examples may be given. Significant reform efforts were focused upon women's education and women's rights. During the 1820s, Emma Willard and Catherine Beecher opened schools in New York and Connecticut, respectively, in order to provide young women with a modern education and to prepare them for productive careers. One of the most impressive of such efforts was Mary Lyon's. A teacher of 20 years' experience, she founded Mount Holyoke Female Seminary in 1837 to provide higher education for women. The seminary later became famous as Mount Holyoke College. It was located in the Massachusetts village of South Hadley, just a few miles from Amherst College, which, in certain respects, provided Mary Lyon with a model. Lyon died 12 years later, in 1849, at the age of 52. Her short life of quiet, unadorned struggle in the service of educational reform helped mold the development of women's colleges across the country, enriching the lives of generations of women yet unborn.

From the earliest years, immigrants to American shores have dreamed of winning salvation, not merely by their own individual efforts, but through cooperation with others in closely knit communities that applied the principle of "all for one and one for all."

These people established their own tiny commonwealths. Some of these were of religious origin, inspired and founded by prophets who brought bands of followers to this country to worship God as they pleased and to live in their own way, free from the cruel persecution of European kings. Others were set up as *utopias*, or model societies whose members might work and play together, grow rich together in small worlds of brotherhood and sisterhood, set apart from the wider world filled, as it was, with cruelty and greed.

Whatever philosophy they followed, communities like these took up land all over the country and cultivated it through a system of cooperative

farming. The participants built societies often experimental in nature, designed as models that the outside world might one day take note of and, perhaps, imitate. By 1850 there were few states—from Maine clear across the country to Iowa, from Wisconsin to Louisiana—in which such model communities were not located. Such communities, to be sure, had been founded long before the Jacksonian age. What is significant is that during the Jacksonian period so many more of them came into existence.

The struggle for the abolition of slavery and for equal rights for colored people was the greatest of all the struggles for social reform generated during the Jacksonian era. Some attention will be paid to it in chapter 6.

* * * *

On March 4, 1829, Anne Royall, a Washington journalist, attended the ceremonies when Andrew Jackson was sworn in as seventh president of the United States. The ceremony took place on the eastern portico of the Capitol. "Not only every seat," wrote Ms. Royall, "but every inch of the platform was crowded, by men, women and children. These had forced the guards, and taken possession. I was shoved and pushed from one place to another, squeezed and be trampled; and at length wedged up about an inch from the door; … as for moving backwards or forwards, it was out of the question."

Andrew Jackson was in the middle of the crush, surrounded by important people like Supreme Court judges and ambassadors from other countries. "He was thin and pale," Ms. Royall wrote, "and his countenance was melancholy." Soon after the ceremony the president left, followed by a huge crowd of shouting people.

Many of these people showed up later for a reception at the White House, fighting with each other for a chance to get near the president and shake his hand. When it was all over, it seemed as though a hurricane had passed: Wreckage was littered all over the floor. "Cut glass and china," said

Ms. Royall, "had been broken in the struggle to get the refreshments."

Jackson's election to the presidency in 1828 marked the coming of age of a political idea—the idea that people had a right to a voice in choosing their rulers, not because they were rich or powerful, but simply because they were people.

In colonial times the right to vote was linked with the ownership of property and the payment of a property tax. It was felt that only propertied people had a "stake" in the community; this "stake," traditionally, was real estate (land) or personal property like ships that carried cargoes across the sea. Propertied people, according to this philosophy, were the ones who ought to rule, who ought to wield power. Poor people existed not to rule but to *be* ruled.

In the short period between 1790 and 1830, this idea of the property qualification as a key element conferring the right to vote went out of fashion. It is true that the right to vote, in 1830, still remained very limited: Most black people and almost all women were barred from its exercise. Nonetheless, a big change was taking place. By 1830 the right to vote and to be a candidate for office was coming to be seen as a white man's *right*, not because he was a wealthy person with broad lands or fine houses and ships, but *because he was a man.*

This was an idea with a big future ahead of it, both in the United States and indeed throughout the whole world. The White House celebration of March 4, 1829, was a dramatic expression of this fact. The people had put the president in the White House. The people's money had built it. They had a right to be there.

Universal manhood suffrage is one of the building blocks of democracy in the modern age. The people of the United States were pioneers in making it a reality.

The theory of democracy holds that final power to make important decisions affecting the life of the people rests with the people themselves, not with those who rule them. The people express their will, the theory goes, by choosing the officials to run the country and to take care of the interests of those who elect them. By voting, the people adopt constitutions or reject them; they set up governments or tear them down.

By such means the people in a democracy shape their institutions and select their agents, from presidents and congresspeople at the top to sheriffs and dogcatchers at the bottom of the ladder of political power and, in many cases, the judges as well.

Perhaps Thomas Jefferson best expressed this democratic theory of popular government when he wrote the Declaration of Independence. The only reason we need government, Jefferson said, is to help us in the struggle for life, freedom and happiness. If rulers abuse their trust, if they commit acts of oppression, robbery, or conquest, the people possess an "inalienable right" to put them down. If people are to be truly free, Jefferson continued, governments must exist upon the basis of a day-by-day scrutiny. If a government shapes up, fine. If not, it should be junked and replaced by a better one.

Between 1790 and 1830, voting began to be viewed as a human right. All men, it was now said, had a right to a voice in affairs of state. It did not matter whether they owned much land or no land, whether they paid high taxes or did not pay taxes at all. It did not matter whether they had money in the bank or no money. Power was in the people; they had the right, born of the American Revolution, to determine their own fate.

This new right assumed first of all the form of universal manhood suffrage. In all parts of the country, the advance of this concept during the early years of the 19th century either lowered the barriers to popular voting or swept many of them away. In the West this movement was even more marked than in the East. Between 1796 and 1821 eight states were admitted to the Union: Ohio, Indiana, Illinois, Tennessee, Missouri, Alabama, Louisiana and Mississippi. Each one established universal white manhood suffrage with only minor restrictions.

Universal white manhood suffrage was an elastic idea; it was linked with the doctrine not merely that all people have rights but that they have *equal* rights. If men had the right to vote, why not women? If whites had the right to vote, why not blacks? It was inevitable that in the course of time people excluded from the suffrage right would raise the demand for it.

Hard upon the heels of the victory of universal white manhood suffrage, women too began to organize and to claim the right to vote. The first women's rights convention was held in 1848 at Seneca Falls, in New York state. "It is the duty of the women of this country," the convention resolved, "to secure to themselves their sacred right to the elective franchise."

Susan B. Anthony was one of the organizers of the women's rights movement. After the Seneca Falls convention was over, she traveled from one end of New York to the other, talking to women about their rights and the need to struggle in order to win them.

A young woman named Caroline Cowles heard Ms. Anthony speak when she visited Canandaigua in the bitter cold of December 1855. The hall was packed. "She talked very plainly about our rights," wrote Caroline in her diary, "and how we should stand up for them, and said the world would never go right until the women had just as much right to vote and rule as the men. She asked us all to come up and sign our names who would promise to do all in our power to bring about that glad day when equal rights should be the law of the land."

Universal manhood suffrage introduced a new kind of responsibility into the political process. Rulers must now face the voters in election campaigns. They must explain their policies and set forth their plans. Henceforth they would have to be *accountable* to the electorate. They were under pressure to shape programs of action that would get them elected and that would produce the kind of reforms that the voters wanted. This produced, too, a new kind of competition among politicians. It is

no accident that the system of political parties as a way of procuring the election of presidents, congresspeople, and city officials emerged fully fledged upon the American scene during the years 1790 to 1830.

Universal manhood suffrage appeared to spread rapidly during the early 19th century. In actuality, it was a change that had been in preparation for many years.

Participation in the political process, in the first place, was far more widespread during the colonial period than might have been expected. America was a land-rich country; many more people owned land here than in Europe. Even ownership of only a few acres might carry with it the right to vote. For this reason, voting in colonial America was a popular institution. Thus when universal manhood suffrage was enacted in state after state, it was important not so much for what it accomplished right away, as for what it promised. Immigration, for example, more than doubled the size of the Massachusetts voting population between 1820 and 1860.

The American revolutionary tradition, in the second place, needs to be stressed in explaining the arrival of universal manhood suffrage. The Revolution was won in a struggle for national independence during which males between the ages of 16 and 60 bore arms and sacrificed much. It wasn't easy, when the war was over, to say "We are happy to have you die for your country in time of war, but you may not have a voice in running it in time of peace."

It may also be said that political leaders who pressed for voting reforms during the 1820s were responding to the democratic spirit of the age. Some of them realized that big changes were going on as immigrants flocked to the United States and as workers began to cluster in the new and ever-expanding industrial towns. Some politicians understood that the demand for voting rights among the newcomers would soon become irresistible. They were anxious to win credit for conceding in timely

Immigration Into the Western Territories by Decade, 1810–1840			
	1810	**1820**	**1830**	**1840**
Old Northwest	270,000	790,000	1,500,000	3,000,000
Old Southwest	710,000	1,200,000	1,800,000	2,575,000

fashion what the people might otherwise decide to take by force.

This was well illustrated in the New York constitutional convention of 1821. Democrats called for this meeting in order to reform the state constitution and to extend voting rights. They knew that tens of thousands of New York tenant farmers wanted the vote; and, too, they were anxious to tap the votes of thousands of immigrants swarming into New York City every year. One speaker at the meeting put it this way: "Why should the men who have had the good fortune to inherit property," he said, "enjoy greater privileges than those … who earn their daily bread by the sweat of their brow? … As honest poverty is no disgrace, it ought to form no obstacle to the full enjoyment of our political rights."

The movement towards universal manhood suffrage when Andrew Jackson became president in 1829 had obvious limitations. Women were shut out, and so too were the slaves and most free black people. By midcentury the electorate was still a minority of the total adult population.

This continuing denial of human rights to great numbers of Americans was, in the course of time, to prove as significant as the victory of manhood suffrage described above. It meant that new movements would be born in a continuing struggle for full democracy.

In 1829, when Anne Royall recorded the riotous scene at the White House reception, the great social transformations of the Jacksonian era were well underway. Some account of these will be given in the pages that follow.

* * * *

At the end of the war with Great Britain in 1783, people began to move in ever-growing numbers into the lands beyond the Appalachians, into the old Northwest and the old Southwest. Kentucky, for example, had enough people to be admitted to the Union as a state in 1792, Ohio in 1803. The land was fertile beyond belief, the lakes and streams were pure and clear, and parakeets with shining green and yellow plumage swarmed by the waters. Midwestern settlers welcomed travelers with coffee, corn bread, venison and pork. One visitor to Indiana thought the women were "silent and reserved"; cabins and settlements abounded with tow-headed children.

The War of 1812 speeded up the westward movement, for it shattered Tecumseh's dream of an all-Indian resistance; and it taught the British that there was no way to win back the Mississippi Valley that they had lost. The figures tell the story: They show how a stream of people was turning into a flood.

After 1815, towns began to grow in the Midwest like, for example, Cincinnati. Here the farmers brought their products for shipment to eastern or southern markets, and here they came to buy the things they needed—like axes, guns, ploughs, clocks and sturdy clothing.

This woodcut illustrates the organization of a New England textile factory in the 1820s and 1830s. The weaving machines are lined up in long rows, three or four abreast, down the length of the shed. The power hookup is to a series of overhead shafts and drums, each drum activating four machines. One mill girl attends to, or "minds," each machine. A male overseer checks the work. The noise, as hundreds of machines clack and whirr, is infernal.

This growing western demand gave a boost to factory production in New England and the central Atlantic states (New York, New Jersey and Pennsylvania). Machines began to be used to carry out tasks, like spinning thread and weaving cloth, that had earlier been done by hand. These machines were brought together into large sheds, or factories, that used first water power and later steam power, to make them run. Little factory towns began to spring up in areas where there were many streams and a steady supply of water.

Francis Cabot Lowell, a Boston merchant, was a pioneer in the development of this new type of industry. Lowell and his Boston associates, who provided much of the money that was needed, set up a factory at Waltham, Massachusetts, in 1813. Here the entire process of cloth production—that is, spinning thread, weaving fabric and dyeing it— was carried on under the same roof. In 1822, when

the war was over, Lowell began something even bigger. He built a town in Massachusetts that he called Lowell, after himself, and brought in young women from the countryside to run his machines. By 1830 the town of Lowell kept 6,000 workers busy turning out 600,000 yards of cloth each week.

One of these Lowell workers was a little girl named Lucy Larcom. She was sent to work in the factory—or mill, as it was called in those days—so that she might help support her widowed mother and her younger brothers and sisters. Many children worked in the mills because their families were too poor to get by without their children's labor. Lucy, like so many other young people, hated it. Life in the midst of the "buzzing and hissing and whistling of pulleys and rollers and spindles and flyers" was dull and tiring for a little girl who would have been happier playing in the fields or studying in school. But, as she wrote, "alas, I could not go.

By the 1830s steamboats carrying passengers and freight had revolutionized the commerce of the Midwest. Steamboat captains often raced their ships against each other, with the delighted passengers laying huge bets. This led to terrible accidents, as crews stoked furnaces and boilers blew up under the enormous pressure.

The little money I could earn—one dollar a week … was needed in the family."

The early mill towns were quite different from the huge industrial cities of our own time. Streets were quiet, flowers bloomed there, and in the spring the buzzing of bees could be heard. Nature, as Lucy wrote, "came very close to the mill gates … There was green grass all around them; violets and geraniums grew by the canals; long stretches of open land between the [factory] buildings and the streets made the town seem country-like."

Eastern factories like Lowell's grew big because they were producing for a big market, not only in the East but across the mountains in the Midwest. But of course such factories could not exist, and they certainly could not grow, without a reliable way of getting their merchandise to the consumer. There had to be a better way than hauling it over the dirt roads and rutted trails that Americans had inherited from an earlier day.

Sure enough, the years following 1814 saw a great improvement in the means of transportation—that is, ways of getting goods to market quickly and easily. The first big step was the steamboat; there were several pioneers here, but the most important of them was Robert Fulton, of Pennsylvania.

Fulton, who was both an artist and an inventor, was living in Paris in 1803 when Robert Livingston arrived to help arrange the Louisiana Purchase. The two men teamed up: Livingston's wealth and Fulton's mechanical ability made a good combination. They floated their first steamboat on the river Seine in Paris in August 1803. The French emperor, Napoleon, was impressed. "This may change the face of the world," he said.

Soon afterward Fulton returned to the United States, where he designed and built a 130-foot-long craft powered by steam. It was named the *Clermont*, after Livingston's country place on the Hudson River. Precisely at 1:00 P.M. on September 10, 1807, the *Clermont* left its wharf in lower Manhattan and moved out into the Hudson for its trial run to Albany and back. A big crowd watched, for a boat driven by steam was a thing that New Yorkers had never seen before. Two huge paddle wheels were hung on each side of the ship; as smoke and sparks belched from the furnace, these wheels began to turn, scattering a fine white spray behind them. People on the shore were holding their sides with laughter, pointing and jeering at the strange sight. But as the *Clermont* picked up speed, one observer tells us, "this feeling gave way to undisguised delight, and cheer after cheer went up from the vast throng."

Steam engines in those days were something new, an invention of the devil. Simple fisherfolk in their sailing craft on the Hudson River were terrified. They saw "what they supposed to be a huge monster, vomiting fire and smoke from its throat and shaking the river with its roar. Some threw themselves flat on the decks of their vessels, where they remained in an agony of terror until the monster had passed, while others made for the shore." Soon, of course, everybody became used to this new magic, which drove boats through the water without the help of oars or sails. By 1830 hundreds of steamboats were gliding over the nation's waterways.

Fulton's *Clermont* marked the dawn of a new technological age, the age of steam. The next step was to put steam engines upon wheels, to lay iron rails across the country and to use these engines to haul passengers and freight. The steam engine, too, was a revolutionary new source of energy that had importance for production as well as transportation. By 1830 hundreds of stationary engines were being installed in factories and upon cotton plantations to

run machines that had previously been operated by water or horse power.

Yet another very important advance in transportation after the end of the War of 1812 was building a network of canals—huge manmade ditches, linked with rivers and filled with water, that could transport bulky stuff like wheat or coal on huge barges hauled by teams of horses. Many great canals were built after 1800, but the greatest of them all was the Erie Canal, which connected the East with the Midwest by the construction of a 350-mile waterway along the Mohawk gap in the Appalachian mountain wall.

Work was begun on this tremendous project on July 4, 1817. Much of the hard labor was done by Irish immigrants who began to reach the country in large numbers when the war ended in 1814. Wherever canals were to be dug or rails to be laid in the years to come, the Irish would be there. Tyrone Power, an English traveler, described them at work:

> *hundreds of fine fellows labouring beneath a sun that … was at times insufferably fierce … wading among stumps of trees, waist-deep in black mud, clearing the spaces pumped out by powerful steam engines; wheeling, digging, hewing, or bearing burdens it made one's shoulders ache to look upon.*

Hundreds died at the diggings in accidents when rock ledges had to be blasted away or of fever, sunstroke and exhaustion. But the work went on. The Erie Canal was opened to traffic along its full route in 1825. The event was announced by the roar of cannon placed in a continuous line at eight-mile intervals from Buffalo to Sandy Hook. The longest canal in the world had been finished in a mere eight years.

The Erie Canal linked the Great Lakes with the Atlantic Ocean. Western foodstuffs and raw materials could now be brought very cheaply to the East, and factory-made goods could be sent the

Major Canals, 1840

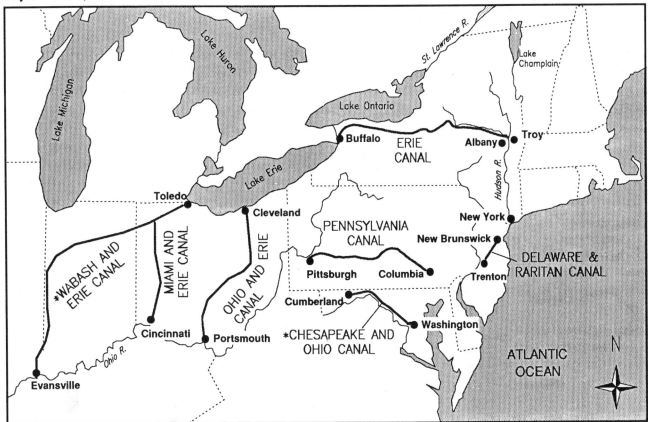

* Canals under construction

other way. The canal also helped to populate the West by providing cheap and easy transportation on passenger boats for tens of thousands of settlers and immigrants. Fares charged were as little as one cent per mile, or less than $4.00 per person for the canal's entire length, from Albany to Buffalo.

In 1814 the American road system was still in miserable shape. Roads were dusty tracks in summer, quagmires in the rainy season. Road travel, too, was slowed down by an almost complete lack of bridges. Big rivers had to be crossed by ferry, which meant a delay of hours.

After the War of 1812 was over, private companies began to improve many roads and to surface them with stone or gravel. They then hung barriers, or turnpikes, across the road and charged the traveler a fee, or toll, for the right to use it; the gateman swung the turnpike open after the fee was paid. One of the greatest of these new, improved

highways was called the Cumberland Road, and it was built by the federal government. The Cumberland Road's starting point was in western Maryland. By 1850, 800 miles had been completed, and the road reached as far as Vandalia, in central Illinois. Already by the 1830s the Cumberland Road was an important stone track linking East and Midwest. "Large wagons," as one traveler noted, "covered with white canvas crawled west passing endless flocks of horses, mules, cattle, hogs and sheep being driven to eastern markets." People also admired the fine stone bridges that carried the road across rivers and streams. "Their thick walls," the traveler said, "round stone buttresses, and carved keystones combine to give them an air of Roman solidity and strength."

An engineer, David Stephenson, saw these great canals and roads as a triumph of human labor. "These great lines of communication," he said, "are

… cut through thick and almost impenetrable forest where [it is possible] to travel for a whole day without encountering a village or even a house." None of this would have been possible without the unbelievable efforts of the immigrants who flocked to American's shores after the War of 1812. From 1815 to 1848, 3,000,000 people fled from Europe and came to the United States to build a new life for themselves. In this short timespan more people reached these shores than the total, European and African combined, who had come during the entire colonial period; and six out of every ten of these immigrants were Irish.

Ireland is a tiny country. It stands at the very western edge of Europe, hammered by the long Atlantic breakers; it is a land of mist, of moor, of endless rain. Too close to England, it became the victim of English greed. Hundreds of years ago the English invaded Ireland, seized its green and fertile acres and turned its people, the Gaels, into landless peasants. By the beginning of the 19th century, most of the Irish were a conquered people living in poverty on a land they no longer owned, toiling for the benefit of English landlords whom they rarely saw.

After 1815 the eyes of many poor Irish people turned across the Atlantic to the young, thriving United States. If they could find money for the ocean crossing they could get good jobs in the New World, digging canals, laying railroad tracks, working in New England factories. American wages would put meat and white bread upon their tables—luxuries almost undreamed of in the Irish cabins.

A tiny trickle of Irish immigrants reached America during the colonial period. After 1815 this trickle turned into a flood. During the 1820s 50,000 Irish crossed the Atlantic; during the 1830s 170,000, or more than three times that number, came. In the 1840s the flood turned into a tidal wave, for in 1845 famine hit Ireland. Most of the people were so poor that only the potatoes that they grew in their tiny garden plots stood between them

and hunger. In 1845 the rot set in; potatoes stored away for winter use turned into a stinking, inedible mess. During the famine years that followed (1847–1854), one million Irish died in the fields and the huts of their native land; one million more quit Ireland forever. They faced a simple choice: emigrate or die.

They sailed in these years for Newfoundland, for Montreal, for Halifax, for New York, Philadelphia, Boston. Many died at sea, but many more survived and came ashore to dig canals, to lay iron rails, to work in the factories.

Many of the mills to which children like Lucy Larcom or Irish immigrants came produced cotton thread and cotton clothing. Not only in the United States but also in Great Britain, these mills used up enormous quantities of raw cotton. By 1850, indeed, cotton was the most valuable crop grown upon American farmlands; and most of it was grown by slaves. How this came to be is one of the most important parts of our story.

In 1789, the year that George Washington was setting up his government in New York City, a young man named Eli Whitney, born and raised in Connecticut, went off to Yale College to get an education. Eli graduated in 1792 and then got a job in South Carolina as a tutor in a planter's family; planters in those days liked to have their children taught at home, and they often hired college graduates to do the job.

On the way to New York to take a ship down the coast, Eli met Catherine Greene. Catherine was born on Block Island, a windswept patch of land that rises out of the sea at the eastern approach to Long Island Sound, and is part of the state of Rhode Island. She was the widow of Nathanael Greene, a famous Revolutionary War general, and the mistress of Mulberry Grove, a plantation near Savannah in Georgia.

Mulberry Grove was a present to General Greene from the people of Georgia, who were very grateful to him for the way that he had fought the British in the South. The general was very pleased with his gift, which included 100 slaves. He planted 100 acres in rice and had a lovely fruit garden where, as he wrote to a friend, he grew "apples, pears, peaches, apricots, nectarines, plums ... figs, pomegranates, and oranges."

Greene did not live long to enjoy his good fortune; he died in 1786, leaving Catherine alone with five small children. Now, in 1792, she was going back to Mulberry Grove after a visit back home in Rhode Island. At the time she was nearly 40 years old, and Whitney was 27. Charmed with the lady's company, he said yes when she invited him to go and stay for a while at Mulberry Grove.

When Mrs. Greene and Whitney arrived, neighboring planters came to visit, and they talked freely about a problem which was bothering them. These Georgia coastal planters were growing a type of cotton known as blackseed. Cotton is simply the fiber, or fuzz, that sticks to the outside of a cotton seed. In the case of blackseed cotton, these fibers are long and silky; all you have to do before you spin them into thread is either pull them off the seed by hand or pass them through a set of rollers.

The problem that the Georgia planters were facing in 1792 was that they were unable to raise enough blackseed cotton to meet the growing demand of the European mills; blackseed cotton grows only in the moist, semitropical lowlands, along a narrow strip of the Georgia and South Carolina coast. There was, indeed, a type of the cotton that *would* grow inland, called greenseed cotton. But the fuzz was so tightly attached to the seed that it was impossible to separate the two without taking weeks of time and lots of labor. "If you can find an easy way to process greenseed," the planters told Whitney, "why, it can be grown all over the South, and it will make fortunes for all of us."

Eli loved to design tools and mechanical gadgets, and in this respect he was an inventor of genius. He set to work on the planters' problem in the spring of 1793. "All agreed," he wrote to his father, "that if a machine could be invented which would clean

This drawing shows a cotton gin being operated on a plantation as the slaves bring in the harvest from the fields and the master and his overseer stand in the background. Hand machines of the type shown did not last for long; they were replaced by much more efficient steam-operated gins.

the cotton [quickly], it would be a great thing both to the country and to the inventor." By the summer of the same year he had produced his first cotton engine, called a "gin" for short.

This machine was a wooden drum mounted in a large box and turned by a crank. Rows of metal hooks were stuck into the surface of the drum. As the hooks turned, they passed through slots in a metal plate and tore into cotton seeds on the other side of the plate. As the drum went on spinning, soon you had bare seeds on one side of the plate, cotton fiber on the other.

Whitney's cotton gin, turned by hand, made it ten times as easy for a person to process greenseed cotton as it was before. But if you used a horse or a steam engine to turn the crank you could "gin" fifty or a hundred times as much cotton in an hour as you could without the machine. Everybody praised Whitney, and he, too, was pleased with his invention. "I shall," as he told his father, "gain some honor as well as profit by [it]." The gin made him famous but not rich. Planters simply built their own models without telling Whitney or paying him the fee that, as the inventor, he was entitled to collect. Soon there were hundreds of gins on Southern plantations run by hand, by horse, by water power, and by steam.

During the long years of slavery, black women comforted and cared for white children while their own babies lay unwatched in the shacks and fields. "All the Pretty Little Horses" is both lullaby and lament that comes down to us from slavery days through oral tradition.

As the years passed, cotton production spread right across the South, all the way from the Georgia and South Carolina coast to Texas. Slaves continued to raise the cotton by hand. Harvesting the crop was skilled work that needed nimble fingers. It required painful effort for long hours and long weeks under the broiling Southern sun.

Solomon Northup, a Louisiana slave, has left a vivid account of the growing of cotton. Northup, originally a free man and a citizen of New York state, was kidnapped from his home in Saratoga Springs in 1841, torn from his wife and children, smuggled off to New Orleans by sea and sold as a slave. After he had toiled ten years on Louisiana plantations, Northup regained his freedom in 1852, returned home and wrote down his story; he died a few years later. His book, *Twelve Years a Slave*, came out as a paperback in 1854 and was widely read in the North. Scholars have hailed it as a first-rate and truthful contribution to American historical literature. It remains in print to this day.

First, wrote Northup, the ground must be prepared in January and February to receive the cotton seed. "The ground is prepared," he wrote,

by throwing up beds or ridges with the plough ... Oxen and mules ... are used ... The women as frequently as the men perform this labor, feeding,

Once ginned and baled, the cotton was shipped off to merchants who exported it to Europe or sold it to American manufacturers, primarily in the North. Cotton bales are here shown piled up at the Charleston, South Carolina, wharf, awaiting export to foreign and domestic ports.

currying and taking care of their teams, and in all respects doing the field and stable work, precisely as do the ploughboys of the North.

When the ground was ready, it was seeded. In March and April, the plough gouged out a little trough along the ridges, "into which a girl usually drops the seed, which she carried in a bag hung around her neck."

Soon the green shoots appeared; it was time to hoe between the ridges, in order to keep the beds free of weeds. Day after dull day, the slaves passed up and down the rows, thinning the plants and scraping away the weeds that, if left alone, would choke them. This went on until July. It was hard

work. "During all these hoeings," wrote Northup, "the overseer follows the slaves on horseback with a whip … If one falls behind, or is a moment idle, he is whipped. In fact the lash is flying from morning until night, the whole day long."

In August the cotton ripened, and harvesting began. Each slave was given a sack to hang around his or her neck, "the mouth of the sack [being] breast high, while the bottom reaches nearly to the ground." During this harvest season, in August and September, "the slaves must be in the field as soon as it is light, and they must stay there until it is too dark to see." All day long they toiled without rest, except for a few minutes at the noonday break: "They are not permitted to be idle," wrote Northup,

81

"until it is too dark to see, and when the moon is full, they must oftentimes labor til the middle of the night."

No matter how tired a slave was at the end of the day, he would carry his baskets to the gin-house, still in fear of the bloody, searing lash. If he had picked less than his quota, he would be lashed. If he had picked more, then he would have that much more to pick the next day. "Whether he has too little or too much," wrote Northup, his approach to the gin- house is always with fear and trembling." And, no matter how late he went to sleep, heaven help the slave who overslept in the morning. "Such an offense," said Northup, "would certainly be attended with not less than twenty lashes."

In 1815 a land rush set in as people swarmed across the mountains into the old Southwest to clear land and to make fortunes from cotton. Wealthy planters and slave traders took with them flocks of slaves. Slaves crowded coastal vessels headed for Mobile and New Orleans, and they were packed into steamboats threading their way south along the Ohio and Mississippi rivers. Bound together by ropes or chains, they wound in weary "coffles" across the overland trails. James K. Paulding, secretary of the Navy, described in 1816 a scene that in the years to come would be common. He saw in Virginia

a little cart drawn by one horse, in which five or six half-naked black children were tumbled like pigs together ... Behind the cart marched three black women, with head, neck, and breasts uncovered, and without shoes or stockings: next came three men, bareheaded and chained together with an ox-chain. Last ... came a white man on horseback.

By 1850 cotton was being grown in a huge belt of land that stretched from the Atlantic coast to Texas. As for black slaves, there were 750,000 of them in 1790, but by 1850 their numbers had increased to 3 1/2 million, or more than four times.

White Americans had thus created one of the largest slave empires known to history. A revolution fought for human rights and human freedom had produced a world in which millions of human beings were not allowed to have any rights at all, where they must work from birth to death for the people who owned them, and must bear children who would suffer the same fate.

Indian "Removal"

As the settlers moved westward to grow tobacco and cotton in the fertile Mississippi Valley, they encountered the native peoples who had been living there for many years. In 1815 there were five Indian nations still living in the southeastern section of the United States. These were the Choctaws, the Chickasaws, the Creeks, the Cherokees and the Seminoles. The Choctaws, the Chickasaws and the Creeks lived in the Mississippi Territory, or the present states of Mississippi and Alabama. The Cherokees were spread throughout the vast and beautiful region of the southern Appalachian Mountains, mostly in the states of Tennessee, North Carolina and Georgia. As for the Seminoles, they were an interracial group of Indians and black slaves who had fled south from the whites during the colonial period and had found refuge in the trackless swamps of Spanish Florida.

Most of these peoples cultivated the soil and were herdsmen and hunters as well. Thomas Lorraine McKenney, who in 1824 became the chief of the Federal Bureau of Indian Affairs, described the Cherokees at that time. They owned, he wrote,

numberless herds of cattle ... horses ... numerous flocks of sheep, goats, and swine ... The[ir] soil is generally rich, producing Indian corn, cotton, tobacco, wheat, oats, indigo, sweet and Irish potatoes ... Apple and peach orchards are quite common, gardens are cultivated, and much attention is paid to them ... Numerous and flourishing villages are seen in every section of their country.

After 1815, Southern planters, land agents, and political leaders were giving much thought to the question of how to uproot these Indian nations, persuade them to give up their lands and get them out of the way. Their aim was to open up the whole area to cotton production, carried forward with gangs of black slaves on big plantations. Many of these people shared the views of federal officials like Andrew Jackson and John C. Calhoun. The Indians, they considered, must be pressured into surrendering all their lands east of the Mississippi River and signing agreements to that effect specially drawn up for them by the federal government. In exchange for what they had lost, the Indians would be given land on the prairies on the western side of the Mississippi in a special Indian Territory set aside for that purpose. There the federal government would provide them with seed, tools and farm animals and help them stake out farms and become full-time farmers. Those that didn't want to farm could go and chase the buffalo.

But the Indian nations fiercely resisted the idea of giving up their lands and going into exile. For many years the pattern of federal-Indian relations was always the same. The federal agents asked the Indian peoples to surrender their lands a little at a time. Piece by piece, the Indians gave them up. They did this because they hoped that if they cooperated with the United States they would be left alone to live in peace on the land that still belonged to them; and this, indeed, is exactly what the federal government promised in the land treaties that it drew up and signed along with the Indian chiefs. These were idle hopes and idle promises. The more the Indians gave, the more they were asked to give. Between 1800 and 1830 the Choctaws, for example, gave up 22,000,000 acres of land, or about four-fifths of the total extent of the state of Mississippi.

The first of these treaties that suggested to the Choctaws the idea of "removal" west of the Mississippi was the Treaty of Doak's Stand, signed in 1820. Andrew Jackson himself was, at the time, chief of the Federal Bureau of Indian Affairs; and his was the master mind behind the agreement. At Doak's Stand the Choctaw chiefs promised that they would give up the very last of their Mississippi lands and move to the Indian Territory.

But for ten years the Treaty of Doak's Stand didn't mean a thing. The fact that a number of chiefs had signed it didn't matter much to the average Choctaw Indian—especially when federal agents and officials were standing around the treaty site, feeding the chiefs whiskey or making them presents of kettles, beads or blankets. Mississippi was where the Choctaws were born and raised; Mississippi was where they planned to die. Mississippi was their motherland, and they weren't going to move.

In 1829, ten years after the Treaty of Doak's Stand was signed, Andrew Jackson became president of the United States. Now he could do more than just *ask* Indians to leave; as commander-in-chief of the armed forces, he had in his hands the power to *make* them go. Throughout the South, in the states of Alabama, Mississippi, North Carolina, Tennessee and Georgia, the cotton planters and land speculators were waiting for him to act. They had, they thought, already waited too long. Why, they asked, should a few "savages" hold up progress?

Shortly after he'd settled in at the White House, Andrew Jackson drew up and sent to Congress an Indian removal bill, with a request that it be enacted into law. This bill gave the president permission to offer all of the Indian peoples in the southeastern portion of the United States land in the Indian Territory in exchange for the lands that they then possessed. The bill said that the president could set aside and spend federal funds in order to provide for the transportation of all the people involved—something between 75,000 and 90,000 of them.

The Indian removal bill sparked a bitter debate in both Houses. Many Congressmen felt that it was both cruel and unjust to uproot the Indians; they charged that the government was planning to carry out its program at the point of the bayonet. The bill passed in both the Senate and the House of Representatives with almost as many people voting against it as voted for it. Jackson then drew up treaties for the tribal chiefs to sign, agreeing that they would give up their lands and "remove" to territory west of the Mississippi.

Andrew Jackson and Martin van Buren, who followed him to the White House in 1837, carried out this plan with almost total success. Indian removal involved one full-scale war against the Seminoles, and all in all several thousand Indians lost their lives as a result of the operation. The cost to the American taxpayer ran to millions of dollars.

"Removal" is not a very good word to describe what Andrew Jackson and Martin van Buren did to the Choctaws, Chickasaws, Creeks, Cherokees, and Seminoles—to say nothing about a number of other tribes who were removed from the old Northwest at about the same time. Many, when told that they must go, left home quietly. Before going, they sat down by the running streams and wept. They stroked the trees, talked to them, kissed their leaves. They went down on their knees and touched their foreheads to the ground. The forests echoed with their lamentation.

Others—especially Creeks, Cherokees and Seminoles—did not go quietly into that dark night known to history as the Trail of Tears. Some stayed in their cabins, some went into hiding, some fled into the woods. Then federal troops and state militia went to look for them, hunted them out with guns and bayonets and made them go, whether they would or not. James Mooney, Indiana-born historian of the Indian peoples, described a scene that became typical when Cherokee removal began in 1837. "Squads of troops," he wrote,

were sent to search out with rifle and bayonet every small cabin hidden away in the coves or by the side of mountain streams ... Families at dinner were startled by the sudden gleam of bayonets in the doorway and rose up to be driven by blows and

Removal of Indian Tribes from the Southeast: 1830-1840

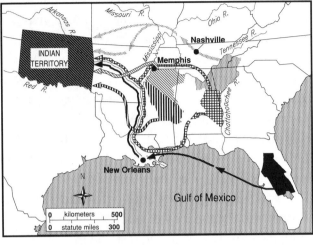

Lands and Routes of Removal

| Cherokee | Choctaw | Seminole |
| Chickasaw | Creek | |

oaths along the trail ... Men were seized in their fields or going along the road, women were taken from their spinning wheels and children from their play.

As they were driven away, some turned their heads for a last look at the homes they were leaving; all they saw was smoke and flames as flocks of whites moved in to loot and burn the cabins and to round up and drive away herds of cattle, goats and swine.

The distance that the Indian peoples had to cover in order to reach the Indian Territory was anywhere from 500 to 1,000 miles, depending on the point from which they started. Transporting tens of thousands of people this way was not an easy job. The government provided only a few wagons; most of the ablebodied had to travel on foot, and this took several months. In the meantime, the federal government had to provide food, shelter, clothing and river transportation, just as it would have done for an army on the march. This was, indeed, up to this time, the biggest and most complicated operation ever undertaken by the federal government.

Much of the job was badly mismanaged. People starved because there was no food, froze because there were no blankets, died of thirst because there was no water. Some of the worst disasters took place when overloaded steamboats collided on the Mississippi and sank with the loss of hundreds of lives. Dreadful epidemics of cholera swept away hundreds who had been rounded up and crammed like cattle into stockades. Old people and children were the special victims. The old died in each other's arms as they huddled together for warmth in the carts. The children walked the frozen trail with bare and bloody feet, and died of exhaustion.

About 15,000 Indian people lost their lives during the long trek. Many died because of broken health, many because of broken hearts. As one of the survivors in the Indian Territory said:

Long time we travel on way to new land. People feel bad when they leave ... Women cry and make sad wails. Children cry and many men cry, and all look sad when friends die, but they say nothing and just put heads down and keep on go towards West. Many days pass and people die very much.

When the Indians were first sent there, the Louisiana Purchase was still just what it had been for hundreds of years before—an expanse of waving grassland, the home of the buffalo that grazed there in uncounted millions and of the nomadic peoples who lived by hunting the herds. West of the 100° meridian of longitude, the land was almost treeless, and the rainfall amounted to only a few inches a year. The summers were a torment of heat, tornadoes, and drought; the winters brought numbing cold, snowstorms and blizzards.

The Louisiana Purchase was the land of the prairies, of the high plains. People in those days called it "the great American desert" and labeled it that way on their maps; a few fur traders and trappers, they thought, might make a living out

there, maybe. But whoever would want to settle in such an awful country?

Beginning in the 1820s, Americans did begin to move out onto the prairies and to blaze trails across them. The lure that pulled people to risk their lives in that harsh land was what lay beyond. To the west and the southwest lay the Spanish borderlands, the vast provinces of New Mexico and California that Spain had claimed in the 16th century but in which only very few Spaniards had settled. Beyond the prairies to the northwest lay the wondrously beautiful Oregon country. Oregon, in the 1820s, was a no-man's-land in which Russians, British and Americans all had claims. Oregon stretched from the Rocky Mountains in the east to the Pacific in the west, from Spanish California in the south to Russian Alaska in the north. British and Americans were content, for the time being, to enjoy what they called "joint occupancy."

The Spanish province of Texas was a special case. There was no prairie barrier between the Mississippi River and the fertile, well-watered lands of the eastern part of the province, only vast stretches of pinewoods. Because eastern Texas was easier to reach, American settlers moved there earlier and faster than they did to Oregon or California. By 1830 there were 20,000 of them raising cattle and cotton in the lovely valleys of the Trinity, the Brazos, the Colorado and the San Antonio rivers. These people brought with them about 1,000 black slaves.

Oregon, California and portions of New Mexico had one thing in common that the high plains lacked—well-wooded lands, abundant water supplies and a fine climate. With territory like this awaiting them, the "Great American Desert" was, for the pioneers, not a place to live or linger but simply an obstacle to cross.

The Santa Fe Trail was the first of the great new routes across the plains that came into use at this time. It led from Independence and Council Grove in western Missouri some 700 miles across what is now the state of Kansas to Santa Fe, capital of New

Mexico, close by the waters of the Rio Grande del Norte. The trail moved west and southwest along the Arkansas, Cimarron and Canadian rivers, skirted the Rockies that rose in snow-capped splendor to the north, and descended gradually into the broad, well-watered valley of the Rio Grande and the province of New Mexico.

The Santa Fe Trail was traveled not so much by pioneers seeking new lands to settle but by merchants carrying cotton goods from the United States, which they hoped to exchange for Mexican silver, furs and buffalo skins. The merchants and their muledrivers banded together in great caravans for protection, and they became skilled in the art of prairie survival. They were a little like the Chinese silk merchants of medieval times who rode their camel caravans from Karakorum in Mongolia, crossing as they went the fearsome wastes of the Gobi Desert and the Takla Makan, the T'ien Shan Mountains or the high Pamirs.

The Oregon Trail was the second of the great travel routes across the prairies during the Jacksonian period. In contrast to the Santa Fe Trail, this was used hardly at all by merchants but mostly by pioneers who dreamed of settling on the Pacific Coast and farming the land. Blazed by Wilson Price Hunt of New Jersey in 1811, the Oregon Trail began to be used by hundreds of people each year in the late thirties and by thousands during the forties. It followed the Missouri River to the Platte River, then westward up the Platte clear across what is now the state of Nebraska to Wind River in Wyoming. Here the path forked. People bound for Oregon followed the Snake and Columbia rivers to the coast. Those bound for California headed down the Humboldt River through Nevada until they reached Carson City and Sacramento. The Oregon Trail, from start to finish, was a grueling experience, 2,000 miles mostly on foot over the grasslands, across the mountainous continental divide in Wyoming, through the deserts or river gorges that lay beyond.

People heading west on the Oregon or Santa Fe trails came together at the beginning of the trip to form their caravans. This happened in one of a number of western Missouri towns like Franklin, Independence, or Council Grove. Leaders were chosen: These had the job of checking the route, choosing river crossings, scouting for campsites, setting up camps and organizing guard duty. Careful preparations had to be made before the caravan took to the trail: Trade goods and food supplies had to be packed onto the overland wagons, barrels filled with water, timber provided for wagon repairs.

The starting time was in the spring. There would be fresh grass along the trail for the cattle to graze upon—the most precious equipment that emigrants took with them to the far west were their horses, mules and cattle. Once they started the caravans crawled along, covering 10, maybe 15 miles in a day. But even at this slow pace there was much work to be done all the time. Wagons sank into the mud when creeks were crossed. The work of many men and many animals was needed to haul them out. From time to time a caravan had to cross a swamp; everybody had to wait while the men cut saplings and gathered brush so that they might build a rough road and then take their spades and give it a covering of dry earth. The pace of the slowest, in these caravans, was the pace of all. A single accident, like the breaking of a wagon's axletree, might mean a long wait while repairs were made.

When afternoon came and a campsite had been reached, the wagons were drawn up in a square or egg-shaped formation. The enclosed space formed a corral for the cattle and the horses. All around, on the outside, campfires were lit and the evening meal prepared. If the weather was fine, people spread their rugs or buffalo skins upon the prairie grass and slept in the open air, under the stars. In some parts of the high plains the air was dry; there were none of the bugs or insects that might have tormented sleepers in other places.

Emigrants crossing the high plains on the Oregon or California trails faced many perils. One of these was attack by hostile Native American bands, skilled horsemen who rode at great speed and matched their bows, arrows and tomahawks against emigrant rifles. This drawing shows an attack as the wagon train is strung out along the line of march.

The prairies had a life and beauty of their own that many travelers found magical. Grassy expanses, green and gold, stirred in the wind like the waves of the sea. Men, women, and children were sailing upon a "prairie ocean," and when there were no rivers to guide them, they steered their course, as at sea, by the compass. In the early summer wildflowers bloomed, mingling so thickly with the grass that children felt as if they were walking on a carpet in paradise.

No part of North America was as blessed with wildlife as the high plains. Francis Parkman traveled the prairies in 1846 just after he had graduated from Harvard. Describing the buffalo herds that he saw upon the Platte, he wrote that

the face of the country was dotted far and wide with countless hundreds of buffalo. They trooped along

in files and columns, bulls, cows, and calves … They scrambled away over the hills to the right and left; and far off, the pale blue swells in the extreme distance were dotted with innumerable specks.

Life on the plains was to be found in a thousand forms. "Gaudy butterflies," wrote Parkman, "fluttered about my horse's head; strangely formed beetles, glittering with metallic lustre, were crawling upon plants that I had never seen before; multitudes of lizards were darting like lightning over the sand."

Sooner or later the caravans met up with Indian people—small hunting parties, war parties, or whole tribes. Josiah Gregg described one such encounter: A Tennessean who crossed the plains from Missouri to Santa Fe many times during the 1830s, he came to love the lonely grasslands more than anything else in life. Gregg described one group of Indians who pitched their tents on the banks of the Cimarron as the caravan passed by. Five hundred wigwams, he wrote, "bespeckled the ample valley before us, and at once gave to its surface the aspect of an immense Indian village. The entire number of Indians, when collected together, could not have been less than two or three thousand."

Francis Parkman, too, observed the plains Indians closely. he described a village on the Platte in which

warriors, women, and children swarmed like bees; hundreds of dogs, of all sizes and colors, ran restlessly about; and, close at hand, the wide shallow stream was alive with boys, girls, and young squaws, splashing, screaming, and laughing in the water.

American travelers on the high plains lived in fear that the Indians might steal their precious supplies and drive off their horses and cattle. They feared, too, the ordeal of heat and drought and the summer storms. Sheets of rain, going on for days, could turn the trail into a river, in which a man must wade up to his ankles or knees. Caravans might be pelted with hailstones larger than a hen's egg; gusts of wind might capsize wagons, tear away their covers and overturn them. People might get lost, killed by lightning or by snakes, swept away while crossing rivers, trampled by horses, destroyed by cholera.

Men, women and children lost their lives on the Oregon and California trails; those passing by counted many gravesites along the way. Some were just mounds of earth; some were marked by a piece of plank with heartbroken messages burned into the wood with a hot iron: "MARY ELLIS. Died May 7, 1845, Aged two months." "JOHN HOOVER. Died June 18, 1849, Aged twelve years. Rest in peace, sweet boy, for thy travels are over."

* * * *

In 1822 Antonio Lopez de Santa Anna, a Mexican general, declared himself for the independence of Mexico and for the creation of a Mexican republic. In 1824 the Mexicans agreed to a new constitution for their country modeled upon the Constitution of the United States. Three centuries of Spanish rule were now over.

The Mexicans, at first, were anxious to attract settlers to the great, empty Spanish borderlands of Texas, and they made it known to North Americans that they would be more than welcome if they came to live in the lands of eastern Texas, in the valleys of the great rivers there that flowed into the Gulf. Many people accepted the invitation and began to move in; the land was cheap and fertile, and the climate was great. But very soon the Mexican mood changed, and the Mexican government became alarmed. The North Americans were bringing slaves with them, in defiance of Mexican law; they demanded *autonomy*, or total self-government; they refused to become Catholic like other Mexicans; and they were bitter about the presence of Mexican troops, who were supposed to keep them in order.

So in 1835 General Antonio Lopez de Santa Anna, who was now the president of Mexico, marched north to teach the Texans a lesson and to set up military rule in the province. The Texans called for their own revolution against Mexico. They declared their independence at the village of Washington in March 1836 and wrote their own constitution, which said, among other things, that it was lawful for Texans to own slaves. In April they defeated Santa Anna's soldiers at the battle of San Jacinto and took Santa Anna prisoner. With their general, Sam Houston, as president, the Texans set up the independent Lone Star Republic and applied for admission to the United States.

Andrew Jackson and Martin van Buren after him were not keen about accepting Texas as an American state. Texas was a huge province; it would come into the Union not only with the small settled area of eastern Texas but with western ter-

On September 13, 1847, American troops under the command of General Winfield Scott stormed Chapultepec Castle after a heavy preliminary bombardment. Thus fell the last major barrier to Mexico City, which capitulated the following day.

ritories as well. Slave states might one day be carved out of these. This was sure to make trouble among people in the northern states, who were becoming more and more angry about the westward expansion of slavery. Then, too, Mexico did not admit or accept the idea of Texan independence. Admission of Texas into the American Union would be sure to lead to war with Mexico.

As the years went by, settlers kept pouring into Texas, and, as before, they brought their slaves with them. Slaveholders in the American government with high positions, like John C. Calhoun, kept on pressing and scheming for the annexation of Texas.

In the presidential election year of 1844, the Democrats chose as their candidate James K. Polk, of Tennessee, with the program "all of Texas, and all of Oregon." The Democrats' plan was to win Northern approval for the acquisition of new slave territories in the South by promising at the same time new free territories for the North. The proposal split the American voters into almost equal halves, for and against. Polk won the election and moved forward to put his program into effect.

In March of 1845, just before Polk had actually arrived in the White House, both Houses of Congress passed a resolution calling for the admission of Texas to the Union. It was a fiery debate. The people who supported the resolution said that it was God's will that the American people should expand across the continent; the Americans, said they, were a chosen people, a superior race with a mission to spread democracy across North America and across the world. As Representative Chesselden Ellis, of New York, told the House, "With Texas and Oregon your brilliant destiny opens before you … You lay the foundations of an empire on the Pacific."

Preparing for war with Mexico, President Polk first came to terms with England about Oregon. The two countries settled their dispute about the Oregon

United States Acquisitions from Mexico, 1848

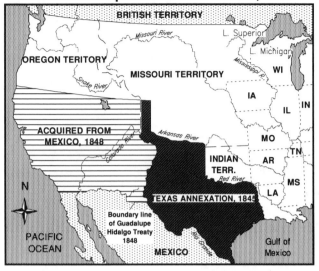

country by dividing it along the 49th parallel of latitude. The northern part went to Great Britain, the southern part to the United States. Then in the spring of 1846 a clash between Mexican and U.S. cavalry patrols on the northern bank of the Rio Grande gave Polk the excuse for war that he was waiting for. "Mexico," he told Congress in a message that he sent in May, "has invaded our territory and shed American blood upon American soil." Congress was caught up in a war fever and voted for war against Mexico. Only a handful of representatives and senators cast votes against it. One of these, Joshua Giddings, of Ohio, told the House, "I will not bathe my hands in the blood of the people of Mexico, nor will I share the guilt of those mur-

ders which have been, and which will be, committed by our army there."

During the years 1846 and 1847, two American armies invaded Mexico. In the north, General Zachary Taylor, who in private life was a Louisiana sugar planter, crossed the Rio Grande and fought the Mexican army on the southern side. General Winfield Scott, who had directed Cherokee removal on the Trail of Tears, launched a thrust from Vera Cruz to the capital, Mexico City. The result was the total defeat of Mexican forces and the surrender of Santa Anna in September 1847.

In February 1848 a treaty of peace was imposed upon Mexico at the village of Guadalupe-Hidalgo, five miles north of Mexico City. Mexico surrendered all of the Spanish borderlands—Texas, New Mexico and California. It was an empire of land running clear across the continent from the Gulf of Mexico in the east to the Pacific Ocean in the west.

People in the United States like Joshua Giddings who opposed the war had said that it was wrong to shed Mexican blood for the sake of grabbing land. At the same time, they warned the people that slaveholders would want to take their slaves into all the lands won by the war. The North, they said, would not allow this to happen. Victory itself, they said, would spark a quarrel between slaveholders and nonslaveholders that might bring an end to the Union itself.

We shall see how these warnings came true.

6

THE SLAVERY CRISIS

*War for the Union and the
Emancipation of the Slaves, 1848–1865*

The Compromise of 1850 and the Anti-slavery Struggle

It was January 24, 1848, just one week before Mexico signed the treaty of Guadelupe-Hidalgo, surrendering California to the Americans. James Marshall was this day directing the building of a sawmill on the land of Captain John Augustus Sutter in the Coloma Valley of central California. Something yellow glittered at the bottom of the mill race that Marshall's men were digging. Marshall scooped up the glittering thing, looked carefully and then spoke softly to his men. "Boys," he said, "I believe I've found gold."

Marshall's discovery triggered a rush of gold seekers to California. They came by ocean on fast clipper ships—a 12,000-mile trip down the coast of South America, around Cape Horn to the seaside village of Yerba Buena, or San Francisco, as it soon came to be called. They came on mules across the swamps of Panama, many of them falling victim to fever and dying by the way. They came by wagon and on foot across the Oregon and California trails.

They came not only from the United States but from faraway Australia and China, from the islands of the Pacific Ocean and from Latin America. Carpenters left their benches, farmers their ploughs, sailors their ships. All downed their tools and were off to California to make their fortunes in the diggings. The Reverend Walter Colton, a U.S. navy Chaplain, described the scene that he saw in November 1848: "Some fifty thousand people," he wrote,

are drifting up and down the slopes of the great Sierra, of every hue, language, and clime ... All are in quest of gold ... Some are with tents, and some without; some have provisions and some are on their last ration; some are carrying crowbars; some, pickaxes and cradles; some, hammers and drills, and powder enough to blow up the rock of Gibraltar!

By December 1849, two years after Marshall's find, the immigrant population of California had exploded from 5,000 to almost 80,000; and, of

VOL. I.]

WILLIAM LLOYD GARRISON AND ISAAC KNAPP, PUBLISHERS.

[NO. 33.

BOSTON, MASSACHUSETTS.]

OUR COUNTRY IS THE WORLD—OUR COUNTRYMEN ARE MANKIND.

[SATURDAY, AUGUST 13, 1831.

The masthead of the *Liberator*, from the issue of August 13, 1831. The woodcut shows a slave auction: Father, mother, and two children are being sold. The auctioneer stands at his desk, which is labeled: SLAVES HORSES & OTHER CATTLE TO BE SOLD AT AUCTION. In the background the United States Capitol is seen; from its dome flies the flag of liberty.

course, it was now a United States territory. A state constitution was drawn up, and the Californians were applying for admission to the Union.

California was the first business that faced Congress when it assembled in December 1849. Northerners felt that slavery should be barred from California and, for that matter, from all the territories that had been won from Mexico; but Southern leaders felt exactly the opposite. Month after month and far into 1850, the debate went on.

This was not the first time that members of Congress had quarreled about slavery in the American territories. In 1819 Missouri asked to be admitted to the Union as a slave state; Northerners spoke against the proposal, and there was a quarrel in Congress, with bitter feelings on both sides. But in the end North and South came to an agreement known as the Missouri Compromise. The Louisiana Purchase territory was split into two parts. In the northern part, said Congress, slavery was "forever" banned. In the southern part it was not.

Working out an agreement between the Northern and Southern sections of the country was one thing in 1820; in 1850 it was going to be much harder. Bit by bit since 1820, Northerners had become uneasily aware that the westward advance of the slave power was both dangerous and wrong. There

was a growing feeling that, at long last, Congress should put a stop to it.

Antislavery societies grew rapidly during the years that followed the Revolution. These societies stimulated antislavery sentiment and championed the liberation of the slaves, particularly in the North. But they were moderate in their aims. They neither desired nor demanded the grant of American citizenship to the freedpeople with the same full and equal rights that white citizens enjoyed. An aggressive and radical movement, championing both freedom and citizenship rights for all slaves in the country without exception, was not launched until the late 1820s.

It began with a young New Englander, William Lloyd Garrison. Garrison was born in Newburyport, Massachusetts, in 1805 and raised by his mother, Frances Maria—Abijah, the father, abandoned Frances Maria and her three children when William was three years old. At the age of 13, Garrison began to serve an apprenticeship with the editor of the Newburyport *Herald* and learned the art of printing. Frances Maria had to work very hard to support the family, and there was no money for education. Living in a tiny attic room, Garrison taught himself by reading all the books that he could beg, borrow or buy. In 1827 he became the editor of a Boston newspaper, the *National*

Philanthropist. The job didn't last long, but it launched him on his career as a newspaper editor.

On July 4, 1829, when he was 24 years old, Garrison gave an Independence Day sermon at the Park Street Church in Boston. It was his own personal declaration of war against American slavery. The pastor of the church, the Reverend Edward Beecher, and his younger sister, Harriet, were in the audience, as well as Lydia Maria Child, already a well-known writer, who would soon turn her pen to the service of the antislavery cause.

The black people of the South, Garrison told his listeners, were human beings held like animals in captivity. Do not turn away from them, he pleaded, do not pass by on the other side. "The slaves," he said "are entitled to the prayers, and sympathies, and charities of the American people." These slaves, he added, were also American citizens. Most of them had been born in this land; they watered its soil with their sweat and tears, and they produced its wealth. "Their children," he cried, "possess the same rights as ours; and it is a crime … to load them with fetters."

In the Park Street Church that day Garrison was attacking the belief, which many people at that time shared, that black people were not, and could never become, American citizens; and that, if indeed they were freed, they should at once be shipped back to Africa. This doctrine was known as *colonizationism.* Colonizationists felt that white people were a superior race who never would, or should, accept Africans as equals. Garrison, on the other hand, was pleading for an America in which blacks and whites would accept each other as brothers and sisters and would live and work together in the same communities.

Garrison's ideas about slavery were important because a small group of New England ministers and writers listened to what he said and shared his worry about the growth of an empire of slavery within the United States; they began a movement to try and make the American people wake up and do something about it. In 1831 Garrison and his friends began to put out an antislavery journal, the *Liberator*, and this became in the following year the official newspaper of the New England Antislavery Society. An American Antislavery Society was organized at a meeting in Philadelphia in 1833; soon antislavery groups, all of them very small at first, were springing up in communities throughout the North.

A young man from Hamden, Connecticut, named Theodore Weld was one of those who did most to carry Garrison's message across the Appalachians and into the Midwest. In 1833 Weld decided to become a minister and to bring the Christian faith to settlers swarming into the Mississippi Valley. He wanted, too, to make Americans understand that the abolition of slavery was the first and the most urgent of Christian duties.

So that year Theodore Weld enrolled as a student at the Lane Theological Seminary, located at Walnut Hills on the outskirts of Cincinnati. "The site of the Seminary," wrote Catharine Beecher, daughter of Lane's president, Lyman Beecher, "is very beautiful. It is located on a farm of one hundred and twenty acres of fine land, with fine groves of trees around it."

In the fall, just after Weld arrived, a terrible cholera epidemic hit the college. Being a very energetic and dedicated person, he at once took the lead in organizing care for students who became sick—schools in those days did not have infirmaries, with nurses and special medical equipment. He turned the college into a hospital and put everybody to work nursing the ill, preparing food, washing and cleaning the patients and the bedclothes. Weld himself worked harder than anybody else, going without sleep for days at a time, comforting the suffering and staying with those who died to the very end.

Weld loved his fellow students very much and was prepared to sacrifice his life for them. The students loved him, too, and thought him a hero. "His hair," as one of them recalled, "was tousled and dark, and his eyes were black and piercing. His face with its deeply etched lines and bushy eyebrows was almost frightening; his voice was rich and mellow." Weld cast an intensely personal spell; the warmth of his smile enchanted people.

Many of Weld's fellow students were Southerners, and he found to his surprise that they either knew nothing about antislavery ideas or were totally opposed to them. So when the cholera epidemic had passed, he set up a debate committee and held a series of debates about slavery on the Lane campus. The discussions continued through the long winter evenings of February 1834. In the end all the students—there were about 100 of them—were won over to the antislavery cause. They formed a Lane Student Antislavery Society; the society's first job was visiting the black people in the Cincinnati ghetto and starting classes there for both children and adults.

As Garrison's followers, the Lane students among them, fanned out across the country to spread the antislavery message, they met a storm of opposition. Speakers were mobbed and jeered at; rotten eggs and even rocks were thrown at them. Mobs broke into their offices, smashed printing presses with sledgehammers and scattered the type. They invaded black ghettoes, smashing windows, ripping doors off their hinges, turning houses into a shambles while the terrified people fled for their very lives. Garrison himself barely escaped being lynched by a crowd of merchants and businessmen in Boston in 1835; Amos Dresser, one of the Lane students, was publicly flogged in Tennessee. Whites rioted in the Cincinnati ghetto in 1836.

Most famous of the antislavery leaders who defied the proslavery mobs was Elijah Lovejoy. A New Englander, Lovejoy graduated from Colby College in Waterville, Maine, in 1826 and then moved to St. Louis, Missouri, resolved to devote his life to the Christian ministry in the West. In the summer of 1834, Andrew Benton, one of the Lane students, visited him and won him to the cause. To the dismay of the St. Louis people, Lovejoy now began to voice antislavery ideas in his newspaper,

the *St. Louis Observer*. In 1836 a crowd of whites snatched a black worker named Frank McIntosh from jail, chained him to a tree on the St. Louis common and burned him alive. Lovejoy visited the scene, then wrote and published a ringing attack upon the "awful barbarity" of McIntosh's murder. At once the mob struck back; they wrecked Lovejoy's office and drove him, his wife, Celia, and their small son from the city. The Lovejoys fled across the Mississippi River and found refuge in the town of Alton, in the free state of Illinois. There Lovejoy began once again to publish his *Observer*.

But the people of Alton had no more patience with Lovejoy's ideas than the people of St. Louis. Between July 1836 and September 1837, mobs dumped Lovejoy's printing press into the river three times; each time Lovejoy sent for a new press and went on printing as before.

By October 1837, the Alton community had had enough. People flocked to a town meeting and demanded with one voice that Lovejoy either quit publishing or quit town. Lovejoy refused to quit. "Is not this a free state?" he asked. "When attacked by a mob at St. Louis, I came here, as to the home of freedom … The mob has pursued me here, and why should I retreat again? There is no way to escape the mob, but to abandon the path of duty; and that, God helping me, I will never do."

A few days later Lovejoy's fourth press arrived by boat; a small group of Lovejoy's antislavery friends unloaded it, placed it in a warehouse and mounted guard. That night the mob stormed the warehouse and set it on fire. Lovejoy was killed by an attacker's bullet, defending his right to have antislavery ideas, to speak about them and to make them known through the press.

The next year, in 1838, a young slave named Frederick Douglass fled from Baltimore to New Bedford, in Massachusetts; he began to earn his living doing odd jobs like sawing wood, loading boats, sweeping chimneys. In 1841 Douglass went to an antislavery meeting on the island of Nantucket. There he talked for the first time about his life as a slave and the sufferings that he had endured. He was a man of powerful build, tall, dark and with a rich, deep voice. William Lloyd Garrison was there, listening. "I never hated slavery so intensely," he said, "as at that moment."

This was the start of Frederick Douglass's career as a speaker for the New England antislavery movement. He traveled through the region for four years, lecturing about slavery and holding his audiences spellbound; some people found it hard to believe the story that he told, but there was no arguing with the welts that scarred his back. In 1845 Douglass published a little book entitled *Narrative of the Life of Frederick Douglass*; soon it was selling in Great Britain and the United States by the tens of thousands. In this *Narrative*, Douglass did not speak just for himself; he brought to Northerners a message from countless numbers of American slaves.

Frederick Douglass was born in 1818 on Maryland's eastern shore; he was the property of Edward Lloyd, a wealthy Talbot County slaveholder. Frederick's mother, Harriet, was a field hand who worked on one of the outlying farms. When her day's work was done she had many miles to walk if she wished to visit her child; Douglass had no recollection of ever having seen her by day. "She was with me in the night," he wrote; "she would lie down with me, and get me to sleep, but long before I waked she was gone." Harriet died when her son was seven years old.

When Frederick was little he was given only light work to do, like driving the cows up from the field in the evening, keeping the chickens out of the vegetable patch, running errands. "I was kept," he wrote, "almost naked—no shoes, no stockings, no jacket, no trousers, nothing on but a coarse linen shirt, reaching only to my knees." He had no bed. When nights were cold, Frederick stole one of the sacks used to hold corn. "I would crawl into the bag," he wrote, "and there sleep on the cold, damp, clay floor, with my head in and my feet out."

Frederick never forgot the first time that he saw a person lashed. The victim was a young woman, his aunt Hester. The overseer stripped Hester from neck to waist, tied her hands and hoisted her up so that she hung by her arms from a beam, her toes barely touching the ground. Then he laid on the lash, and soon "the warm red blood came dripping to the floor." The frightened child, thinking that it would be his turn next, hid in a closet. "The scene," he wrote, "struck me with awful force. It was the blood-stained gate, the entrance to the hell of slavery, through which I was about to pass."

In 1825 Frederick was sent to Baltimore to live with Hugh and Sophia Auld, who were relatives of Colonel Lloyd; his job was to take care of the Aulds' little son, Thomas, and to serve as Thomas's personal slave. Sophia Auld began to teach Frederick his alphabet, but her husband at once put a stop to this. The law, said Hugh, made it a crime to teach slaves to read; a slave who knew how to read would not want to be a slave anymore.

Frederick saw at once that reading marked the trail from slavery to freedom; he began to fight his own secret battle for education. The white children in his neighborhood were poor and also hungry. Whenever he was sent on an errand, Frederick took a book with him and some bread. The white boys gave him knowledge, he gave them food; and once he had learned to read, he learned to write in the same way. "My copybook," he wrote, "was the board fence, brick wall, and pavement; my pen was a lump of chalk."

By the time Douglass was 12, he was reading all the books that he could lay his hands upon, including books about slavery. As Hugh Auld had feared, the more he read, the more he came to hate slaveholders. "I could regard them," he said, "in no other light than a band of successful robbers, who had left their homes, and gone to Africa, and stolen us from our homes, and in a strange land reduced us to slavery. I loathed them as being the meanest as well as the most wicked of men."

When Congress assembled in December 1849 to debate the future of California and the lands won from Mexico, the mood of the North had changed;

it was now quite different from what it had been 30 years before, when the question of Missouri was being debated. Years of brave, quiet and patient work by the men and women of the antislavery movement had borne fruit. Gone were the pro-slavery mobs with their jeers and stones and sledgehammers and firebrands. People found themselves in agreement with the antislavery movement on one point at least: Slavery's advance into the western lands must be checked.

In August 1850, after long months of debate, Congress passed a set of new laws that, it was hoped, would satisfy both North and South. This was the Compromise of 1850. Two new states were to be added to the Union, one with slavery (Texas) and one without (California). Next, Congress outlawed the slave trade in Washington, D.C. This was something that antislavery people had been asking for a long time. It seemed revolting to them that slaves were being driven like dumb brutes through the streets of the nation's capital itself; that they were being advertised for sale in Washington's newspapers; and that they were herded into pens within a stone's throw of the White House.

To offset this concession to the North, Congress passed a new Fugitive Slave Act. From now on the federal government itself would have the duty to hunt for slaves who had fled the South and to return them to their owners.

Slaves fought back against bondage in different ways: They hid during work hours, they burned barns, broke ploughs, fought with overseers who tried to lash them, murdered masters and even committed suicide. But flight was what slaves dreamed about most and what they talked about most in the years after the Civil War, when they were old. Some of them fled to swamps, caves, hills and thickets that lay close to their plantation homes. In most cases hunger forced them to go back sooner or later; but they spent days, weeks and even months in these hideouts. Black women bore and raised children there.

Some slaves played for higher stakes: Every year hundreds of them ran away in the hope that they would be able to leave the South for good. Many of these people traveled clear across the North and did not stop until they had reached Canada. The reason for this was that the U.S. Constitution gave slaveowners the right to hunt for fugitives in all the Northern states and in all the free territories, and to drag them back to the South when they were found. Thus the number of fugitives who, like Frederick Douglass, remained in the North was small. Between 1800 and 1850 the black population in Canada grew from 4,000 to about 55,000. Most of these people had once been American slaves or were the children of American slaves born on Canadian soil.

Advertisements for fugitives filled Southern newspapers and were also posted at country stores and steamboat landings in the North. Runaways were described by sex, age, height, clothing, color of hair and, above all, by their scars or mutilations. There was, unfortunately, no shortage of people ready to grab runaways in the hope of getting a fat reward.

$100 REWARD

RANAWAY from my plantation in Bolivar County, Mississippi, a Negro man named MAY, aged 40 years, 5 feet 10 or 11 inches high, copper colored, and very straight ... Has some scars on his back that show above the skin plain, caused by the whip ...

Black fugitives had to be brave. They might lose their way, starve or freeze to death, die of snakebite, or drown in the swamps. White militiamen patrolled the plantation lands each night on the lookout for runaways; fleeing slaves who fell into their hands were certain to receive savage punishment on the spot. Slavecatchers even hunted with dogs that sometimes fell upon their human quarry and tore them to pieces.

A fugitive who was captured alive was likely to face torture when taken home. Esther Easter, a Tennessee slave, witnessed one such punishment when she was a child. "A runaway," she recalled, "was brought back and there was a public whipping, so's the slaves could see what happens when they tries to get away. The runaway was chained to the whipping post, and I was full of misery when I see the lash cutting deep into that boy's skin. He swell up like a dead horse."

Men and women who fled had to struggle not only against hardship and danger but against inner pain. Some left families behind them—all that they had in this world, all that they loved best—perhaps forever. Many more people would have fled the South if they had not been bound by ties such as these. This, too, is the reason that when some ran, they did not run alone but in family groups.

Until the 1830s, the slaveowner did not have too much of a problem in recapturing runaways. He tracked the slaves, found them, put manacles on them and dragged them home. But as the years passed, resistance began to grow. The sight of runaways was enough to melt all but the most hardened hearts. These were starving, worn-out people, clothed in stinking rags, shivering in the winter cold, shoeless and with bleeding feet. Many came alone, but more often than not they came in family groups, Jack and Lucy, Louis and Ellen, John and Mary, leading their little children by the hand or carrying them in their arms. Sometimes they came in bands, several families together, and three generations of the same family—grandfather, parents, and children.

The very presence of these fugitives on free soil was a cry for help. How could a true Christian turn away, when he had learned the first lesson of the gospel at his mother's knee, had been taught that when you help the poor, the sick, and those in need, you help Jesus himself? These fugitives, too, aroused not only compassion but admiration. The more they struggled and suffered on the path to freedom, the more the resolve grew in many of

them to die if need be but not to be retaken. When overtaken by the slavecatchers, some of them killed first their children and then themselves, but they did not surrender.

People, therefore, came to the help of the fugitives: They hid them in cellars and barns and attics, and they transported them in carts, hidden under a load of hay. Naturally enough, those who helped runaways soon got to know who else in their neighborhood and in nearby communities could be relied upon to help, too. Informal networks sprang up. People who helped fugitives became *agents*, their homes became *stops*, and the path that the runaways traveled from one stop to the next became the secret escape route, the *Underground Railroad*.

Some agents made no secret that they were helping fugitives, but these were a tiny minority. Most agents kept quiet about their activities. Federal law, and in some cases state law, made it a crime to help fugitives. Before 1850 the penalty was a $500 fine, which in those days was a very large sum of money. After 1850 this was increased to $1,000 and six months in jail. In addition to this, of course, slaveowners could take to court and sue for damages people who helped fugitives. These damages were fixed by the law of 1850 at $1,000 for every fugitive whom a person helped.

The great period of the Underground Railroad was between 1840 and 1860. The fugitives passed along many trails that led from the Ohio River and the Pennsylvania border to Canada— across Ohio, Indiana, Illinois and the New England states. Thanks to the growing feeling against slavery and the growing resistance to slavecatching in many Northern communities, retrieving runaways in the free states had come almost to a standstill by 1850. Slaveowners in pursuit of slaves could expect no help from the local police and little if any cooperation from local citizens. At the very least they could expect difficulty and delay and maybe even violence.

The Fugitive Slave Act of 1850 changed all this. From now on, catching runaways became the job of the federal government itself. Special judges, called commissioners, were appointed to administer the new law. If a slave were seized and a commissioner felt that he needed help to prevent that person being set free by antislavery people, he had the authority to call out United States troops to guard the prisoner. This was an entirely new provision of the law; until 1850 slaveowners had been obliged to catch fugitive slaves themselves, with no help from the federal authorities and very little from local sheriffs or police.

Slaveholders defended this provision of the law on the grounds that it was authorized by the Constitution, which stated that "persons held to service or labor" ought to be "delivered up on claim of the party" to whom that service might be due. Antislavery people did not agree: The Constitution, they said, was never intended to sanction slavecatching by the federal government itself.

Americans were given a lesson in the practical meaning of the new law in April 1851. Thomas Sims, a Georgia runaway, was seized in Boston. Three hundred federal soldiers guarded him as he was marched to the Boston docks, placed on board a ship, and sent back South. Northerners seethed with rage at the sight of the federal government under the thumb of slavecatchers—a tool to take away from black human beings their God-given right to life, liberty and the pursuit of happiness.

Harriet Beecher Stowe was a New England woman who shared these feelings. She had, as she said, "a mother's heart, bursting with anguish excited by the cruelty and injustice our nation is showing the slave." Early in 1851 she sat down to write a short piece about slavery, which she hoped to publish in an antislavery magazine. The short piece turned, as the months went by, into a long novel. It was published in March 1852 under the title *Uncle Tom's Cabin*, and it became an instant success. People are still reading it, not only in the United States but all over the world; few other books in human history have enjoyed so wide a circulation.

The first part of *Uncle Tom's Cabin* deals with George and Eliza, married slaves who have a small son, Harry. Finding out that her owner plans to sell the child, Eliza grabs her boy and flees northward toward the Ohio River through the cold spring night. Slavecatchers follow her. Eliza resolves to win her freedom or die. Leaping from floe to floe, she crosses the icebound stream with Harry in her arms. When she reaches the northern bank, antislavery people take her in. She and George are reunited and proceed on their way to Canada, fighting off at gunpoint the slavecatchers who pursue them.

With these first scenes of her book Mrs. Stowe drew a true picture of the slave trade, of the Underground Railroad, of the heroism of the fugitives. It was a message that thrilled people. Overnight she made antislavery sympathies the property of millions, and fueled the Northern belief that the growing power of the slaveholders was not only dangerous but also wrong.

The quarrel between the North and South broke out again in 1854 over the question of Kansas, and it did so with a bitterness that was fiercer than ever before. This was due in no small measure to the feelings aroused by the Fugitive Slave Act and *Uncle Tom's Cabin*. This new quarrel would lead, finally, to blows.

HARRIET BEECHER STOWE

Harriet Beecher was born in Litchfield, Connecticut, in 1811, daughter of a famous revivalist preacher the Reverend Lyman Beecher. Harriet's mother died when she was five; she grew up in a house full of boys—three older brothers and two younger ones. She suffered from being a little sister who always had to tag along behind somebody else. When Lyman Beecher took the boys on fishing trips, Harriet was left to pass the day by herself. "It was so still," she recalled, "no tramping or laughing, wrestling boys—no singing and shouting; and perhaps only a seam on a sheet to be oversewed as the sole means of beguiling the hours of absence."

Most precious of her childhood memories was the lovely Connecticut Valley at whose border she lived. "I remember," she wrote later, "standing in the door of our house and looking over a distant horizon where Mount Tom reared its round blue head against the sky, and the Great and Little Ponds … gleamed out amid a steel-blue sea of distant pine groves."

When Harriet was 14 she was sent away to be a pupil at the Female Academy in Hartford, where her older sister, Catharine, was principal. Soon she became a teacher in her sister's school. Life was lonely and sad. She made few friends and was tormented by homesickness.

In 1832, when Harriet was 21, Lyman Beecher accepted a position as president of Lane Theological Seminary, in Cincinnati, Ohio. Catharine decided to go with her father and to set up a new Female Institute there. Harriet obediently pulled up stakes and tagged along after her big sister.

Lane Seminary was located at Walnut Hills, a couple of miles outside Cincinnati. At first Harriet lived in her father's house on the college campus. Four years later, in 1836, she moved into her own home close by, after marrying Calvin Ellis Stowe, Lane's Bible professor. But marriage did not provide Harriet with the independence that she yearned for. The Stowes lived at Walnut Hills for 14 years, always in the shadow of want.

Their plight was due to a financial crisis at the college. This came about when the students, under the leadership of Theodore Weld—who would later be one of the country's leading antislavery organizers—set up the Lane Antislavery Society. The college trustees banned this society and forbade any discussion of slavery on campus. The Lane students then packed their bags and left. Lane Seminary limped on with only a handful of students and little financial support from outside donors.

During the Lane years, from 1836 to 1850, Harriet bore seven children; the experience was made bitter by poverty. "How little comfort had I in being a mother!" she lamented. The struggle to survive took up all her energies. It was a narrow, wretched and dull existence. By 1850 she was, as she wrote, "a little bit of a woman … about as thin and dry as a pinch of snuff; never very much to look at in my best days, and looking like a used up article now."

Throughout the Lane years antislavery struggles were central to Harriet's midwestern experience. She had witnessed the conflict between the students and the Lane trustees that led to the near destruction of the college. She knew James G. Birney, an exslaveholder who had launched an antislavery journal, the *Philanthropist*, in Cincinnati in 1836 and had his press smashed by the mob when the townspeople unleashed an orgy of violence against the black people of the town ghetto.

Harriet had many opportunities, too, to learn about slavery from exslaves themselves. Black wash clothes. Most had been born in the South and had at one time been slaves. Harriet worked alongside them and questioned them carefully. She learned endless details about bondage and its impact upon the lives of ordinary people.

During the 1830s and the 1840s fugitive slaves followed many trails through Ohio as they went northward to Canada and freedom. One of the freedom trails led through Walnut Hills. Harriet came into contact with the activists who sheltered the fugitives and gave them aid. One of these, the Reverend John Rankin, a Southerner from Tennessee, lived on a bluff above the Ohio River. He was famous among antislavery people for befriending Eliza Harris, whose story he himself told to Harriet. This was the same Eliza who appeared as a fugitive heroine in *Uncle Tom's Cabin*.

Harriet's brother, the Reverend Edward Beecher, was a leader of the antislavery struggle in Illinois. Edward was Harriet's favorite brother; she loved him for his sympathy with human beings, his sturdy common sense and his deep antislavery convictions. She agreed with Edward when he wrote that "Americans must act now to abolish slavery or else face God's punishment for their crime." But how was a woman, burdened with household duties and the care of small children, to become involved in such a struggle? "No one," Harriet told her husband, Calvin, "can have the system of slavery brought before him without an irrepressible desire to *do* something, and what is there to be done?"

One day in 1849, Calvin returned from a trip to the East with the welcome news that he had been offered a professorship at Bowdoin College, in Brunswick, Maine. The long years of impoverished exile from New England were now over. Harriet reached Brunswick in May 1850. She was pregnant for the eighth time, and she busied herself settling into the Titcomb House.

Charles Edward Stowe was born a few weeks later, in July; and in September the Fugitive Slave Act became law. Isabel, Edward's wife, wrote to Harriet, urging her to speak out against it. "If I could use a pen as you can," said she, "I would write something that would make this whole nation feel what an accursed thing slavery is."

Early in 1851, as Charles Edward lay in the cradle, Harriet, at long last, took up her pen. Now, finally, she was free to do something about slavery by writing. The dam that for years had blocked the tender heart, the soaring imagination and the creative mind, was broken. Long pent-up feelings, thoughts and dreams came roaring through the breach.

Uncle Tom's Cabin was written as a serial story appearing in weekly installments in the antislavery paper the *National Era*, beginning in June of 1851; it was published as a book in March of 1852. The work made Harriet almost instantly famous, not only in the United States but also throughout the world.

Kansas and the Rise of the Republican Party, 1854–1860

The peace bought by the Compromise of 1850 lasted for only a short while; the conflict of the two sections, North and South, broke out again in 1854 over the issue of the western lands.

In 1819 a bitter dispute had erupted in Washington, D.C. when Missouri applied for admission to the Union as a slave state. Northerners objected: Missouri was part of the Louisiana Territory, land bought from France on the western bank of the Mississippi. If slavery could leap across the Mississippi, where would it end? Was Congress going to allow slaveholders to take their slaves anywhere in America?

After much discussion, Congress reached an agreement known as the Missouri Compromise. Congress decided that throughout the greater portion of the Louisiana Purchase land, slavery would be forever banned. An exception was made for Missouri itself, as well as a small portion of the Louisiana Territory that lay south of the parallel of latitude 36º30' which was located at Missouri's southern border.

So matters stood until 1854. Two new states were admitted to the Union from the Louisiana Territory, notably Arkansas in 1836 and Iowa in 1846. Most of the territory remained unorganized. Louisiana Territory was a realm of icy winters and torrid summers—a sea of grassland where little water fell, where trees grew only along watercourses, where the buffalo lived and roamed by the millions, followed and hunted by many Native American tribes.

Such was the territory west of Iowa and Missouri, whose time for settlement had come by 1853. Railroads were starting to creep westward across Iowa and Missouri. In just a few years they would reach the unorganized territory that lay beyond. Governments had to be set up so that roads and railroads could be built, so that settlers could move in, and Native American titles to the land could be transferred to white people.

At the end of 1853, Stephen Arnold Douglas, the U.S. senator from Illinois, took the lead in accomplishing this purpose. Douglas was an important person, the leader of the Democratic party and chairman of the Senate's Committee of Territories. Late in 1853 and early in 1854, he steered through Congress a bill known as the Kansas-Nebraska Act; it dealt with most of the Louisiana Purchase area north of 36º30', where slavery had been forever banned by the Missouri Compromise.

Under the Kansas-Nebraska Act, this territory was split into two separate territories, Kansas and Nebraska. After May 1854, when the act was passed, Kansas settlers were given a choice: They might bring slaves with them into Kansas; and they might write a state constitution adopting or banning slavery, as they chose.

This idea was labeled *popular sovereignty*, or "settlers' choice," and it was closely identified with

Compromise of 1850 and Kansas-Nebraska Act of 1854

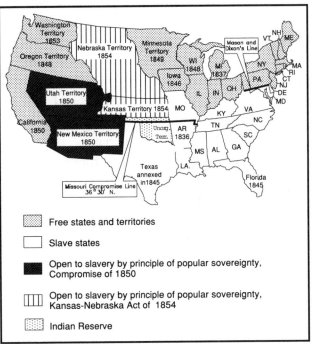

- Free states and territories
- Slave states
- Open to slavery by principle of popular sovereignty, Compromise of 1850
- Open to slavery by principle of popular sovereignty, Kansas-Nebraska Act of 1854
- Indian Reserve

the name of Stephen Douglas, its most articulate champion. Popular sovereignty took the decision about slavery and where it might go out of the hands of Congress and placed it in the hands of the Kansas settlers themselves. Congress was, in effect, washing its hands of the issue, saying "Let's have a race, proslavery against antislavery settlers. Whoever gets there fastest with the mostest wins."

Thus organized, Kansas Territory stretched all the way from the Missouri border in the east to the Rocky Mountains in the west. Broad rivers flowed through fertile valleys that needed, as one traveler wrote, "nothing but the plough to convert them into fruitful fields." Beyond these valleys lay the prairie, "the beautiful, undulating prairie, here and there a grove of walnut, hickory, oak, or sugar maple … stretching its velvety surface of grass as far as the horizon."

The Kansas-Nebraska Act produced a tempest of opposition throughout the North; but Douglas controlled enough votes to secure passage of his bill by slim majorities. Railroad politics and speculators' greed had a lot to do with this bill, whose enactment led within a few years to the outbreak of the Civil War.

Congress had money enough to subsidize a single transcontinental railroad; the issue was the route that this railroad should take: Should it go through the northern, central, or southern part of the Louisiana prairies? Since land values would at once rise wherever the rails were laid, land speculators and railroad shareholders had a major interest in the outcome. The final choice—a track through the central part of the country, by way of Missouri—was the result of a compromise between Northern and Southern interests. Southern Congressmen gave their votes for the act in return for a removal of the old ban upon slavery in the new territory.

Even before the Kansas-Nebraska Act was passed (May 1854), Southerners had begun to take steps to make sure that they would beat the Northerners to the gun and set up a government in Kansas controlled by the proslavery interest. Societies called Blue Lodges were organized all over Missouri to launch a movement for the settlement of eastern Kansas; similar societies were organized in other Southern states. Societies to boost emigration to Kansas were also organized in the North. During the late summer and fall, both pro- and antislavery settlers trickled into the territory.

In March 1855, elections were held in Kansas in order to create a territorial legislature. Proslavery people streamed across the border from Missouri. Organized into companies, they marched with their own bands, drums, banners, horses, wagons and tents. They beat up or chased away antislavery voters and elected a proslavery assembly. The assembly at once produced a constitution declaring that slavery was lawful; that anybody who spoke against slavery, or even helped a slave to escape, might be put to death.

Thus the slaveholders launched a reign of terror in Kansas; the people, mostly Missourians, who were the strong-arm men for this new slavery regime, called themselves Border Ruffians. Border Ruffians were rough-looking people, their "hair uncut and uncombed," as one traveler wrote, with "unshaven faces and unwashed hands." The handles of long-bladed knives stuck out from the tops of their boots; swords and revolvers dangled from their belts. They crossed the border from Missouri at will to raid the settlements of the free-state people. They waylaid men and women on the trails, stole their possessions, beat and killed them. Their purpose was so to terrorize antislavery settlers that either they would not dare to resist or they would be driven from the territory.

Free-state people, meanwhile, held a meeting in October 1855 at their own settlement of Lawrence. They, too, drafted a state constitution; and, of course, it banned slavery. By 1856 there were two territorial governments in Kansas, one in favor of slavery and one against it. Open warfare broke out between the two groups when the proslavery people raided and looted Lawrence in May 1856 and left much of it in ruins. Violence and death as Americans fought each other—such was the fruit of "popular sovereignty" in Kansas.

Anger at the passage of the Kansas-Nebraska Act swept across the North like a flame. Town by town, state by state, people met together, set up committees and created a new political party—the Republican party. This new party united the voters around a single demand: *End the violence in Kansas, stop the spread of slavery into the western territories.*

As their presidential candidate in the 1856 elections, the Republicans chose John C. Fremont, a Southerner who had won fame for his explorations in the far West. Popular response throughout the North was instantaneous. Within two short years of its formation, the Republicans had won 1,300,000 votes for Fremont. His rival, the Democrat James Buchanan, of Pennsylvania, won 1,800,000 votes. This election showed that by the mid-1850s the antislavery message was reaching not just a few thousand people but millions. These people, to be sure, cared little about the lives or the suffering or the fate of blacks; but for the first time in American history they identified slavery itself as an enemy that must, at all costs, be checked.

The outcome of this election, the rise of the Republican party as a vehicle for resistance to slavery, and the violence in Kansas created a crisis for proslavery people. The Kansas-Nebraska Act, which they had hoped would lead to an extension of slavery and its influence, had had the opposite result: It had produced, instead, a tempest of opposition that challenged the very existence of slavery. How, some of them asked, was this opposition to be subdued?

The instrument that they found at hand was a family of four black slaves: Dred Scott, his wife, Harriet, and their two children, Eliza and Lizzie. In March of 1857, these four people stood quietly in the very center of the American stage.

Dred Scott and Harriet were Missouri slaves who had been taken by their owners to live for a while in the Louisiana Purchase territory, in what is now the state of Minnesota. There the two met, and there their children were born.

On being brought back to Missouri in 1838 Dred Scott went to court and sued his owner for freedom—his own freedom and the freedom of his family. The grounds for the suit were that the adults had been taken to federal territory where slavery was forever banned and that the children had been born on free land or on a ship sailing the free waters of the Mississippi.

In 1852 the supreme court of the state of Missouri put, it seemed, an end to the suit. A slave who went to free territory, said the court, could certainly claim his freedom. But if he came back to Missouri, the state had a right to reverse that claim. Scott's antislavery backers were disappointed with this decision, but they refused to take no for an answer. They pushed the case up into the federal courts; they wanted a decision, if need be, from the Supreme Court of the United States itself.

The case first came before the Supreme Court in 1856, in a year when the demand that the spread of slavery be halted was being raised by millions. The chief justice at that time was Roger B. Taney, frail, bent, hollow-cheeked, 80 years of age, and himself a Maryland slaveholder. The Court was dominated by Southerners.

In November of that year James Buchanan was elected president; he was the head of the Democratic party and committed to the expansion of slavery in Kansas. On March 4, 1857, Buchanan gave his inaugural address and referred to the Dred Scott case. To the decision of the Court, said he, whatever it was, "I shall cheerfully submit … May we not, then, hope that the long agitation on this subject is approaching its end. Most happy will it be for the country when the public mind shall be diverted from this question."

Two days later, Roger Taney handed down his decision in the Dred Scott case. It was designed, just as Buchanan knew it would be, to quiet "the long agitation" in Kansas.

Taney's decision carried a double punch. Blacks, he said, had no right to sue for freedom in a federal court. They were not, never had been and never could become American citizens. They could claim no rights under the federal constitution. They must be content with whatever rights state law might give them. The final decision in the Dred Scott case, he said, had been made by the supreme court of Missouri. The Scotts were slaves.

Taney had now decided the case; but he went on. The Missouri Compromise, under which the Scotts claimed their freedom, he said, was itself unconstitutional. His reasoning was simple enough. In federal territories the U.S. government was obliged to enforce the Bill of Rights, but to enforce it for white people, not for black. Blacks were subjects, not citizens; they had no rights at all in the eyes of federal law. No person, said the Bill of Rights, shall be deprived of life, liberty, or property without due process of law. Slaves were the property of white men. No Congress had the right to declare that such property could be "liberated" in the federal territories. Such a thing was forbidden by the Constitution itself.

Democrats hailed Taney's decision with delight. It did far more than return the Scotts to slavery: It legitimized the proslavery constitution in Kansas, and it threw all of the American territories, wherever they might be, open to the advance of slavery. Surely, Buchanan thought to himself, this decision will indeed "quiet the agitation" in the North! "Slavery," as he now wrote to Congress, "exists in Kansas by virtue of the Constitution of the United States; Kansas is ... as much a slave state as Georgia or South Carolina." It followed that he was well within his rights to send federal troops to Kansas to put down antislavery "disturbances."

Most Northerners had no use for Taney's decision, but many of them were still confused about slavery in the territories. Did Congress really have a right to ban slavery there? Or should the settlers themselves be allowed to choose? It would not be a bad guess to say that in 1858 at least one-half of all Northern electors felt that Douglas's position was still a reasonable one: With respect to slavery, not the Supreme Court, not the Congress, but the people themselves should choose whether they wanted it or not.

In 1858 Stephen Douglas's six-year term of office as U.S. senator for Illinois ran out, and he planned to run for reelection. This meant traveling all over Illinois and making speeches during the summer, in time for the voting, which would take place in November.

The Illinois Republicans picked their best man to run against Douglas. This Republican candidate wasn't very well known even in Illinois, and he wasn't known at all outside of the state. His name was Abraham Lincoln. Lincoln's mother and father were very poor people from Kentucky, who had left their home years before, crossed the Ohio and settled in Illinois. Lincoln had educated himself, taken up the practice of law and settled down in the state capital at Springfield. The Republicans described him to the electors as "an intelligent, shrewd, and well-balanced man." He was 49 years of age in 1858. One observer recalled at that time

that "his clothes hung awkwardly upon his giant frame; his face was of a dark pallor without the slightest tinge of color; his seamed and rugged features bore the furrows of hardship and struggle; his deep-set eyes looked sad and anxious."

Lincoln's plan was to use the election campaign to explain to the people of Illinois the difference between Douglas's position on slavery and his own. So he invited the "little giant," as people called his opponent, to meet with him during the campaign in different parts of the state and to conduct a public debate. "Will it be agreeable to you," he wrote to Douglas on July 24, "for you and myself to divide time, and address the same audiences?" Douglas agreed. Between August and October, the two men met seven times and debated their positions in front of thousands of people. These Lincoln-Douglas debates were the first political speeches ever to be taken down in shorthand. Journalists went along with the candidates and sent back a complete record of the debates by telegraph to their newspapers. In this way people not only in Illinois but also all over the North were able to follow the great duel of words and to grasp the difference between the candidates' positions.

The first of these debates were held at Ottawa, Illinois. People poured into town on horseback, on foot, in wagons and by train. "Flags, mottoes and devices," one correspondent wrote, "fluttered and stared from every street corner." Roughly 10,000 people turned up and stood sweating in the summer heat, listening to the men on the platform in the public square, striving to catch every word. Lincoln and Douglas shouted at the top of their lungs, battling to make their voices carry to the very edge of the huge throng, to be heard above the neighing and stamping of horses, the barking of dogs, the shrieks of children, the laughter and clapping and shouting of the people.

In the debates it became clear that Lincoln and Douglas agreed that blacks were inferior to whites and that, if any of them were freed, they should be sent back to Africa as soon as possible. The central difference between them was this: Douglas did not care whether blacks were slaves or not, and he didn't care if whites chose to take them into the territories. Lincoln, on the other hand, insisted that slavery was wrong; its growth, therefore, must be checked. If slavery were allowed to advance, asked Lincoln, where would it end? Would all America from Canada to Cape Horn, and the Caribbean Islands as well, come under the rule of the slavemasters? Douglas, charged Lincoln, "is blowing out the moral lights around us, when he contends that whoever wants slaves has a right to hold them … [H]e is in every possible way preparing the public mind, by his vast influence, for making the institution of slavery perpetual and national."

Douglas won the election and returned to the United States Senate. Lincoln was a winner, too. The debates made his name a household word throughout the North. He had stated the Republican position simply and clearly. Republicans began to think of him as their candidate for the presidency in 1860.

In October 1859, just one year after the debates had taken place, John Brown with 21 followers, some black and some white, seized the armory at Harper's Ferry in Virginia. The armory was a depot in which the federal government manufactured guns and stored them. This was the first step in a plan that Brown had been long preparing, to free the slaves. "He stooped as he walked," one of his friends remembered, "and went looking on the ground almost all the time … His features were sharp, nose prominent, eyes were black or very dark grey."

How was it possible, Brown asked himself, that a handful of slavemasters, 200,000 at most, could rule and control four million slaves? The slaveholders, he told himself, had guns, military patrols and overseers to destroy resistance and to suppress revolt. The slaves, on the other hand, were hemmed in on separate plantations and scattered over a vast area. It was impossible for them to

United States Marines are shown battering in the doors of the engine house at Harper's Ferry at dawn on October 18, 1859. One marine, mortally wounded, lies in the foreground. The fire from the guns of John Brown's men is seen spurting from holes in the engine-house door.

move, to meet, to communicate and to plan. They had no guns.

Brown concluded that leadership and weapons for the black freedom struggle had to come from the outside. He dreamed of setting up a free republic in the Appalachian Mountains, of turning the hills into a fortress plunged like a stone dagger into the vitals of the land of slavery. Fugitives and their families, he hoped, would flee to this mountain stronghold. Here they would arm themselves, organize a struggle to defend their freedom and, in the end, topple planter rule.

No slave uprising took place at Harper's Ferry; Brown and his men were soon besieged in the armory. Colonel Robert E. Lee arrived with a company of U.S. Marines. Oliver and Watson, two of Brown's sons, were killed in the battle that followed; Brown himself, badly wounded, was taken prisoner. Tried at Charlestown, Virginia, for trying to organize a slave revolt, he was found guilty and sentenced to hang. John Brown did not feel guilty. "To have interfered as I have done," he told the court, "in behalf of His despised poor, is no wrong, but right." Early in December the old man was drawn from the jail in a wagon, sitting upon his own coffin, and taken to the gallows.

Two months later, Abraham Lincoln made a speech in New York City. Brown, he told his audience, was only a crazy man who fancied that

The Union and the Confederacy

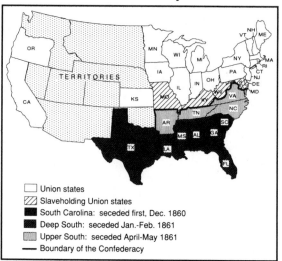

Union states
Slaveholding Union states
South Carolina: seceded first, Dec. 1860
Deep South: seceded Jan.-Feb. 1861
Upper South: seceded April-May 1861
Boundary of the Confederacy

Heaven itself had ordered him to free the slaves. Lincoln went out of his way to tell the South that the Republicans did not feel as Brown did, that they had no plans to organize revolts or to liberate slaves. Republicans had only one concern, Lincoln told the Southerners: to make sure that slavery would not expand one single inch further in federal territories. Republicans had no desire at all to interfere with slavery where it already existed in the Southern states.

Assurances such as these could in no way calm Southern fears. The slaveholders saw that American public opinion was turning against them, that after long years of indifference millions were challenging the slaveholders' right to use the machinery of the federal government for their own purposes. Southern spokespeople now warned the North that if the Republicans won the 1860 elections—and the power to put their antislavery program into action—the South would quit the Union.

In the summer of 1860, the Republican party chose Abraham Lincoln as its candidate for the presidency. Everybody knew that this was going to be no ordinary election. The only question before the people, Lincoln told them, was slavery; an end must be put to the slaveholders' race into the western lands. "You," he told the Southerners, "think that slavery is right. We think that it is wrong. That is the essence of the difference between us."

The North voted for Lincoln as a single bloc; he won the election. The slaveholders at once began to lead the Southern states out of the Union. South Carolina was the first to go; Georgia, Florida, Mississippi, Alabama, Texas and Louisiana trooped after her. Delegates from these states set up the Confederate States of America at Montgomery, Alabama, in February of 1861, with Jefferson Davis as president. They declared slavery to be "the cornerstone" of the Southern way of life.

On April 12, 1861, the Confederate commander-in-chief, Pierre Beauregard, turned his guns on Fort Sumter, a newly built federal stronghold in Charleston, South Carolina, harbor. Harbor batteries began a cannonade before dawn. By midmorning on April 13, the fort was blazing: "The roaring and crackling of the flames," wrote Abner Doubleday, second in command at the fort, "the dense masses of whirling smoke, the bursting of the enemy's shells and our own which were exploding in the burning rooms … the sound of masonry falling in every direction, made the fort a pandemonium."

Later that day the tiny garrison surrendered; they saluted their flag, packed their bags, and were allowed to sail away. The war had begun.

Virginia now cast its lot with the Confederacy, and the capital was moved to Richmond.

Civil War and the Emancipation of the Slaves, 1861–1865

Like many another long and terrible struggle, the Civil War began in a lighthearted mood. The bands played, the men marched in their bright uniforms, the girls flocked around. In the South they sang:

Soldier boy, oh soldier boy, a soldier boy for me!
If ever I get married a soldier's wife I'll be.

And in the North:

Johnny is my darling,
  My darling, my darling,
Johnny is my darling,
  The Union volunteer.

What were they fighting for? Southerners saw it as a war for independence and equal rights—the right, that is, to have slaves and to take them anywhere in the Union that they pleased. Few Northerners at the opening of the struggle thought of it as a war to end slavery. No, it was a war to save the Union, and to teach the rebels a lesson. For both sides, North and South, it was to be a white man's war in a white man's country. As for the blacks, let them go on working quietly as they had always worked—in the fields, the factories, the ships and the docks. Free black people in the North tried to volunteer for the army, but the whites would have none of it. "Keep out of this," they said; "this is a white man's war."

In July 1861, Northern troops moved into Virginia under General Irvin McDowell with the aim of taking Richmond. Civilians in their best Sunday clothes tagged along with the army, carrying picnic hampers. Everyone was in a holiday mood. It was going to be so easy! A summer campaign would be enought to put the rebellion down; then everybody could go back to their home fires before winter set in.

Twenty-five miles southwest of Washington, Pierre Beauregard and Thomas (Stonewall) Jackson stopped the Yankees cold at Manassas in what came to be known as the First Battle of Bull Run. The Union men streamed back to the capital, hanging their heads in shame. "Yankee Doodle wheeled about," the South sang,

And scampered off at full run,
And such a race was never seen
As that he ran at Bull Run.

During most of 1861, North and South were not so much fighting as making their preparations for the battles to come. After Bull Run Lincoln replaced McDowell with General George Mc-Clellan, who spent the rest of the year building up the army on the eastern front—they called it the Army of the Potomac—and strengthening the defenses around Washington. McClellan delighted in military music, parades and marching soldiers. He was popular with his men, who called him "the young Napoleon." Under McClellan's loving care, the Army of the Potomac swelled in numbers and spent its time drilling, singing and marching.

When the war began Lincoln declared a blockade of Southern shores and harbors. As the blockade tightened, overseas trade, the windpipe of the Confederate states, began to be choked off. Jefferson Davis knew that Great Britain alone could break that blockade; if Britain would ally with the Confederacy, the South could dream of victory in the war. Southern soldiers, too, understood how important an English alliance was for their cause. In 1862 they were singing a little song:

Oh Johnny Bull, my Jo John, let's take the field
  together,
And hunt the Yankee Doodles home in spite of wind
  and weather.

In 1862 the war began in earnest. On the wide western front, between the Mississippi and the Appalachians, Ulysses Grant and George Thomas moved south through Kentucky, taking Forts Henry and Donelson. Their advance put the Confederacy in deep trouble; but General Albert S. Johnston counterattacked and hurled his army at Grant's when they were camped near the Tennessee River, at the village of Shiloh. At the end of a single day's battle, 25,000 Americans were killed or maimed; a hard rain fell upon living, dying and dead. For Ulysses Grant it was victory of a sort: He had held his ground, refused to panic, and had driven the enemy away.

When Abraham Lincoln was given the news of Shiloh he was living in his own numb agony of

General Lee's Wooing

O Ma-ry-land, my Ma-ry-land, I bring thee pre-sents fine;

A dia-mond sword with jew-elled hilt, A flask of Bour-bon wine.

I bring thee sheets of ghost-ly white To deck thy bri-dal bed;

And gar-lands of the pur-ple eve And gar-ments go-ry red.

2. My Maryland, my Maryland,
    Sweet land upon the shore,
  Bring out thy stalwart yeomanry,
    Make clean the threshing floor.
  My ready wains lie stretching far
    Across the fertile plain,
  And I among the reapers stand
    To gather in the grain.

3. My Maryland, my Maryland,
    I fondly wait to see
  Thy banner flaunting in the breeze,
    Beneath the trysting tree.
  While all my gallant company
    Of gentlemen with spurs,
  Come tramping, tramping o'er the hills,
    And tramping through the furze.

4. My Maryland, my Maryland,
    I feel the leaden rain,
  I see the winged messenger,
    Come hurling to my brain.
  I feathered with thy golden hair,
    'Tis feathered now in vain,
  I spurn the hand that loosed the shaft
    And curse thee in my pain.

5. My Maryland, my Maryland,
    Alas the ruthless day,
  That sees my gallant buttonwoods
    Ride galloping away;
  And ruthless for my chivalry,
    Proud gentlemen with spurs,
  Whose bones lie stark upon the hills,
    And stark among the furze.

This song was composed by a soldier after the battle of Antietam, September 17, 1862. These verses illuminate in a single flash the meaning of that struggle, in which 6,000 men lost their lives. Lee himself tells the story. He invades Maryland, bringing the ghastly gifts of war; his soldiers are reapers, eager to glean the harvest of death. Thrust back by the "leaden rain" of Northern bullets, the general laments his army's defeat and the death of his soldiers whose bones will whiten upon the Maryland hills. The last word of the song, *furze*, sounds the same as *firs*. It is an old word for *gorse*—a shrub that bloomed in the Maryland countryside.

grief. A few days earlier, a cold rain had fallen while Willie Lincoln was riding his pony; the child became sick and died. Lincoln in the White House gazed long upon the face of his son, murmuring, "It is hard, hard, hard, to have him die."

One week after Shiloh, Union forces seized New Orleans, gateway to the Mississippi and the South's largest port. Battleships sailed up the river under the very mouths of the Confederate guns. Union soldiers and sailors made fund of the rebels' panic-stricken flight from the city:

O a wonder it was to see them run,
  A wonderful thing to see,

and the Yankees sailed up without shooting a gun,
    And captured their great city.

But the Union's hour of danger was at hand. In March General McClellan moved his army down the Virginia coast, landed it between the York and James rivers and prepared to attack Richmond. The Confederacy put General Robert E. Lee in command of its forces. Lee beat off McClellan in the Seven Days' Fight and then moved to the attack. Racing northward in July, he crossed the Potomac early in September and headed toward Pennsylvania.

The world held its breath and watched. A Southern victory now would mean that Britain's government would recognize the Confederacy as an independent nation. Southern cotton would once more feed British looms, and Southern armies would fight with British guns. If Lincoln dared to stop British ships sailing into Southern ports, he would bring about the war with Britain that he dreaded. With such help from abroad the South might be able to go on fighting for years; it might even win. As for Britain, it would be a big chance to weaken, and maybe even to destroy, a nation that was fast growing to be her most formidable commercial rival.

General George McClellan rallied the Union's forces and hastened to meet Lee 55 miles northwest of the capital, at Antietam Creek, in Maryland. A horrible struggle took place on September 17, 1862, that cost the American people 6,000 dead and 20,000 wounded and missing. The Southern offensive was halted, but there was no Union victory. Lee's army, badly mauled, was obliged to retreat. Long lines limped south, carrying with them their wounded and their dying, leaving bloody tracks in the dust.

Five days later, on September 22, 1862, Lincoln issued the first Emancipation Proclamation. End the rebellion before January 1, 1863, he told the Confederacy. If you do not, I, as commander-in-chief of the armed forces of the United States, will emancipate your slaves: They "shall be then, henceforward, and forever free."

This was Lincoln's master stroke. At Antietam the Union had come close to defeat. Beaten to its knees, it faced a long and terrible struggle for survival. By freeing the slaves as an act of war, Abraham Lincoln had called the blacks into the struggle in order to save the nation. His great decision arose not from generosity or antislavery conviction but from dire necessity. His supreme loyalty was to the Union. If he could not save the Union without freeing the slaves, so be it. He set aside constitutional scruples and the convictions of a lifetime to accomplish his end. It was a revolutionary act.

On January 1, 1863, Lincoln issued a second Emancipation Proclamation to confirm the first. From now on, the Civil War was a war to end slavery. So great was the feeling in Europe against slavery that no European government, least of all the British, would dare to help the South. By giving the American nation the greatest of war aims—human liberty—Lincoln had turned aside the menace of British intervention. The logic of his act obliged him not merely to free the slaves but to arm black people as well. Three years earlier he had denounced John Brown as a madman. He would now bring black people into the army by the tens of thousands, on a scale that would have left Brown speechless had he lived to see it.

Blacks thought of January 1, 1863, as a second July 4. Meetings were held everywhere to celebrate the occasion. In Washington, D.C., huge throngs marched in front of the White House while the president stood at the window. In England the workers held meetings to show their support for Lincoln. They had suffered much due to unemployment, partly resulting from the lack of American cotton to feed the spinning machines and looms; even so they were happy. The United States at last had a war aim that British workers welcomed with all their hearts.

This woodcut made early in 1863 shows slaves freed by the Emancipation Proclamation flocking to the Northern lines at New Bern, North Carolina. Women with small children ride in the ox-drawn wagons, which are also piled with household goods; the column, stretching off into the distance, is flanked by a line of soldiers with a mounted officer at their head. At the right, men, women and older children are shown on foot.

Frederick Douglass, famous by this time, urged his people to rally to the Union cause. "The iron gate of our prison," he told them, "stands open. One gallant rush from the North will fling it wide, while four millions of our brothers and sisters will march out to liberty. The chance is now given you to end in a day the bondage of centuries."

Soon black troops were marching to war. They sang

Old John Brown's body is a-mouldering in the dust,
Old John Brown's rifle's red with blood spots turned to rust,
Old John Brown's pike has made its last unflinching thrust,
His soul is marching on!

The first African-American regiment to fight under the federal flag was a band of volunteers recruited throughout the North by Frederick Douglass and the governor of Massachusetts, John Andrew. This was the famous 54th Massachusetts, in which two of Douglass's own sons fought. Its colonel was young Robert Gould Shaw, a white officer of deep antislavery convictions. The regiment covered itself with glory in the assault upon Fort Wagner, one of the strongholds involved in the defense of Charleston, in July 1863. The soldiers of the 54th thus blazed the way for 200,000 colored troops who followed them into the armed forces.

THE FIFTY-FOURTH MASSACHUSETTS INFANTRY (COLORED) AND ROBERT GOULD SHAW

In 1862 Lieutenant Robert Gould Shaw, of the Massachusetts Volunteer Infantry, was stationed at Harper's Ferry, West Virginia, and then at Charles Town, where John Brown had been tried and hanged three years earlier. Shaw's Charles Town headquarters were in the office of Andrew Hunter, the state prosecutor who had conducted the case against Brown and had won his conviction.

Lieutenant Shaw found that Hunter's files were crammed with documents about Brown. These made fascinating reading. For the first time the young lieutenant became aware of the full dimensions of John Brown's plan: To set up a base in the South to which thousands of black fugitives might come, and where the youngest and bravest of these might be armed and equipped to fight for their people's freedom.

By the summer of 1862 Lieutenant Shaw had reached the conclusion that John Brown was right: Slavery could only be overthrown if the black people themselves were called in as allies in the struggle. He expressed impatience that the War Department had as yet taken no steps to raise Negro troops. Is it not extraordinary, he wrote to a family friend, that "the government won't make use of the instrument that would finish the war sooner than anything else—that is the slaves?"

During 1862 Lieutenant Shaw gained much battlefield experience. In September of that year he fought at Antietam, the critical engagement in Maryland, not very far from Harper's Ferry, where the Union army halted General Lee in his tracks and paved the way for Lincoln's Emancipation Proclamation.

By the end of 1862 Lieutenant Shaw, hardened veteran that he now was, had won great popularity with the men whom he commanded. He was conscious, too, of his value to a regiment that had lost many of its best leaders in action. Like a good soldier, he felt deep loyalty to his outfit. "A man," he wrote to his father, Francis Shaw, "should be reluctant to leave a regiment in which he has gone through as much as we have in this."

On January 1, 1863, Lincoln proclaimed the emancipation of the slaves. Nobody welcomed this more than John Andrew, governor of Massachusetts. Andrew was a member of a Massachusetts antislavery circle that included a number of political and literary leaders, such as the Massachusetts senator Charles Sumner and Robert Shaw's father, Francis. Andrew shared with Frederick Douglass and John Brown the view that black people would only win freedom arms in hand and that their contribution was a key to Union victory.

Governor Andrew, accordingly, took the initiative in organizing the Union's first African-American regiment. In finding soldiers to lead it he turned, at the end of January 1863, to Francis Shaw. He was looking, he wrote his friend, for young men "of military experience, of firm antislavery principles … having faith in the capacity of colored men for military service. I would like," he said, "to offer the colonelcy of such a Regiment to your son."

The elder Shaw at once hastened to Virginia to bring Governor Andrew's invitation to his son. A painful conflict tore the young man's soul. He was a captain in the Massachusetts volunteers, bound by ties of long, honorable service. He was now invited not only to abandon his command but to assume a new one that involved enormous risks— risks of failure, ostracism, contempt. It is hard to realize that the mass of white people in those days

When the 54th Massachusetts stormed Fort Wagner in July 1863, it paved the way for men of color, both free and fugitive slaves, to join the Union army and put on the uniform. Black soldiers such as the one shown above fought in segregated regiments.

had zero expectations about blacks. A racist nation believed that blacks were capable of nothing, least of all fighting.

After considerable reflection, Robert Gould Shaw rejected Andrew's invitation; he would neither lead the governor's new black regiment nor participate in any way in its formation.

Francis Shaw returned home deeply saddened by his son's decision. He and his wife had held lifelong antislavery convictions; they would have liked nothing better than that their son, too, contribute by his deeds to the antislavery cause.

Overnight Robert Gould Shaw changed his mind and wired his acceptance of the governor's offer. To his girl friend, Annie Haggerty of Lenox, he

wrote that "a Negro army [is] of the greatest importance to our country at this time."

Next month, February of 1863, the 54th Massachusetts Infantry (Colored) was commissioned; recruiting and training got under way. One of the men who traveled throughout the North to find recruits was Frederick Douglass himself.

By the end of May, the training period was over. The 54th, with Robert Shaw at its head, marched through Boston amid a great crowd of people and sailed away to the South. One month later it prepared itself for an attack, along with white troops, upon Charleston, South Carolina.

The 54th Massachusetts formed ranks at dusk upon Morris Island beach and readied themselves for an assault upon Fort Wagner, one and a half miles away. Fort Wagner was a stronghold built by the rebels to help with the defense of Charleston; the 54th had accepted the commanding general's invitation to lead the attack. White soldiers gazed with awe upon a sight entirely new to their eyes, "a thousand black men [standing] like giant statues of marble, upon the snow-white sands of the beach, waiting the order to advance."

The attack began. Robert Gould Shaw led his men up over the ramparts to engage in close combat with the defenders of the fort. "Here," as an observer wrote, "the brave Shaw, with scores of his black warriors, went down, fighting desperately ..." They buried him along with his African-American comrades in a trench below the ramparts. Today the Atlantic waters have closed over the ruins of the fort and the anonymous grave at its foot.

Some 1,500 Union troops in all lost their lives in this vain engagement. Seven weeks later, the Confederate forces abandoned the fort after Union guns had begun to batter it to pieces.

On Boston Common a bronze memorial created by the renowned Irish-American sculptor Augustus Saint-Gaudens keeps green the memory of the black volunteers of Massachusetts and their young colonel. The 54th Regiment, as one writer said, "made Fort Wagner such a name to the colored race as Bunker Hill has been ... to the white Yankees."

The war went on. Once more in the spring of 1863, the Army of the Potomac moved south through Virginia to attack Richmond. Once more Lee checked it, this time at Chancellorsville; once more he moved over to the attack, racing up the beautiful Shenandoah Valley toward Pennsylvania. Once more, as the gray tide swept forward, the Union rallied its forces, this time under General George Meade. Once more the two armies collided on the battlefield, at Gettysburg. Three days of blood at the beginning of July, and Lee's army was broken. Once more the columns limped back south, drawing their wounded and dying comrades after them. Meade let them go; his army was too battered and too weary to pursue.

Even as Lee's retreat began, news came that Ulysses Grant, in one of the war's greatest campaigns, had seized the fortress town of Vicksburg, on the Mississippi. The Union navy now controlled the entire river, and Texas and Louisiana had been cut off from the rest of the Confederacy.

Some 6,000 Americans died at Gettysburg, and 40,000 were wounded. These figures are even more terrible than they seem. Most surgeons didn't yet know about the new medical doctrine taught by a Viennese doctor, Carl Semmelweiss, that they should wash their hands and knives before each operation. Antiseptics were unknown; eight out of ten patients operated upon in field hospitals during the Civil War did not survive their ordeal and died of gangrene or blood poisoning. Carl Schurz, an American general, described the situation at Gettysburg. The "field hospitals" were only barns and sheds crammed with "moaning, wailing human beings." Hour after hour carts and ambulances filled with the wounded kept rolling in. "There," wrote Schurz, "stood the surgeons, their sleeves rolled up to their elbow, their knives not seldom held between their teeth ... around them pools of blood and amputated arms or legs in heaps."

This was a war fought over a vast country; battle lines stretched along rivers, over hills and fields, for hundreds of miles. Soldiers for the most part had to travel to and from the front on foot. In winter, rain turned the roads into a sea of mud, in which whole armies became bogged down. As a Northern soldier described the winter campaign in Virginia in 1863, "night ushered in a storm of wind and pouring rain, harder for that moving army to encounter than a hundred thousand enemies; a driving rain that drenched and chilled the poor shelterless men and horses."

As for the summer, no one who went through the war ever forgot the dust. John De Forest, another Northern soldier, wrote that "the movement of so many thousands of feet throws up ... dense and prodigious clouds ... The faces become grimed out of all human semblance; the eyelashes loaded, the hair discolored, and the uniform turns to the color of the earth."

In the Civil War Americans fought and killed Americans; and this was bad enough. But sometimes blood brothers killed each other. One family of three brothers came from Philadelphia; two of the brothers went to and settled in New Orleans before the war broke out and then enlisted in the Confederate army; the youngest, who had stayed in Philadelphia, joined the Union forces. At the battle of Fredericksburg in 1862, the Confederates overran the Union lines. One of the boys from New Orleans "reached the body of his dead enemy, turned it over ... and to his horror beheld the corpse of his youngest brother, his woolen shirt stained with a stream of blood that oozed from a bullet hole above the heart."

Abandoned on the battlefield, some wounded men died slowly and alone. They prepared themselves by taking from their pockets the photographs and letters of their loved ones and looking at them. To remember happiness in a time of suffering added to a man's torment, but it also gave comfort at the moment of death.

In November 1863, a war cemetery at Gettysburg was dedicated in a ceremony with flags, prayers, speeches and music. The whole affair went on for hours. The president of the United States was

The plantation patrols had been instituted during the days of slavery, in order to prevent slaves from escaping. Mounted and armed, small squads of men patrolled the roads by night, seizing and whipping black people without passes. After the Emancipation Proclamation, the patrols became even more vigilant and cruel than before. When the war was over, patrolmen donned hoods and robes and joined terrorist organizations, of which the Ku Klux Klan was one.

there, and he spoke for less than one minute. Let us, he said, "highly resolve that these dead shall not have died in vain—that this nation, under God, shall have a new birth of freedom—and that government of the people, by the people, for the people, shall not perish from the earth."

In 1864 it was the North's turn to attack. Lincoln summoned Ulysses Grant to Washington and gave him supreme command of the Union forces. Grant's plan was for the Army of the Potomac to pin Lee down in Virginia while the Army of the Cumberland approached from the rear. William Sherman moved down the railroad line from Chattanooga, in Tennessee, to Atlanta, then slashed straight through Georgia, 250 miles to Savannah.

Turning north, he came up through the Carolinas to take Lee in the rear.

As for Grant himself, he headed south toward Richmond through the tangled forest called the Wilderness. "I mean to follow Lee," he said, "wherever he goes." In two months of campaigning that spring, Grant lost 60,000 men. But there seemed to be no end to the blue-clad swarm that came to fight on Southern soil, and to find a grave there.

For Lee the end came early in April. He abandoned Richmond and met with Grant to arrange surrender. Then, on Palm Sunday, 1865, he rode out among his men and told them that the war was over.

THE SOUTH

Revolution and Counterrevolution, 1865–1877

On the evening of April 14, 1865, just five days after Lee's surrender, Abraham Lincoln and Mary, his wife, attended a play at Ford's Theater in Washington. In the middle of the performance a young Southerner and professional actor, John Wilkes Booth, slipped into the presidential box and fired a bullet point blank into Lincoln's head.

Unconscious, Lincoln was carried to a house across the street. On going in, Gideon Welles, secretary of the Navy, met a doctor coming out; the wound was fatal, the doctor told him. The president would soon die. "The giant sufferer," wrote Welles, "lay extended diagonally across the bed, which was not long enough for him ... His slow, full respiration lifted the clothes with each breath that he took."

Mrs. Lincoln, with friends about her, stayed in a room in the front of the house. "About once an hour," wrote Welles, "she would repair to the bedside of her dying husband and with lamentation and tears remain until overcome with emotion." The speaker of the House of Representatives and members of the cabinet stood around.

The night was dark and cloudy; rain fell in a drizzle. A crowd of weeping people thronged the street outside.

Gideon Welles settled in for an all-night watch, listening, as he said, "to the heavy groans and witnessing the wasting life of the good and great man who was expiring before me."

A little after dawn Welles felt faint and left the house, walking hatless in the rain for 15 minutes. People stopped him and asked how the president did. "Intense grief was on every countenance," he wrote; "the colored people especially—and there were at this time more of them, perhaps, than of whites—were overwhelmed with grief."

In the early dawn of April 15, Abraham Lincoln died.

Lincoln's death came at a climactic moment in the nation's history. It marked the end of the military struggle against slavery and the beginning of a new and equally bitter struggle over the future

Abraham Lincoln died on April 15, 1865, in a house across the street from Ford's Theater. This picture shows him surrounded by his family and members of the cabinet. Mrs. Lincoln is kneeling; Lincoln's son Robert, hiding his face in his hands, stands at the head of the bed behind his father. Charles Sumner is directly to the right. Gideon Welles, secretary of the Navy, sits at the foot of the bed.

of the South and its people, including the millions of slaves who had so recently been freed.

When Lincoln died the debate about the future of the South was just beginning. Neither the Republicans in Congress nor the president himself had as yet found answers to the question that faced them: How to treat a defeated people, how to rebuild a shattered society. Lincoln and the Republicans were bitterly divided over this. As the president himself had said, "We, the loyal people, differ among ourselves as to the mode, manner, and means of reconstruction."

Lincoln died at the moment of Northern victory. Huge areas of the South lay in waste; plantations were idle and in ruins. Virginia's lovely Shenan-

doah Valley was so scorched and stripped by marching armies that, as General Sheridan said, "a crow could not fly over it without taking his rations with him."

Fine cities like Richmond and Atlanta were beds of cinders, cellars half filled with bricks and rubbish, broken and blackened walls, impassable streets. Small towns and villages were crumbled and crushed. John Trowbridge, a Northern farmer and schoolteacher, visited Charles Town, West Virginia, where John Brown had been hanged as a traitor. The jail that had held him was in ashes; the courthouse where he had been tried "was a ruin abandoned to rats and toads ... In the floorless hall of justice rank weeds were growing."

Four years of war and the defeat of the Confederacy had inflicted great suffering upon the people of the South; they had lost their finest youth upon the battlefields; the only fruits of their struggle were hardship and poverty. Veterans, often sick and crippled, were coming home with despair in their hearts.

The collapse of the Confederacy brought freedom to millions of black slaves who had also suffered much. Fugitives from the plantations had downed their tools and sought freedom with the Union armies. Many of these people, men, women and children, were still following the troops, camping in makeshift shacks, often starving and sick.

Black people, too, had left the plantations and had taken to the roads to look for husbands, wives and children torn from them by slavery and war. For some the search would go on for years. "I have a mother in the world," wrote the Reverend E. W. Johnson in 1879 to whoever might read his appeal, "I know not where. She used to belong to Philip Mathias in Elbert County, Georgia, and she left her children there about twenty-three years ago, and I have never heard of her since … Her name was Martha, and I heard that she was carried off to Mississippi by speculators."

Lincoln died at a moment when decisions had to be made that would shape the lives of countless people, black and white, who were still unborn. The South was a conquered country; the Union held the whole Southern world in its hands. What was the South's future to be? The crisis of the battlefield was over; new and even more difficult struggles confronted the American nation.

Andrew Johnson and Reconstruction, 1865–1866

At this critical moment Andrew Johnson, the vice president, moved to the center of the national stage. Born in North Carolina the son of poor parents, Johnson was apprenticed to a tailor at the age of 14; two years later he crossed the mountains

Andrew Johnson, 16th president of the United States.

into eastern Tennessee and started a tailor's shop of his own. The boy had little education, and he did not learn to read until he was 19; his wife, Eliza McCardle, was his teacher.

Hard work, ambition and courage did the rest. Johnson bought a farm, entered politics and began to rise in the world. When the Civil War broke out he was a Jacksonian Democrat and the governor of Tennessee. He battled with the secessionists, the people who wanted to take Tenneseee out of the Union. Unsuccessful in this struggle, he was obliged to quit Tennessee.

In 1862 Union troops occupied the state; Andrew Johnson came back with them as military governor. In 1864 he received the reward for his services to the Northern cause when he was nominated as vice president on Lincoln's Republican Union ticket. John Trowbridge described him in 1865 as "a man below medium height, sufficiently stout, with a well-developed head, strong features, dark, iron-gray hair … deep sunk eyes, with a wrinkled, care-worn look about them."

Johnson personally was a brave man; he was in no way as wise a person as Lincoln, nor as skillful a politician. He neither foresaw nor understood the crisis that would arise if he went ahead with a Southern reconstruction plan without consulting the Republicans in Congress and winning their support. Yet this is what he now did. Between May to December of 1865, when Congress was not in session, he dictated all by himself the terms upon which the Confederate states might return to the Union.

Johnson's terms were generous enough. The theory under which he operated was that the Southern states had never really been "out of the Union." Secession was no more than a temporary disturbance in the normal relationship between the states and the federal government. This normal relationship, in his view, ought now to be restored with as little fuss as possible.

President Johnson appointed provisional governors in each of the Southern states and instructed them to call together constitutional conventions. These conventions then cancelled the declarations, or "ordinances," of secession that had been passed when the war broke out. They also drew up written statements ratifying the 13th Amendment, which declared that slavery had been abolished.

Under Johnson's plan white Southerners who had taken up arms could be pardoned for rebellion if they took a pledge renewing their allegiance to the United States. Nobody was excluded from this offer, not even the Confederacy's topflight political and military leaders. They too would be pardoned if each of them wrote a personal letter to Andrew Johnson at the White House and asked to be forgiven. All those who were pardoned received in return their full rights as American citizens, including the right to run for Congress and to vote in federal elections.

Not a few Confederate leaders had been panic stricken when Robert E. Lee surrendered in April. They were defeated rebels; what, they wondered, was going to happen to them now? They received an answer to their question when President Johnson announced his reconstruction plan. Nobody, it seemed, was going to be tried for rebellion, much

less hanged like John Brown had been. Confederate politicians and military leaders relaxed and began to breathe more easily.

Soon petitions from leading rebels seeking forgiveness began to pour into the White House; many of these people even came to Washington themselves in order to present their cases. The president insisted upon talking to each and every one of them personally. As a Tennessee politician he had never made any secret of his hatred for slaveholders; it flattered him that Southern aristocrats were coming hat in hand to seek favors from the poor white boy who now lived in the big White House.

All summer long Andrew Johnson signed pardons and conducted interviews. Crowds of Southern generals and politicians waited patiently in the summer heat to see the president. John Towbridge witnessed the scene. "Some were walking to and fro," he wrote, "some were conversing in groups; others were lounging on chairs, window-seats … One was paring his nails; another was fanning himself with his hat; a third was asleep. A fourth was sitting in a window, spitting tobacco-juice at an urn three yards off."

By the end of 1865 almost all the Southern states had set up new governments, withdrawn their secession ordinances and agreed to the abolition of slavery. Andrew Johnson was satisfied with what he had achieved. As far as he was concerned, reconstruction of the South was now an accomplished fact. Nothing further remained to be done.

The results were seen when elections for Congress were held in November. Leading rebels arrived in Washington. This time they came not as humble petitioners seeking pardon but as Congressmen. Southern white voters had elected to Congress as their representatives and senators nine high-ranking Confederate military officers, six members of the Confederate cabinet, and dozens of men who had sat in the Confederate Congress. Alexander Stevens, vice president of the Confederate States of America, headed the South's congressional team.

As Johnson's reconstruction policy unfolded during the summer and fall of 1865, Republican leaders stood in the wings and watched with dismay. Had they fought the war, they asked themselves, and won it, only to witness the restoration of planter and rebel rule in the South? What of the wartime promises to the black people of freedom and citizenship?

The president's reconstruction policy, indeed, had little to offer blacks. Johnson shared the detestation of many poor Southern whites for slaveholders and for the whole plantation aristocracy. But he also shared the feelings of almost all Southern whites about slaves: He regarded them with hatred and contempt. Johnson demanded from the pardoned white Southerners no guarantees that the freed people would be fairly treated. None were given.

Johnson was, above all, opposed to the idea that the black people had a right to own land and to become independent farmers. During the war the Union had begun to seize big plantations and to divide them up among the slaves; in Georgia and South Carolina, 480,000 acres of land passed into the hands of the freedpeople when in January 1865, General William Sherman issued a famous decree, Field Order #15. In other places black people took over plantations that planters had abandoned, and began to operate them for themselves.

When Johnson became president he put a stop to these land divisions. He ordered that all such plantations be restored, as far as possible, to their white owners.

This decree spelled disaster for the former slaves. It meant that they would remain poor and landless. They would be obliged to toil on land that they did not own so that white people, not they, might draw a profit from their labor.

Johnson's policy of keeping the land in the hands of the whites was good news to the planters. Fears that the plantations would be taken over by the freedpeople began to evaporate. For sure, planters told themselves, the blacks were now free; but they still had to work for a living. It was simply a matter of rounding them up, especially the young and ablebodied ones, and putting them to work.

Starting in November 1865, in Mississippi, the Southern states, as reconstructed by Johnson, proceeded to define the future of black people by writing laws to regulate their behavior. These laws, Black Codes, as they were called, were to apply not to all the people in the state but only to colored people or, as the laws labeled them, "freedmen, free negroes and mulattoes."

The Black Codes forbade blacks from owning land, leasing it from others, or moving to town to take nonfarm jobs. Blacks must have a farm job, the codes said, and they must enter into written contracts with their white employers. People leaving their work without permission might be chased and dragged back. The Mississippi Code, for example, said that sheriffs "shall … arrest and carry back to his or her legal employer any freedman, free negro or mulatto who shall have quit the service of his or her employer … without good cause."

Black people who refused to sign a work contract were labeled "vagrants." Vagrancy was made a crime punishable by fine and imprisonment. Vagrants too poor to pay the fine could be turned over to the first person who paid the fine and other costs. This money could then be deducted from future wages.

The Black Codes, enacted in late 1865 and early 1866, gave a clear picture of the future that faced the black people of the South under presidential reconstruction. As landless, voteless, rightless farm laborers, they would be free in name only.

On September 6, 1865, Congressman Thaddeus Stevens spoke out publicly against the president's reconstruction policy. In a speech that he gave to his constituents at Lancaster, Pennsylvania, Stevens outlined a quite different concept of reconstruction. What he set before his listeners was a bold plan for the transformation of the whole Southern society.

Thaddeus Stevens was born in 1792 on a rock-strewn Vermont farm, the second of the four sons of Sarah Stevens. His father was a cobbler who abandoned the family while the boys were still quite little; Sarah raised them by herself. She supported her children by earning her living as a houseworker and a nurse.

Sarah Stevens was a woman of courage and of iron will who vowed that, come what might, her two oldest children should have a college education. The oldest boy, Joshua, remained a cobbler like his father; Thad went to Darmouth College. On graduation, he moved to Pennsylvania and set up a law office at Gettysburg.

During the 1830s Stevens bought an ironworks, became a wealthy ironmaster and was active in Pennsylvania politics. He fought for the right of black men to vote in state elections, and he defended fugitive slaves in court. In 1847 he ran for Congress and was elected on the issue of barring slavery from the territories won by war from Mexico. In 1854 he joined the Republicans; the voters sent him back to Congress on the Republican ticket in 1858. During the war years he served as leader of the Republican majority in the House; he championed measures both to arm the slaves and to seize the estates of the rebellious planters.

Thad Stevens was a stern-looking man who walked with a limp and wore a red wig. He believed that black people had a right to equality and to full citizenship in the American republic. The vision of interracial democracy in America and the commitment to struggle for it possessed his soul.

The slaveholders, Stevens told the people of Lancaster, had taken the South out of the Union; they had committed treason, and they had shown themselves to be enemies of democracy. The Union had taken up arms and defeated them. Congress alone had the authority to set the terms under which the Southern people might be readmitted to the Union that they had sought to destroy.

Land, said Stevens, was the key to the reconstruction of the South. "It is impossible," he said, that any practical equality of rights can exist where only a few thousand men monopolize the whole landed property." To transform the South and to make it democratic, Congress must insist upon the confiscation of the big estates; it must put an end to planter power and rule.

Stevens, it must be noted, believed that only the wealthy and powerful planters ought to have their lands taken away. They were the ones who had taken the South out of the Union and must bear the chief blame for the rebellion. "The poor, the ignorant, and the coerced," he said, "should be forgiven. They followed the example and the teachings of their wealthy and intelligent neighbors. The rebellion would never have originated with them."

Stevens was proposing that Congress initiate and carry out a social revolution in the South. "The foundations of Southern institutions," he said, "must be broken up and relaid." Let the land be divided up among the black people, who had so long toiled upon it without reward, and among the poor white people who had never received their fair share. Build a democratic society with free farmers, black and white, made strong and independent by the ownership of land. If you fail to do this, he told Republicans, "*all our blood and treasure will have been spent in vain.*"

It might be objected, Stevens went on, that the confiscation of the big estates, "driving the rebels to exile or to honest labor," would be harsh; it would cause suffering to innocent women and children. Stevens agreed; but he pointed out that Lincoln himself was a colonizationist who believed that the freedpeople should be taken from their homes and settled in a foreign land. "It is far easier," he said, "and more beneficial to exile 70,000 proud and defiant rebels, than to expatriate four millions of laborers, native to the soil and loyal to the Government."

Stevens stressed that the program he advocated was revolutionary. "This plan," he said, "would work a radical reorganization in Southern institutions, habits, and manners." Land reform and the destruction of planter rule were the essence of the reconstruction of the South that he envisaged. Since he wished to tear up slavery by the roots and to destroy all its evil fruits, Republicans labeled his kind of program "root and branch reconstruction." People in general who opposed Johnson's policies, whether or not they agreed with Stevens' ideas, were soon being called *Radicals.*

When Congress reassembled in December 1865, the Republican majority was in an angry mood. First they slammed the doors in the face of the "representatives" who had arrived from the South. "When a man puts a knife to my throat, and I succeed in conquering him, shall I be so foolish," they asked, "as at once to restore him to his former position, knife and all?"

This exclusion of the Southerners was a direct challenge to all that the president had done. The Republicans then set up a joint committee of the House and the Senate, called the Committee of Fifteen, with a mandate to hold hearings and to shape a reconstruction program that could later be submitted to Congress for examination and adoption.

This done, Congress at once turned its attention to the plight of the black people in Johnson's reconstructed South. The Republicans knew all about the Black Codes then being enacted. In addition they were well aware of the contents of Carl Schurz's "Report on the Condition of the South."

Carl Schurz was a major general in the Union army who resigned his commission in the spring of 1865, at the end of the war. Andrew Johnson then invited him to make a tour of the deep South in order to gather information and to advise on what ought to be done.

For Schurz this was a mission of such urgency that he felt it impossible to refuse. Leaving New York early in July, he spent the summer touring South Carolina, Georgia, Alabama, Mississippi and Louisiana; he was back in Washington by the first week of October. The president received him

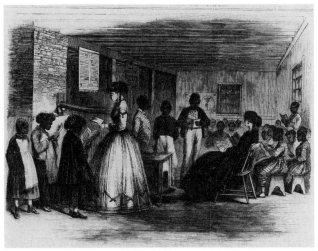

This engraving shows a Richmond, Virginia, freedpeople's school in 1866. It was run by two sisters, with support from the Freedmen's Bureau.

coldly; the dispatches that Schurz had been sending in from the field were not at all to his liking. The president assured Schurz that there was no need to prepare a formal report.

Schurz, on the contrary, was convinced that his findings ought to be laid before Congress and the general public. "I thought it due to the country that the truth should be known," he wrote. Soon the report was ready, and the president reluctantly transmitted a copy to the Senate on December 19, one week after Congress had reassembled. By the end of the month the report had been printed and was circulating in an edition of 100,000 copies.

Rapid withdrawal of Union military forces during 1865, Schurz wrote, combined with restoration of power to the planter class, had delivered the exslaves into the hands of their enemies. Southern blacks were now "completely without power to protect themselves."

The Southern planters, Schurz continued, believed that "the blacks at large belonged to the whites at large," and that force must be used to compel them to work submissively for the whites. Throughout the deep South, he reported, black people—men, women and children—were daily the victims of naked violence. Armed patrols were beating and killing black people whom they caught off the plantations; some were even burned alive.

Numbers of whites in the deep South, Schurz said, perceived blacks as Union sympathizers and therefore an enemy in their midst. Veterans regarded them as scapegoats, the ones who had brought war to the South and who were responsible for all their sufferings. They sought vengeance for their defeat with acts of atrocious cruelty upon the bodies of their black victims with no fear at all that they would be called to account for their deeds.

Schurz buttressed these findings with field reports submitted by army officers. He cited many terrible examples. At Bladon Springs, Alabama, for instance, a freedman was chained to a pine tree and burned to death. In Choctaw County, Alabama, a preacher stated in the pulpit that the roads stunk with the dead bodies of servants who had fled from their masters. Captain W. A. Poillon, who headed the Freedmen's Bureau in Mobile, Alabama, summed up the situation. "Murder," he wrote, "with his ghastly train stalks abroad at noonday and revels in undisputed carnage. The bewildered and terrified freedmen know not what to do. To leave the plantation is death … The lash and murder are resorted to to intimidate those whom fear … alone causes to remain."

Early in February 1866, Congress sat in debate and enacted a bill to extend the life of the Freedmen's Bureau. The Republicans felt that the bureau was an instrument well fitted, if strengthened and expanded, to check the lawlessness that Carl Schurz had described.

The Freedmen's Bureau was a federal agency set up just before Lincoln's death in order to provide emergency relief for starving, landless and jobless Southerners. The bureau was under the control of the U.S. army and operated primarily in the battle zones. It helped freedpeople find jobs, it regulated wage rates, and it ran courts to settle disputes in which exslaves became involved.

One of the bureau's most important contributions was in education. With the coming of peace and freedom, Southern blacks began to show a passion for learning that amazed observers. They flocked to schools set up by an army of Northern teachers and ministers who came south with funds provided by Northern aid societies. Classes were held in old buildings, tumbledown sheds, or the open air. "The pews of colored churches," wrote John Trowbridge, "or plain benches in the vestries, or old chairs with boards laid across them in some loft over a shop, or out-of-doors on the grass in summer—was the usual scene of the freedmen's schools."

Classes were not just for children. People of all ages and both sexes came to them. "Six years and sixty," said Trowbridge, "may be seen, side by side, learning to read from the same chart or book. Perhaps a bright little negro boy or girl is teaching a white-haired old man, or bent old woman in spectacles, their letters. There are few more affecting sights than these old people beginning the child's task so late in life, often after their eyesight has failed."

The second Freedmen's Bureau bill, enacted in February 1866, gave the bureau the power to operate throughout the South. The bureau was authorized to punish white people who deprived blacks of their right to life, liberty and property "on account of race, color, or previous condition of servitude." The bill provided, too, for the distribution of land and farm equipment and for the building of schools.

Andrew Johnson vetoed this bill on February 19 and sent it back to Congress with a message explaining why. He did not want blacks to receive special favors and special protection from the federal government. "The idea on which the slaves were assisted to freedom," Johnson wrote, "was that on becoming free they would be a self-sustaining population." Lots of planters and capitalists, he said, were eager for their services. Let the black people go to work, earn wages and build their own schools. They will succeed, he said, "only through their own merits and exertions."

Congress tried to override this veto but failed. Some Republicans still hoped that it would prove possible to cooperate with the president. They recoiled from the political crisis that would surely arise from a confrontation between the Republican majority in Congress and the chief executive.

The Republicans swallowed their defeat, then returned to the attack. They prepared a new bill that focused exclusively upon the protection of the civil rights of African-Americans. In March 1866 Congress passed an act to confer citizenship upon America's four million blacks and to bring them directly under the protection of the federal government.

This civil rights act was the first of its kind in the history of the United States. The act declared that "all persons born in the United States and not subject to any foreign power ... are hereby declared to be citizens of the United States."

From now on black people possessed, as Americans, "inalienable rights," which the federal government itself was obliged to protect. Any person anywhere within the United States who trampled upon those rights was henceforth liable to be convicted in a federal court and imprisoned in a federal jail.

Henceforth all American citizens, of every race and color, "without regard to any previous condition of slavery," were to enjoy in every state and territory exactly the same rights and to be subject to the same penalties. With these words Congress swept away the Black Codes and all laws that, taking away the rights of black people or exposing them to cruel and unusual punishments, made them victims of racial discrimination.

Andrew Johnson vetoed the act on March 27, 1866. I will not sign this bill, the president told Congress. The black people are ignorant; they are not yet worthy to receive the "prize" of citizenship. They need to give proof of their "fitness" for so great an honor.

Beyond that, said the president, the civil rights bill was unconstitutional. The powers that it conferred upon the federal government flowed from the 13th Amendment, which authorized Congress to protect the right to freedom by "appropriate legislation." There was, he said, no necessity for such a law, since "slavery has been abolished, and at present nowhere exists within the jurisdiction of the United States; nor has there been ... any attempt to revive it by the people or the States."

Congress immediately passed the act over the president's veto. Just as some Republicans had feared, the political crisis deepened. Lawmakers and chief executive were now in open opposition to each other. Johnson publicly called the Republicans a band of radicals and traitors. Republicans began to think of the president as a rebel agent sitting in the White House.

In April 1866, the Joint Committee on Reconstruction reported its recommendations to Congress. The Southern states, said the committee, should be required to ratify one more constitutional amendment, the 14th, before they were readmitted to the Union.

The committee had spent many weeks preparing this amendment. Sections 1 and 5 produced a fundamental change in the Constitution.

Section 1 declared that "all persons" born in the United States were "citizens of the United States and of the State wherein they reside."

With these words the 14th Amendment wrote the Civil Rights Act of 1866 into the United States Constitution. There were good reasons for doing this. The Republicans foresaw that the representatives from the Southern states, when readmitted to Congress, might form an alliance with Northern Democrats to repeal the Civil Rights Act. Even if they did not, the Supreme Court might overturn it on the grounds that it was unconstitutional—just as President Johnson had tried to do in his veto message. Therefore they decided that the Civil Rights Act must become part of the fundamental law of the land—beyond the power of presidents, or courts, or congressional majorities to overturn.

There is a majestic meaning behind the wording of the 14th Amendment. American citizenship

This drawing appeared in *Harper's Weekly*, November 16, 1867, when Congressional Reconstruction was in full swing.

belongs not just to white people but to black people, too: to people, indeed, of every race and every color who inhabit this country. Freedom is a birthright. It belongs to every child of African-American parentage as well as to every white child. Government in a democratic country is duty-bound to treat all alike, to discriminate against none.

Section 5 of the 14th Amendment decreed that "Congress shall have power to enforce, by appropriate legislation, the provisions of this article."

With these few words the federal government was endowed with the ultimate authority in the United States to enforce and to protect the rights of American citizens in general and of the black people in particular. No such authority had existed before the Civil War. Previous to that time citizenship and its rights were to be protected and enforced almost exclusively by the states. For the first time, now, in 1868, the Constitution declared that protection of the rights of all Americans—men, women and children, young and old, black and white—was a central purpose of the federal government itself.

The 14th amendment here gave legal force to the dream that Thomas Jefferson had expressed in the Declaration of Independence: the only reason why governmens ought to be set up, and the only reason why they should be permitted to survive, is to help secure to mankind "certain inalienable rights ... life, liberty, and the pursuit of happiness."

For these reasons the 14th Amendment must rank with the Declaration of Independence itself as a vitally important element in the constitutional legacy of the American people.

Congress approved the 14th Amendment and submitted it to the states for ratification. Meet these terms, Congress told the Southerners, guarantee protection for the fundamental rights of the colored people. We will then open the doors of the Capitol and admit your representatives.

These were, undoubtedly, moderate terms. They did not challenge the existence of the state governments that Johnson had set up, nor the wealthy planters' continuing monopoly of the South's productive lands. They were far indeed from the vision of social change that Stevens had set forth at Lancaster the previous year.

These terms, moderate as they were, were not to the liking of the white Southern leaders. Each of the Southern states refused to ratify the 14th Amendment and in doing so they received the open support of Andrew Johnson.

The two sides took their case to the electorate in the fall of 1866. A vote for the Democrats was a vote for Johnson, a vote for the Republicans a vote for the 14th Amendment. The result was a Republican landslide; Republicans won nearly three-quarters of the seats in the House and two-thirds of the seats in the Senate.

Early in 1867, the Republicans swept aside the state governments that President Johnson had brought into being in the South and proceeded to put their own policies into effect. The era that followed, 1867–1877, is known as Congressional Reconstruction.

Congressional Reconstruction, 1867–1877

Congress came into session in January 1867 in a determined mood. Laws passed in March wiped out the state governments that President Johnson had set up two years before. The South was broken up into five military districts and returned to army rule, each district under its own commander.

The states of the planter South had rejected the terms offered by Congress for readmission to the Union: that by ratifying the 14th Amendment they gave a guarantee to protect the rights of all Ameircan citizens, black as well as white, who lived within their boundaries.

Congress now took action itself to set up state governments in the South that would agree to the 14th Amendment. Under Congressional instructions the commanders of the five military districts drew up lists of qualified voters in their regions; these lists, of course, included black male citizens. The voters then elected delegates to constitutional conventions which were held in every one of the states.

Now, for the first time, black and white delegates sat together in convention halls, worked out state constitutions and submitted these to the voters for their approval. Elections were then held for state legislatures and governors. New state authorities came into being. When the state legislatures ratified the 14th Amendment, these states were readmitted to the Union and were allowed to send representatives and senators to Congress.

Now, for the first time, black men made their appearance as lawmakers on Capitol Hill. The first black ever to sit in the U.S. Senate was Hiram Revels, of Mississippi, who took his seat in place of Jefferson Davis in February 1870. Revels, born a free man in North Carolina, attended college at Bloomington, Illinois, and then became a minister. When he made his maiden speech in the Senate, the galleries were packed to overflowing. "Never," wrote a journalist, "since the birth of the Republic has such an audience been assembled under one single roof. It embraced the greatest and the least American citizens."

Three years after the passage of the Reconstruction acts of March 1867, Congressional Reconstruction was complete. All the Southern states had been readmitted to the Union; all of them had ratified not only the 14th Amendment, but the 15th Amendment as well. This amendment forbade the states from barring anybody from voting "on account of race, color, or previous condition of servitude."

Congressional Reconstruction accomplished, for a fleeting moment, a transformation of race relations in the South, one in which political power was transferred from the old slaveholding minority, which had held it so long and used it so cruelly, to a new coalition of ordinary Southerners.

The black people who emerged as leaders in this movement were both exslaves and members of the South's free black community: lawyers, ministers and teachers. They learned rapidly how to make laws and to run states. Edward King, a Northern journalist, visited Columbia, South Carolina, in 1873 and described the legislature then in session. "The House, when I visited it," he wrote,

was composed of 83 colored members, all of whom were Republicans, and 41 whites; the Senate consisted of 15 colored men, ten white Republicans, and eight white Democrats. The President of the Senate and the Speaker of the House, both colored, were elegant and accomplished men, highly educated, who would have creditably presided over any commonwealth's legislative assembly.

Some whites were amused at the sight of black people making laws and threw insults at them, calling them "ignorant," "coarse," or "rude." King's observations were interesting. "The Negro," he wrote,

does not allow himself to be abashed by hostile criticism. When he gets a sentence tangled, or cannot follow the thread of his own thought in words, he will gravely open a book ... and, after seeming to consult it for some minutes, will resume. He has been gaining time for a new start.

Andrew Johnson vetoed all the Reconstruction acts of 1867 and 1868. Congress passed the acts over his veto. The establishment of new Southern governments based upon a broad interracial suffrage was a bitter humiliation for the president whose own plans were thus rejected and set aside.

Congress found that Andrew Johnson, now leader of the opposition, was a man to be feared. As chief executive he alone was empowered to carry out the laws that Congress passed. He had the power to hold up and to sabotage the policies that the Republicans were beginning to unfold. In the last summer of 1867, for example, he removed the district commanders whom he suspected of supporting the programs of Congress. And early in

Members of the KKK, hooded and armed, as they appeared in 1868.

1868, he fired Secretary of War Edwin Stanton, the one ally that the congressional Republicans had in Johnson's cabinet.

Stanton's removal was carried out in defiance of the Tenure of Office Act of March 1867, by which Congress forbade the president to remove cabinet members without the approval of the Senate. The Republicans decided that the stalemate between Congress and president must be broken by getting rid of Johnson. They wished to replace him with an executive committed to working with Congress, not against it.

The Founding Fathers had never envisioned the possibility of a deadlock between president and Congress. The Constitution said nothing about how such a crisis ought to be handled. The Republicans acted under a provision of the Constitution that authorized the removal of a president from office if he had been tried and convicted of "treason, bribery, or other high crimes and misdemeanors." The whole process is known as *impeachment*; it is an ancient practice imported from England.

The House of Representatives drew up the formal accusation, or indictment, against the president. The main charge was that he had illegally dismissed Stanton from his post and that he had conspired with others for this purpose.

The actual trial was conducted before the U.S. Senate, sitting as a court of law; it opened on March 23, 1868. William Crook, presidential bodyguard, sat in the Senate gallery and watched. Later he described how he felt. "When," he wrote,

from my seat in the gallery, I looked down on the Senate chamber, I had a moment almost of terror ... For the first time in the history of the United States a President was on trial for more than his life. [He was on trial] for his place in the judgement of his countrymen and of history.

In May 1868 the Senate found Johnson guilty, but the vote was one short of the two-thirds majority that was necessary for conviction under the Constitution. So Andrew Johnson was allowed to finish out his term of office. Less than a year later Ulysses Grant, the North's greatest Civil War general, succeeded him as president.

The state governments set up by Congress in 1867 and 1868 took over the job of rebuilding the South after the devastation of the war. They constructed roads, bridges and railroads. They dredged harbors and cleared them of sunken vessels. They established new hospitals and asylums. They passed laws guaranteeing to both black and white citizens access to theaters, public transportation and schools.

All of this aroused the bitter hostility of the pro-Johnson Southern Democrats. They accused the new governments of being a corrupt alliance of "shiftless niggers," *carpetbaggers*—by whom they meant Northern whites—and *scalawags*—by whom they meant Southern Unionists. They attacked the new authorities for unfair taxation and extravagant spending.

Much of this talk was political propaganda. There was, to be sure, a certain amount of corruption in high places; but modern historians have rejected many of the wild charges that the Democrats made. The new Southern governments, indeed, were remarkably honest by comparison with state governments in the North at the same time; they were much more honest than the so-called Democratic "Redeemer" governments that took over in the South after Congressional reconstruction had collapsed.

The Overthrow of the Reconstruction Governments, 1869–1876

Congressional Reconstruction was an experiment in interracial cooperation and democratic rule that had barely made a beginning before it was brought to an end. At the very moment that the new state regimes came into being, their enemies began to lay plans for their overthrow. In 1867 a Southern-wide meeting was held at Nashville, Tennessee,

This drawing by Thomas Nash, a famous cartoonist, appeared in *Harper's Weekly* in 1872. As well as a drawing can, it summarizes the political aims of the KKK.

and the Ku Klux Klan was set up. The most powerful of a number of secret organizations that came into being at that time, the KKK's objective was to kill or drive out black Republican leaders and to break the power of black voters by using the weapons of terror and intimidation. The KKK enjoyed the support of many Confederate veterans across the South. "White supremacy," or racism, was their watchword.

In 1868 violence was unleashed. Meeting places, churches and schools were burned to the ground. Political leaders and teachers were assassinated. Hundreds of black people attending political gatherings or prayer meetings were attacked and mowed down in cold blood. Black voters were warned to stay away from the polls on pain of death.

Robert Gleeds, an exslave and state senator in Mississippi, stated what the Klan's objectives were. "We believe it had two objects," he reported.

One was political, and the other was to hold the black man in subjection to the white man and to have white supremacy in the South. A paper published in Alabama said in plain words. "We must kill or drive away the leading Negroes and only let the humble and submissive remain." That was in 1868 … I spoke of it often—the idea of a party being built up on the principle of the open slaughter of human beings. It was startling to me.

In October 1868, B. F. Randolph, state senator from Orangeburg County, South Carolina, and chairman of the state committee of the Republican party, was assassinated in broad daylight at a political meeting. Randolph's death was one of the first of thousands of killings that took place across the South in the years that followed for the purpose of carrying out the objectives that the Klan had set for itself. As Robert Gleeds had said, murder, terror and the midnight raid now became the prime weapons of white supremacist politics.

The rank and file of the Klan mobs were Confederate veterans and poor white people. The leaders were men of property and standing. In October 1869, a gang attacked the home of Abram Colby, a member of the Georgia legislature, and broke down the door. "They took me out of bed," Colby said, "took me to the woods and whipped me three hours or more and left me for dead." The mob used "sticks and straps that had buckles on the ends of them" to inflict thousands of blows that left him crippled for life. The leaders of the gang, Colby told Congress, were "first-class men in our town. One is a lawyer, one a doctor, and some are farmers."

This conservative counterattack against the new Reconstruction governments was fearfully effective; the governments began to crumble. By 1872, when the KKK officially went out of existence, Democrats had been successful in seizing power in Virginia, North Carolina, Georgia and Tennessee. The governments that they set up were called *Redeemer* governments because they claimed to have "redeemed" their states from the unholy rule of Negroes, carpetbaggers and scalawags.

President Grant took steps to end Klan violence. The Force Acts of 1871 and 1872 made it a federal offense to use violence to keep people from the polls and to deprive them of their voting rights under the 15th Amendment. Federal troops were sent back into the South, and leading Klansmen were prosecuted and jailed.

Grant's action, however, was weak and ineffective. The violence and the terror went on. Four years later, by the end of 1876, the Redeemers had taken power in all the Southern states except Florida, South Carolina and Louisiana.

The KKK and the counterrevolution that it organized is only part of the reason why Congressional Reconstruction in the South collapsed so rapidly. During the 1870s the Republican party in Washington faced two alternatives. One of these was to continue the effort to reorganize the South and to build democracy there. This was the hardest choice to make; it required a continuing struggle, under federal leadership, that might perhaps take decades. Final victory over the slave society and its inhuman racist practices would demand those policies of land distribution and the destruction of planter power that Thaddeus Stevens had asked for at Lancaster in 1865.

The other alternative facing the Republicans was to admit defeat and to make the best terms that they could with the Southern planters—the old elite who, in spite of the war, still possessed their lands and still controlled many thousands of black workers.

This is what the Republicans chose to do. By the 1870s the times were changing. The older antislavery generation was passing away; the party was now dominated by a new breed of men. These were mediocre, timid politicians who had little patience with continuing disorder in the South and wished to end it as rapidly as possible. Their decision was embodied in what is known to history as the Compromise of 1877.

The Compromise of 1877

In the presidential election of 1876, the Republican candidate was Rutherford B. Hayes, of

Ohio; the Democratic candidate was Samuel J. Tilden, of New York. A total of 185 electoral votes were necessary for victory. When the returns came in the tally was as follows: 185 for Hayes, 184 for Tilden.

Hayes counted as part of his electoral total the 19 electoral votes awarded him by the state election boards in Louisiana, South Carolina and Florida. These three states were the only ones in all of the South where Republican regimes still existed, thanks to the continuing presence of federal troops.

The Democrats hotly disputed the returns from these states. If they could be awarded the electoral votes in just one of these three, they would win the election.

Faced with the Democratic challenge, Congress appointed an electoral commission to investigate the returns from the three states in dispute. The commission was composed of five representatives, five senators, and five Supreme Court justices. It so happened that seven of these commissioners were Democrats, and eight were Republicans. The commission, predictably enough, awarded the disputed votes to Hayes by an 8–7 vote. The Republican swing man was an associate justice of the United States Supreme Court, Joseph Philo Bradley.

Congress was then asked to approve the result. It did so, but only after lengthy behind-the-scenes negotiations. The Congressional Democrats were in a position to apply a good deal of political pressure. By resort to procedural delays and endless debates, they threatened to hold up the presidential inauguration indefinitely.

By March of 1877, the two sides had worked out a sectional agreement, the Compromise of 1877—a compromise that, in its own way, was every bit as important as the compromises of 1820 and 1850. This largely informal and unpublicized agreement decided the fate of the South and, indirectly, of the United States itself, for generations to come.

The Republicans promised to make available federal funds for the building of Southern railroads and other internal improvements. They also promised the Southern Democrats that they would have *home rule*. This was a pledge that the Republicans would leave undisturbed the Redeemer governments of the 1870s; the federal authorities would make no further efforts to prevent Southern whites from governing the South as they saw fit. A part, but only a small part, of this pledge, was the Republican commitment to withdraw federal troops from South Carolina, Louisiana and Florida after the new president had been inaugurated.

The Democrats, on their side, withdrew their opposition to Hayes being declared victor in the election; they promised continuing cooperation with the Republicans in Congress in the passage of legislation and the conduct of the nation's affairs.

True to his word, President Rutherford Hayes withdrew the troops from Louisiana, South Carolina and Florida after his inauguration in 1877. The Republican regimes in these three states promptly collapsed. Reconstruction was at an end.

* * * *

The Compromise of 1877 was a betrayal of the cause for which the Civil War had been fought. It marked a return to the reconstruction policies of Andrew Johnson and their triumph. In spite of the 15th Amendment, black people would no longer be allowed to vote in the South, except to the extent that the Democratic party found such voting necessary or desirable. Within a quarter of a century, black voting rights throughout the South had been virtually destroyed; the black vote had become negligible. As for the 14th Amendment as a guarantee for the protection of the wider rights and freedom of the exslaves, it soon became a dead letter.

By 1900 black people in the South enjoyed few, if any, rights, that whites felt bound to respect. Many years would pass before the struggle for these rights would once more be resumed.

8

THE WEST
Cattlemen and Indian Wars, 1865–1890

Mexicans were the first people in America to raise cattle; they inherited breeds brought here from Spain. Some of these animals escaped to the prairies and became as wild as the bears, panthers and wolves. These *cimarrones* ("strangers," or "wild ones") mixed with other types of cattle imported from Spain to create a new breed with long-spreading horns and coats of many colors. Many years before English-speaking people arrived, Mexican *vaqueros*, or "herders" (from Spanish *vaca*, "cow"), were raising these Longhorn cattle in the thickets and prairies on both sides of the Rio Grande, in the vast and beautiful Spanish provinces of Coahuila and Texas.

During the 1830s, English-speaking colonists migrating to the coastal regions of Texas began to raise cattle; but the North Americans knew nothing about the special skills that they needed in order to herd the animals that lived and grazed upon the open prairies; they had to learn these skills from the Mexican *vaqueros* among whom they lived. The vocabulary of American cattle-raising is full of Spanish words provided by the Spanish-speaking people who first practiced these skills upon American soil. The rawhide rope that they used for lassoing cattle the Mexicans called *la reata*, "lariat." The slipknot in the rope was called a *lazo*, or "lasso." "Stampede" is the English form of the Spanish *estampida*, and so on.

The lasso was a basic tool for herding, catching and controlling range cattle. Basil Hall, an English traveler who visited Texas in 1824, was amazed at the skill with which the *vaqueros* used it. They could, he wrote, "place their lasso on any particular part [of the animal's body] they please—over the horns, round the neck or body, or they can include all four legs, or two, or any one of the four." The secret of the *vaquero*'s skill was that he had been practicing with the lasso ever since he was a child. "I have often seen little boys," Hall wrote, "actively employed in lassoing cats and entangling the legs of every dog that was unfortunate enough to pass within reach."

The English-speaking colonists in Texas learned much from the Mexican cowboys; and they also stole the Mexican cattle where they grazed in the great borderland area between the Nueces River and the Rio Grande. With these stolen animals they first built up their own herds; but, unlike the Mexicans, they only allowed carefully selected bulls to mate with the cows. These Texan longhorns were the toughest of creatures. As J. Frank Dobie, a Texas writer and cattleman, put it, the longhorns "with their steel hoofs, their long legs, their thick skins, their powerful horns, could walk the roughest ground, cross the widest deserts, climb the highest mountains, swim the widest rivers, fight off the fiercest band of wolves, endure cold, thirst, hunger and punishment as few beasts of the earth have ever shown themselves capable of enduring."

The Texans raised their longhorn cattle along many rivers that flowed southward from the *Llano Estacado* (the Edwards Plateau) and the Indian territory into the Gulf of Mexico. But the cradle of the Texan cattle kingdom was the very southernmost tip of the state—a vast, diamond-shaped area with San Antonio, Corpus Christi, Brownsville and Laredo as its four points. Conditions there for the raising of cattle were close to perfect. Clumps of timber gave shade from the sun, the climate was mild, and the grass was plentiful.

The Great Plains and the Cattle Kingdom

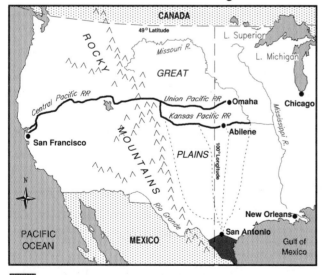

▨ Cradle of the cattle kingdom
⋯⋯ Cattle trails
▬ Transcontinental railroads (central routes)

The region was seldom if ever touched by blizzard or snow, and there was enough water. The San Antonio valley lay at the heart of this region; it was far away from the southern part of the high plains, from which for generations the warlike Comanche bands had been raiding settlements in New Mexico and upper Texas, stealing cayuses (ponies) and killing people.

In the years just before the Civil War, the Texas cattle business began to prosper. Herders drove their longhorns over the Shawnee trail that led from Texas to Missouri; steamboats carried the steers across the Gulf of New Orleans; herds were even driven on foot all the way to New York City. But when the war came these drives ended. Ranchers and their hands joined the Confederate army and went off to fight the Yankees. As for the cattle, there was nobody left to take care of them and during the four years of war they grazed upon the prairies and multiplied. The cattle population of southern Texas doubled. When the veterans came back home they found their stock, much of it un-branded, roaming the plains and thickets.

With the war over, these cattle were a great opportunity for their owners. Immigrants were once more swarming into the United States to work in the factories and to lay the railroad lines thrusting toward the West. The industrial cities of the North were swelling with people as they expanded operations to meet a rising demand for steel, iron rails, steam engines, cotton clothing and leather shoes. These industrial workers needed huge amounts of meat to keep them going; money, clearly enough, was to be made out of the Texas herds if they could be rounded up and shipped to the Northern market.

But, the ranchers asked themselves, how were their cattle to be transported in such large numbers across the thousand miles or more of farmlands that separated them from city consumers? By 1866 the Missouri Pacific Railroad, with its eastern base at St. Louis, had pushed its rails as far west as Sedalia, almost to the border of Kansas. Perhaps, the Texans thought to themselves, the way to market their

Cattle that grazed upon the unfenced grasslands of the West had to be rounded up periodically in order to brand and count them or to separate the calves from the herd. For such purposes they were driven into a corral, or enclosure. This drawing, made in 1875, probably shows cattle being corraled after having made the trip from Texas to a reservation on the northern plains, close to the Rocky Mountains. Note the number of Native Americans involved in the operation.

cattle was to drive them over the trail to Sedalia, then ship them to St. Louis by railroad. At St. Louis the animals could be slaughtered and the meat distributed, again by railroad, to Eastern markets.

In the year of 1866, 200,000 longhorns headed north across Indian territory toward Sedalia. Soon the herders ran into trouble. Indian people demanded payment for all the grass that the longhorns ate along the way; rifles in hand, angry Missouri farmers blocked the path and insisted that the herds turn back. They knew that Texas cattle were infested with ticks. As one poet put it so vividly, "The ticks were there by millions,/I tell the very truth,/for they covered up the cattle/just like shingles on a roof." Before the Civil War these ticks had carried the dreaded Spanish cattle fever to the Missouri herds and wiped many of them out. The ranchers, too, had to cope with rustlers who stampeded the herds at night: Some of the cowboys

fought pitched battles with these raiders and died gun in hand, defending their steers.

Few longhorns arrived in Sedalia that year. It was discouraging news for Texas cattlemen. The Northern market seemed farther off than ever.

In 1867 a young livestock dealer from Illinois, Joseph G. McCoy, began to think about the problem. There must be some way, McCoy thought, to bring together people who wanted to sell cattle and people who wanted to buy them. There must, he thought, be some way to set up a center in which "the Southern drover and the Northern buyer would meet on an equal footing, and both be undisturbed by mobs and swindling thieves." McCoy then turned his attention to the Kansas Pacific Railroad; in 1867 this railroad was driving its steel rails from St. Joseph, on the Missouri border, clear across the state of Kansas, far out onto the open prairies. Why not, McCoy thought to himself, establish a market center on the Kansas Pacific, way out on the prairie far to the west of the Missouri farmlands? Then the herders could drive their cattle northward over the grassland trails without interference from Missouri farmers or thieves. Eager buyers would be waiting at the railhead; the steers could be shipped in cattle cars back to Chicago or St. Louis.

As a reception center for the Texas cattle, McCoy chose Abilene in Dickinson County, Kansas. He set to work to build enclosures well supplied with water where the ranchers might bring their cattle and keep them until they were sold and ready to be shipped east. He sent word to Texas that if the ranchers drove their herds northward over the prairie to Abilene, they would find fine corrals (from the Spanish *corral*, a yard for cattle) and eager buyers. This was good news to the Texans; it gave promise, as McCoy wrote, "that the day of fair dealing had dawned for Texas drovers, and the era of mobs and brutal murder [had] ended forever."

That year 35,000 longhorns arrived in Abilene; they were sold and shipped to the new slaughterhouses and meat-packing plants of Chicago. The trail from Texas that the cattle now began to tread lay far to the west of the old Sedalia trail; it was a buffalo path that buffalo and their Indian hunters had used for countless years. Americans called it the Chisholm trail, after Jesse Chisholm, the first white man to move south over it with his wagons when the Civil War ended. The trail led clear from the Nueces River, due north across Texas and the Indian territory, till it hit the railheads in Kansas.

Abilene was the first of the new cattle towns, and the Chisholm trail the first of the post-war prairie trails. From 1867 for nearly 25 years, millions of longhorns threaded their way along these trails to Kansas in one of the greatest animal migrations on record. Mexican as well as American cattlemen used the trails, and some of the cowboys who worked for Texas ranchers were Mexican. Mexican feelings about the trails, in their enormous length, found expression in a famous *corrido*, or cattleman's song: "Cuando salimos pa' Kiansis/

con una grande partida,/¡Ah, que camino tan largo!/No contaba con mi vida. [When we left for Kansas with a great herd, how long a trail it was! I never thought I'd make it.]"

One after the other cowtowns now began to spring up along the Kansas railroad lines— Ellsworth, Dodge City, Salina, Wichita. Villages with a few huts became centers where cattle bawled, where stockyards spread, where cowboys milled in the streets.

What was a cowboy's life really like? No one has left a more vivid record than Andy Adams, whose *Log of a Cowboy* was published in 1903. Andy was born in Indiana; shortly after the Civil War ended, he and his family moved to Texas. Andy's two older brothers left home to become cowboys, and Andy, too, was fascinated by the thought of life on the open plains, herding cattle. In 1882, at the age of 18, Andy took a job as a cowboy with a drover named Don Lovell and rode north with Lovell's Circle Dot herd. Andy's boss had instructions to drive the herd all the way from the Rio Grande to the Blackfoot Indian reservation in Montana, a distance of over 1,200 miles. The Circle Dot herd would follow the trail northward for more than three months.

It was April and time for the spring drive when Andy left home. The Adams family stood at the gate to say good-bye. Andy's mother and sisters wept; his father said, "You are the third son to have left our roof, but your father's blessing goes with you." With a lump in his throat, the young man mounted his horse and rode away.

Herds driven up the trail numbered anywhere from 1,000 to 3,000 head of cattle; more than this would be dangerous in a stampede, and they'd be too strung out to control easily. An experienced cattleman—the trail boss—was in charge of the cowboys riding with the herd, who numbered from 10 to 18 men, depending upon the number of animals to be driven. A cook with the chuck wagon and a horse wrangler completed the party. The horse wrangler gave most of his time to caring for

This drawing shows cattle bedded down for the night beside a stream. The cowboys ride quietly around the herd, on the alert for any disturbance that might produce panic and a stampede. Three members of the patrol may be seen in the distance, in addition to the man in the foreground.

the horses that had to be taken along, for there were many of them. Cowboys needed fresh horses to ride by night as well as by day; extra horses, too, were needed in case of loss, theft, or accident. On the plains a cowboy without a horse was of no use to anybody, including himself.

When the Circle Dot herd hit the trail in April 1882, it was strung out in a thin line, like a winding snake, for over a mile. Cowboys rode in the lead, out on both flanks and in the rear. Everybody moved along at an easy pace. As Flood, the trail boss, told his men, "The secret of trailing cattle is never to let the herd know that they are under restraint." The cattle were allowed to move on at their own pace, grazing as they went. The cowboys kept them under watch, making sure that none strayed from the line and that other cattle from the range did not slip into the column.

Men and cattle were now moving northward over the open grasslands of the high plains, far to

the west of agricultural settlements. This was the country that an earlier generation had called "the great American desert." It stretched roughly from the 100º meridian of longitude westward to the Rockies, from Texas in the south to the Canadian border and beyond. The winters were icy cold, the summers were a time of torrid heat, of drought and drenching thunderstorms. Not enough rain fell year round to sustain the growth of forests; but there was water enough in streams and waterholes to quench the thirst of both cattle and men. As the cowboys with their herds moved northward along the trails after 1867, they inherited this grasslands empire for a lttle while. The vast open plains themselves became America's cattle kingdom.

Shortly after dawn each day the men broke camp, roused the cattle from the bedding ground and got them moving. Headed north, often under a fierce sun, driving winds, or drenching rain, the cowboys remained in the saddle all day. When evening came

Buffalo graze in a river valley on the high plains.

the cattle were bedded down for the night at a campsite chosen in advance. The men ate their supper, sat around the fire for a while and unrolled their blankets. Even then a cowboy's duty was not done. Like soldiers in time of war, cowboys also had to perform guard duty through the hours of darkness. Each man with his buddy served a two-hour shift. They kept watch for hostile Indians, cattle rustlers and horse thieves. If, of course, there was a real emergency, like a storm or a stampede, everybody was up all night. Cowboys, they told Andy, were expected to get their sleep during the winter. This was supposed to be a joke, but it was also true. In those days on the Texas ranches, when the cattle grazed on the open range, there wasn't very much for a ranch hand to do during the winter except doze in the bunkhouse by the fire.

During night duty, the two guards rode in opposite directions in a huge circle round the sleeping herd. "The guards," wrote Andy, "usually sing or whistle continuously, so that the sleeping herd may know that a friend and not an enemy is keeping watch." The songs that the cowboys sang, and that the cattle liked best, were lullabies, love songs and hymns. The most beautiful songs ever written in the English language were sung to sleeping cattle.

Life on the trail was, for the most part, dull and exhausting. It could also be dangerous. Lightning killed many men in the fierce summer storms that came up swiftly and without warning on the plains. During the course of a single trip many rivers had to be forded; these flowed fast, especially in the spring or after a torrential downpour. Cattle, horses and men were swept away in the swirling waters or lost in the mill if the lead cattle panicked and turned back in midstream. When the Circle Dot herd was crossing one river, Andy tells how he heard a cry of mingled anguish and terror rising above the sound of bawling cattle, rushing waters and laughing men. "It dawned on my mind," he wrote, "that someone had lost his seat, and that terrified cry was for help." Wade Scholar, one of the cowboys, was missing. A dozen pairs of eyes scanned the waters in vain; strong currents had sucked him down to his death.

The peril that cowboys feared most was a stampede. Longhorn cattle were the hardiest of creatures, and also the most timid. The least thing, especially at night—a strange smell, a stranger's voice, a change in barometric pressure, a sudden shout, the striking of a match, or flickering lightning—could throw them into a panic. In a single bound a thousand steers would leap to their feet, mill around and streak away. "The cattle," as Adams described it, "might be lying on the ground in quiet … Suddenly one common impulse brought them to their feet and started them on a wild, headlong rush through the darkness. Away they went in a frantic, stumbling, panic-stricken plunging mass with little bluish flames flickering at the tips of their horns."

When cattle stampeded there was little that cowboys could do except stay with the herd. Their one hope was to turn the cattle and make them run in a circle; then they could run harmlessly round and round, until they were tired out. A rampaging herd generated a heat so fierce that it sometimes blistered the faces of men riding nearby. Sometimes the cattle scattered over a huge area, and it took several days to round them up again. Some animals were found so badly damaged that they had to be killed; others were found crushed flat by the pounding hooves that had passed over their carcasses; still others, perhaps hundreds, plunged to their deaths over cliffs or river bluffs.

Once in a while the cowboys had to go looking for a missing comrade; he might be found dead with his neck broken after having been thrown from his horse, or lying with shattered body at the foot of a precipice. As for the cowboys' feelings about a stampede, Frank Desprez said it for everybody in his poem "Lasca," which tells of a stampede down by the Rio Grande in which his girl friend, Lasca, died.

The air was heavy, the night was hot,
I sat by her side, and forgot, forgot;
Forgot the herd that were taking their rest,
Forgot that the air was close oppressed,
That the Texas norther comes sudden and soon,
In the dead of night or the blaze of noon;
That once let the herd at its breath take fright,
Nothing on earth can stop their flight;
And woe to the rider and woe to the steed,
that falls in front of their mad stampede!

After weeks and months on the trail, cattle and cowboys reached their destination; the men were paid off and the horses were sold. The railhead towns, of course, were primarily market and transportation centers where millions of cattle changed hands and were packed into cattle cars and shipped to Chicago. But money was to be made in these towns from cowboys as well as from cattle. After weeks of drudgery and danger, the cowboys had money jingling in their pockets; they were wild for amusement, liquor, women's companionship. Lots of seedy characters swarmed to these towns to help the herders spend their hard-earned cash— barkeepers, gamblers, con men, storekeepers, madams, pimps and prostitutes. The cowboys danced, gambled, drank, quarreled, and used their six-shooters freely. Men perished in the gunfights and duels that took place in the cowtowns. Such incidents have made good theater for movies and television, but they are not really what cowboy life was about. Life on the trail was infinitely more dangerous than a couple of days in town. The Chisholm trail was marked at frequent intervals with mounds; these were the nameless graves of

This print shows the kind of trip organized by Western railroad companies during the 1870s so that sportsmen might shoot the buffalo. The men take aim from the roofs of the coaches, from the windows and from the engine cab, with minimal effort and risk to themselves.

Texas horsemen who fell victim to the perils of the cowboy's path.

During the 1870s Texas longhorns not only moved up to the Kansas railheads; the entire high plains area became their grazing ground. This northward movement of the longhorns was speeded by the destruction of the buffalo that took place in the decade 1871–1882. Up until the 1870s, the buffalo were the most numerous of all the wild creatures that lived upon the high plains. Their numbers were beyond counting—60 million, perhaps, would be a moderate guess. For thousands of years these buffalo had provided the Indian hunters of the plains with their living. The plains Indians knew well that the buffalo was the source of their existence; to them this animal was sacred. Indian hunters did not kill the buffalo wantonly, or for sport; they took only what they needed to sustain their own life. When they killed, nothing was wasted, and every part of the carcass—flesh, sinew,

blood, horns, and bones—was used. Buffalo skins were made into robes, tents, lariats, saddles, and canoes. Buffalo horns were shaped into ladles and spoons. Buffalo bones became war clubs; sinews and tendons were used to string Indian bows. Even the buffalo's tail was used—to swat flies and brush away mosquitoes. So careful were the Indians to conserve the buffalo that, even though they killed many, the herds did not diminish. Indians lived off the *increase* of the herds; they did not destroy the herds themselves.

In the early 1870s Americans began to slaughter the buffalo in appalling numbers. Railroad crews building new lines across the plains needed meat; so did the soldiers who manned the forts that now began to dot the plains. Buffalo hunting became a fashionable sport among the wealthy. Monied people, including European aristocrats and their servants, were hauled out onto the plains in luxurious railroad coaches. All day they enjoyed the shoot ("Hand me my gun, James." "Good shot, sir!"); at dusk they retired to the coaches for an evening of dining, wining and card playing. Professional buffalo hunters made their appearances in large numbers. After 1870 there was a rising market for buffalo hides back East. The strong, elastic hides were admirable material out of which to make drive belts. Hundreds of these belts were used in the big factories to hook up the machines with the main source of powers.

So it was that during the 1870s buffalo hunting and buffalo skinning became a big craze—for meat, amusement and, above all, for money. During these years hundreds of hunters moved out onto the prairies for the kill. The result was a total sacrifice of the buffalo herds on the altar of human greed. As an army officer, Colonel Dodge, put it, "The buffalo melted away like snow before a summer's sun." The hunters delighted in death. One of them surveyed a field of buffalo corpses: "This is the prettiest sight I ever beheld," he said. Most of the hunters took from the carcasses only what they wanted, which was little enough. They stripped the animals of their hides and left the flesh to rot. As Black Elk, a chief of the Oglala Sioux, put it, "The white men did not kill them in order to eat … they took only the hides to sell. Sometimes they did not even take the hides, only the tongues."

The buffalo herds grazed upon the open prairies, upon land that was "open range"—the property, that is, of the American nation and of the United States government as an agent of the people. The buffalo in their millions belonged to the nation. Why then did not the federal government limit this mindless slaughter?

Destruction of the buffalo herds fitted in well with federal plans for ending Indian resistance to the advance of the white man in the West. Buffalo hunters, as General Sheridan told the Texas legislature, deserved the nation's thanks. "It is a well-known fact," said the general, "that an army losing its base of supplies is at a great disadvantage. … For the sake of peace let the [buffalo hunters] kill, skin, and sell until the buffalo are exterminated. Then your prairies will be covered with cattle and the cowboy." From the Canadian border to the Rio Grande, the job was done by 1882; only a few hundred pitiable survivors were left. Chief Seattle, of the Dwamish people, has made the final judgment, not only for himself but for all of us. "What is man without the beasts?" he asked. "If all the beasts were gone, man would die from great loneliness of spirit, for whatever happens to the beasts also happens to man. All things are connected. Whatever befalls the earth befalls the sons of the earth."

By 1882 the buffalo were gone, the power of the Indian peoples on the High Plains was broken. Longhorns could now graze on the open range, not only in Texas and Kansas, but in Nebraska, Wyoming, Colorado, the Dakotas and Montana as well. The cattle flooded like water onto the northern plains, and the cowboys came with them. The early 1880s were a boomtime for the cattle business. Investors in both the East and in Europe began to dream of easy riches from the buying and selling of range cattle. Judge Sherwood of Connecticut, one of many boosters, wrote that "The profits are enormous. There is no business like it in the world, and the whole secret of it is, it costs nothing to feed the cattle. They grow without eating your money. They literally raise themselves." Dozens of cattle companies were now formed; they were owned by absentee businessmen and bankers who hired managers to run their ranches for them. A new breed of cattlemen now began to appear in the West. These people made their headquarters at the luxurious Cheyenne Club in Cheyenne, Wyoming. They played tennis, sipped iced champagne, changed their clothes before the evening meal and talked cattle. They were a far cry from the ordinary working cowboys whom they employed to fence the range, to round up and brand the cattle, and to drive them to the railheads.

By 1885 the market was glutted with too many cattle; the big companies were in trouble, because

The Colorado Trail

1. Eyes like the morn-ing star, Cheeks like a rose, Ann-ie was a pret-ty girl, God Al-might-y knows;

Weep all you lit-tle rains, Wail, winds, wail, All a-long, a-long, a-long, the Col-o-rad-o Trail.

2. Ride all the lonely night,
Ride all the day,
Keep those herds a-rollin' on,
Rollin' on their way;
Weep all you little rains,
Wail, winds, wail,
All along, along, along,
The Colorado Trail.

Repeat Verse 1

3. Ride through the stormy night,
Dark is the sky,
Wish I'd stayed in Abilene,
Nice and warm and dry;
Weep all you little rains,
Wail, winds, wail,
All along, along, along,
The Colorado Trail.

Repeat Verse 1

On night patrol, the cowboy croons this song to lull the cattle to sleep. He has sung it many times on the trail, and he will sing it many times again.

their heavy investments and falling prices made it impossible to pay dividends. The knockout came in the two winter months of January 1886 and January 1887. Terrible blizzards hit the high plains in two successive years and brought death to millions of longhorns. "The cattle," as one rancher wrote, "turn their heads from the blast, and huddle down like a flock of sheep … The close-packed mass is now blanketed with snow and sleet … The cattle are drifting with the cruel storm guided only by the course of the freezing gale." Death came to many as they fell into ravines, "tumbling upon each other in a sickening heap of struggling, bellowing, half-frozen, crippled, smothering beasts." Some found shelter in deep ravines, where they slowly starved to death. Other stumbled on till they reached the limits of their endurance, then fell, froze and died. Some cowboys followed the herds and died with them. "They are lost," wrote one, "all lost together, out here upon the pitiless plains."

In March 1887 the snows melted. Rivers flooding across the prairies carried with them countless carcasses day after day, rolling over and over as they went. Canyons and ravines were piled deep with the corpses; every breeze that blew upon the plains was tainted with the stench of decay.

This disaster spelled the end of the open-range cattle business. Tending cattle on the high plains became a year-round job; the romance of the trail came to a sudden end. Henceforth ranches were fenced with barbed wire, and feed and shelter for the winter were provided. Cattleworkers raised and harvested hay in summer, fed hay to their beasts in winter, built barns and cattle sheds, strung fences, kept buildings and machines in repair. The open range, divided up between cattle ranches and advancing farmers, vanished.

What happened after 1890 to the cowboys who only a few years before had been singing "Don't fence me in"? Some, broken in spirit by the horrors

140

of the blizzard, never worked again. Others quit the cattle business and moved on to other jobs; they became farmers, joined up with the army, went to work in the lumber woods or the stockyards. They had contributed much to America's wealth, but they themselves did not grow rich. As one old trail hand, G. D. Burrows, said, "I put in eighteen or twenty years on the trail, and all I had in the final outcome was the highheeled boots, the striped pants, and about $4.80 of other clothing."

Chief Joseph and the Nez Perces Bands: A Freedom Struggle of 1877

During the 1870s the federal government was involved in a series of wars with Native American peoples throughout the West. The Indians fought back as best they could against the white invader who came to seize their lands or to wipe out the animals that were the foundation of their existence. The army had a single objective in these campaigns: To round up the bands, to put an end to their resistance and to herd them on to the reservations set aside for them.

Many of the tribes lived in small bands numbering a couple of hundred braves at most, owning a few guns and little ammunition, fighting for the most part with bows and arrows and tomahawks. Against them the United States brought hundreds of blue-coated soldiers armed with cannon, guns, ammunition and plentiful supplies. Faced with such overwhelming power, some peoples accepted defeat, gave up their freedom and became prisoners on the reservations.

Others did not go so quietly; they chose the warpath. These the army regarded as outlaws to be hunted down, men, women and children, babies on their cradle boards. They lived and died as patriots, fighting for their freedom.

Most extraordinary of all these Indian Wars in the West was the struggle of Young Joseph and the Wallowa River bands of the Nez Perces in 1877. It is a story that takes us to the Snake River and Idaho.

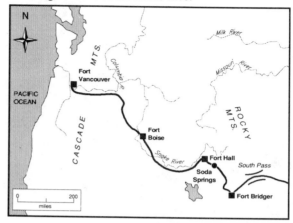

The Oregon Trail and the Snake River

It tells of a people who lived beyond the buffalo range but who were, nonetheless, buffalo hunters and whose destiny was linked to the people of the high plains.

Idaho is Snake River country. The great river rises upon the eastern fringe of the state, beyond the rampart of the Rocky Mountains that defines its border. Cascading down from the heights, the Snake River winds westward clear across Idaho in an arc that extends the full width of the state. Then the river turns abruptly to the north, flowing along a course that forms for nearly 200 miles the boundary between Idaho and Oregon. Here the last half of the Snake's journey lies through the stupendous gorge of Hell's Canyon. Turning westward once more, the river flows away in a gentle curve through southeastern Washington and finally mingles its waters with those of the Columbia River at Walla Walla.

The Snake River is shaped like the Big Dipper in the night sky or the cup of an outstretched hand. It defines and, as it were, contains the state of Idaho. Idaho, indeed, is that wondrously beautiful stretch of America that lies between the Snake River on the south and the west and the high wall of the Rocky Mountains on the east and the north. A land of infinite variety—of sand, sagebrush and volcanic rock, of glaciated valleys and alpine meadows, of timber-covered hills—its irrigated lowlands are blessed with the most fertile soil on earth.

The young man shown here, resplendent in his native costume, was photographed by Edward S. Curtis, famed photographer of native American peoples, around 1900. The child was a member of the Flathead tribe who lived in Idaho and shared a common culture with the Nez Perces, even though their languages were different.

Native American peoples explored the far West and settled there thousands of years ago. Among them was a group who made their home in central Idaho, in the region between the Salmon and Clearwater rivers, tributaries of the Snake. Whites who encountered them early in the 19th century called these peoples the *Nez Perces*, or pierced noses, from the decorative shells they wore in their nostrils.

Several Nez Perces bands made their home to the west of Hell's Canyon, in the Wallowa Mountains of northeastern Oregon. Their land was bounded by the Powder River in the south, the Blue Mountains in the west and the Snake River in the east. These, the so-called Lower Nez Perces, numbering perhaps not more than 800 souls in all, are the subject of our story.

Hunters and gatherers like the Nez Perces were obliged of necessity to follow a wandering existence. When winter came, they sheltered in the lowland valleys where they had built earthern lodges. For the rest of the year they lived in temporary camps, wherever the search for food might take them.

In spring the people moved into the hills. There they ranged over a wide territory in search of wild fruits, berries, vegetables and nuts. When meadows blazed purple with camas lilies in flower, they gathered in the meadows and dug up the bulbs with pointed sticks. Fisherpeople, when spring came, went down to the lonely river waters to await the spawning salmon; they caught, cleaned and cured the harvest, storing it against the wintertime. Hunters made arduous journeys, searching amid the rocky, forested highlands for game and deer. Children played an important part in many of these activities. Some of them had skill in fashioning traps or catching fish with their bare hands.

During the 18th century the Nez Perces acquired horses from the Spanish settlements in New Mexico and began to rear hardy, fleet-of-foot and beautiful steeds of their own. They began to trade in furs with the British and the Americans, getting guns and other goods in return.

In 1836 the Reverend Henry Spalding, a Presbyterian minister, arrived in Idaho. He and his wife, Eliza, built a mission house at Lapwai, on the Clearwater River. Soon this hardworking couple were teaching the Nez Perces the secrets of reading and writing and the planting of field and garden crops, in addition, of course, to instructing them in the Bible.

The first coming of white people like the Spaldings to Idaho brought few changes in the life of the Nez Perces. Most whites during the 1830s and 1840s came to Idaho not to stay but to pass through. Their eyes were fixed upon the fertile and well-watered lands of the Pacific Coast. The route to this promised land, the Oregon trail, took them over the sandy plain where the Snake River flowed, far to the south of the Wallowa Mountains.

Chief of the Lower Nez Perces during the mid-century years was Old Joseph, a sturdy, strong-willed man with an immeasurable love for his native land. In 1855 he, along with other Nez Perces chiefs, signed a treaty with the federal government. By this treaty, the United States recognized that most of what is now northern and central Idaho, bounded by the Bitterroot Mountains in the east and the Snake Valley in the west, belonged to the Nez Perces peoples. This vast reservation area included the home of the Lower Nez Perces, lying between the Blue Mountains and the Snake.

Very soon things began to change. In 1861 a party of white men, trespassers on Nez Perces lands, discovered gold at Oro Fino, in the mountains north of the Clearwater River. The news set the West ablaze. Whites began to flock to Idaho to stay. They raised violent hands against the Native American peoples "in their way," attacking them upon their own lands, chasing them off, bullying and murdering them with impunity.

In 1863 federal commissioners arrived to enforce a new Indian policy. They drew the boundary lines of a new reservation, infinitely smaller than the old one. Here, they said, all the Nez Perces must come and live. They demanded that Chief Joseph abandon the Wallowa Valley; this Valley was only a tiny part of the vast area that the Nez Perces were now being asked to surrender to the whites. A treaty was placed before the Nez Perces chiefs, and they were invited to sign on the dotted line.

Old Joseph refused and went back home. Several years later he was on his dying bed. His son, Young Joseph, was with him. "I saw he was dying," the young man remembered. "I took his hand in mine. He said … 'When I am gone think of your country. You are the chief of these people. They look to you to guide them. Always remember that your father

Route of Nez Perce Long March

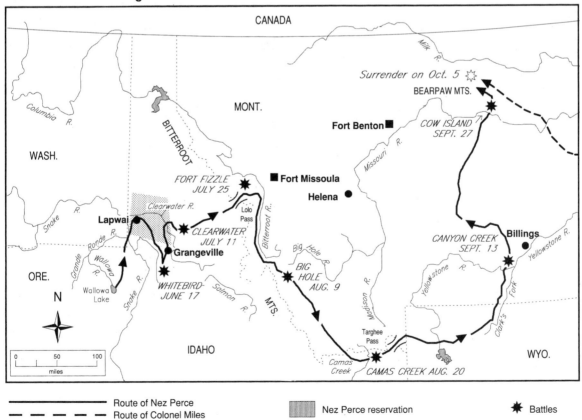

never sold his country. You must stop your ears whenever you are asked to sign a treaty selling your home … This country holds your father's body. Never sell the bones of your father and your mother.'"

Young Joseph pressed his father's hand. "I will protect your grave with my life," he said. The old man smiled and passed away. "I buried him," said the young chief, "in that beautiful valley of Winding Waters. I love that land more than all the rest of the world."

By the early 1870s, just as the old chief had predicted, white settlers were moving into the Wallowa Valley and squatting upon the land. They demanded that the natives be driven away. Officials in Washington, D.C. refused, saying that the Wallowa lands must be retained as a home for the Nez Perces. President Grant confirmed this position by an order issued in 1873. But two years later, federal officials changed their mind and reversed their position. General Oliver Otis Howard was sent out to Idaho with the mission of persuading young Joseph and the bands of which he was the leader to give up the Wallowa country and to move to the Lapwai Reservation. Howard was a distinguished soldier who had fought right through the Civil War and had commanded the Army of the Tennessee in 1864. He had lost his right arm in military service.

Young Joseph and other members of the Wallowa Valley bands met with Howard at Lapwai in November 1876. The young chief, by common consent, spoke for all. He was, at the time, 36 years of age, six foot tall, and bore himself with quiet dignity. Joseph's black hair fell upon his shoulders in a double braid. Dark brown eyes were set in a broad and open face.

The young chief addressed himself to Howard. Neither his father, his people, nor himself, he said, had ever agreed to give up their ancestral lands—ever. They wanted nothing from the white man. They wanted only to be left in peace to live, as they had always lived, upon their native earth.

General Howard delivered the United States ultimatum. You must leave the Wallowa Valley, he told Joseph. Come in to Lapwai of your own free will; if not, we will bring you in by force. You have until the middle of June 1877.

The Wallowa Valley bands gave in. Early in the month of June they reached a campsite outside Lapwai; there they paused for a day or two to rest. They were exhausted by the long struggle that they had been obliged to wage in order to drive their horses and cattle down from the hills and to bring them across the Snake River, swollen by the spring floods into a raging torrent. Many animals had been swept away.

Suddenly the suppressed rage of the braves at their accumulated wrongs erupted like a volcano. Three of them went off and massacred four whites notorious for their ill treatment of Nez Perces people. Returning to camp, the braves boasted of their deeds and taunted other braves with cowardice because they would submit tamely to wrongs without seeking revenge. Yet another war party set out. Returning to camp after an expedition to round up cattle, Joseph found that the people had abandoned any thought of obeying the white man's deadline for coming in to Lapwai. They had all fled southward to White Bird Canyon. He followed them.

General Howard, at the head of federal troops and Idaho volunteers, set off in hot pursuit. The Nez Perces bands fought them off, scattering their pursuers like chaff. Their success strengthened Howard's resolve to destroy them. Nez Perces resistance, he knew, could not go unpunished. It would embolden Native Americans throughout the West to defy federal authority and to rise in revolt.

Leadership of the Nez Perces bands now went to the war chiefs. They understood well enough that more federal troops would come after them and that there would be no peace for them in Idaho short of surrender; if they wished to live in freedom, they must abandon their native land.

They decided, therefore, to embark upon the long and dangerous journey to Montana. Surely there, they thought, they could hunt the buffalo and live in peace.

The whole people, accordingly, crossed the Continental Divide late in July. Men, women, children and herds all made the perilous crossing over the Bitterroot Mountains, along the Lolo trail. Federal forces toiled after them, far to the rear.

On the eastern side of the mountains the bands descended into the Bitterroot Valley and moved south. They wished, they told the white settlers, to walk through the valley in peace. They would not harm anybody, and they would pay for what they took. They rested here for a while, in the illusion that the war was over.

Foolish Indians, to think that the United States would give up so easily! At dawn on August 9, a force of 200 men under Colonel John Gibbon attacked the Nez Perces camp in a meadow by the Big Hole River. The camp, of course, was occupied not merely by soldiers but by all the Nez Perces people—men, women and children. The Nez Perces braves rallied, beat off the attack, and drove Gibbon's men back to where they had started, across the river. Swarming after them in a counterattack, the warriors pinned the federal troops down and held them while the people under Joseph's direction struck camp, packed up and headed south. The Nez Perces as well as the federal forces suffered heavily in this engagement. Most of the Indian casualties were women and children.

The Big Hole battle shattered the Nez Perces' illusion that they would be allowed to live in peace in Montana or, for that matter, anywhere in the United States. Now they set themselves a new objective: They would head for Canada. In that haven alone would they find the right to pursue life, liberty and happiness. Canada became the goal for these Native Americans as, before the Civil War, it had been for the fugitive slaves.

For the third time, the bands crossed the Continental Divide at the Targhee Pass, fled eastward through Yellowstone Park, then turned north toward Canada. Always the federal troops were in

Chief Joseph, as he appeared at the age of 37, shortly after the Nez Perces surrendered in 1877 at the Bear Paws. The face has a striking beauty; it is etched with lines of sorrow and fatigue [photograph by Edward S. Curtis].

hot pursuit; the braves had to fight ceaseless rear-guard actions.

At the end of September, the bands reached the Bear Paw Mountains in northern Montana. There, in a deep hollow in the plains at the edge of the hills, they paused to rest. The Canadian frontier was a mere 30 miles away. Winter was coming, and a thick blanket of snow covered the ground. The people were exhausted by the long, unrelenting struggle. The children were hungry. Many of the animals had died, many others were starving.

Here Colonel Nelson Miles with a force of 400 cavalry and infantry intercepted the Nez Perces and caught them by surprise with a sudden attack.

Driven off in bitter fighting that inflicted heavy casualties upon the whites, Colonel Miles withdrew and settled down for a siege. He opened talks with Chief Joseph and urged him to surrender. Promises wer made: If the Nez Perces gave up there would be no punishment for their resistance. They would receive food and blankets. They would be sent back to Idaho.

Early in October General Howard arrived and joined Miles. Joseph, with five of his warriors, rode out to meet the white officers. "Hear me, my chiefs," he said. "The little children are freezing to death. My people, some of them, have run away to the hills and have no blankets, no food; no one knows where they are—perhaps freezing to death." A cold wind blew across the field. "I want to have time to look for my children," Joseph continued. "Maybe I shall find them dead. Hear me, my chiefs. I am tired; my heart is sick and sad. From where the sun now stands, I will fight no more forever."

Joseph and his people surrendered; but the federal government did not keep its promise to return them to Lapwai. They lived out their lives in painful exile on distant reservations. Joseph himself carried on to the very end his struggle for the right to go back to the Wallowa Valley. He died at the Colville reservation in Washington state in 1904. The agency physician, as one historian writes, "reported simply that he had died of a broken heart."

* * * *

The Nez Perces bands carried out a fighting retreat from Lapwai to the Bear Paws for 1,700 miles across some of the most rugged country in the United States. Seven hundred and fifty men, women and children defied seemingly hopeless odds. Time and again they put to rout the United States troops and volunteers sent against them. Native Americans have waged many battles for their freedom; the struggle of the Nez Perces speaks for them all. It is, at the same time, almost unique, not only in the annals of this country, but also in the history of the world.

9

THE AMERICAN COLOSSUS

Industry, Immigration and Empire, 1865–1914

By defeating the South the North won the freedom to open up and develop the vast region that lay west of the Mississippi— from the Canadian border to the Rio Grande, from the high plains to the Pacific Ocean. As soon as the war had ended, the railroads moved rapidly into this western area. From 1869 to 1893, no less than five transcontinental lines were built spanning the plains, hills and deserts from the Mississippi Valley to the Pacific coast.

In this epic of railroad construction the story of the Union Pacific is the best known. To build the first great transcontinental line along the central route from Omaha, Nebraska, to San Francisco, two companies were formed and began work at the same time: the Central Pacific Company, which started in California and moved east across the Sierras; and the Union Pacific Company, which started in Nebraska and moved west across the Rockies. The Union Pacific moved faster than its rival, laying hundreds of miles of track across the gently sloping plains. It faced at first no special problems except building

bridges, fighting off Indian attacks, and bringing up supplies.

The Central Pacific Company could not move nearly as fast. From the beginning its engineers— the most famous of whom was Theodore Judah— faced unbelievable difficulties. Crossing the Sierras meant that the rails had to snake their way along narrow river gorges and had to be laid up steep inclines. Sometimes it was impossible to go either over or around the hills, so tunnels had to be driven through them. Dozens of these tunnels, some several miles long, had to be blasted through the rock. Often this rock was so hard that even large charges of dynamite didn't help much; the work went forward at a snail's pace, not more, maybe, than a few feet per day. Gorges had to be spanned hundreds of feet above the waters that foamed in the channel below, and huge crevasses or depressions had to be crossed. The engineers had to design iron bridges and enormous wooden trestles over which the rails might go.

The whole railroad-building activity took place in an atmosphere of feverish haste as the two com-

At the right of the picture one team unloads wooden *sleepers* and steel rails; to the left gangs lay the track and spike the rails down. Native Americans—a man, woman and child—look on.

panies raced to see which could lay the most track; and this, of course, was more than just a friendly game. In order to encourage the two companies to tackle their gigantic task, the United States government had agreed to pay them thousands of dollars for each mile of railroad track that they laid;

Early Pacific Railroad Lines, 1865-1884

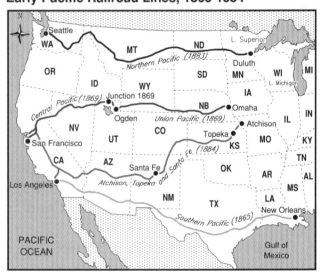

naturally it paid more money for building in hilly country, because that type of construction was more difficult, costly and time consuming. In addition, the federal government promised to give the two companies thousands of acres of land lying on either side of the tracks. This meant that the builders could make money by selling this land to people who would swarm west to farm it. So it's no wonder that the job got done in a short time. Work on the Central Pacific-Union Pacific line started in 1864; the last spike was driven in 1869, only five years later.

The Union Pacific brought in 10,000 men to lay its line, most of them Irish, many of them Civil War veterans, both Union and Confederate. Armed with picks, shovels and sledgehammers, these workers graded and cleared the track, positioned the crossties or "sleepers," laid the rails and spiked them into place. As for the Central Pacific, it recruited 10,000 Chinese immigrants. The Chinese began arriving in this country in 1850 to dig for

This drawing shows the emigrant waiting room of the Union Pacific Railroad at Omaha, Nebraska, in 1877. Some of the emigrants were heading West to stake out farms; others were gold diggers, bound for the Black Hills on the western border of South Dakota. By 1890, gold to the value of $45,000,000 had been mined there.

gold; the Chinese, in fact, called America *Gum Shan*, or "Gold Mountain." Toward the end of the Civil War they had moved into railroad building. Thus the Central Pacific part of the line across the Sierras and the deserts of Nevada and Utah was built almost entirely by the Chinese, with a little help from their Irish friends.

Irish and Chinese workers suffered equally in thrusting the ribbon of iron and steel across the continent. There is no complete record of the number of people killed in the building of the great transcontinental lines, but it ran into thousands. Men died in the explosions that were set to blast tunnels and to cut paths along rocky gorges; and they were buried in the landslides and rockfalls that followed such explosions. In the heat of summer, they dropped dead of exhaustion, or they froze in the icy winters. Pitched battles were fought with the

Indians, and lives were lost. The native peoples fought against the railroad builders without mercy; they knew well enough that iron and steel and steam marked a new age in which the ancient life-styles were doomed. The Indians, too, were killed in large numbers when federal troops rounded them up and cleared them from the path of the tracks. Men, women and children alike died in these federal sweeps.

The building of the Union Pacific and other transcontinental lines was one of the most important things that ever happened in American history. Before the coming of the steel rails, there were no roads of any type at all across the continent. The only way to go from the Mississippi Valley to California by land was to follow the trails and passes blazed by the buffalo and the Indians and followed so painfully by the early pioneers with

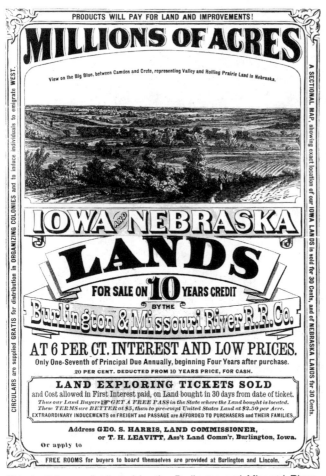

This leaflet was distributed by the Burlington and Missouri River Railroad Company to promote the sale and development of Iowa and Nebraska lands that it owned on both sides of the railroad line. The company makes promises to tempt the land-hungry immigrant: rolling, well-wooded prairies, generous credit, a free railroad pass to view the land, cheap transportation for purchasers, their families and freight.

their covered wagons and their oxen. Now for the first time, in 1870, large numbers of people and freight in huge amounts could be hauled across 2,000 miles of Western mountains, plains and deserts. Trips that in the past had taken months could now be accomplished in a couple of days. The new roads of iron and steel opened up the vast empire of the far West for settlement; they made available bottomless resources of coal, timber and iron for use in Eastern factories, and wheat and meat to feed the rapidly growing army of American workers.

The transcontinental railroad lines helped to bring about a great leap forward both in the number of factories that were operating east of the Missis-

sippi and in their size. It is impossible to build railroads without enormous supplies of iron and steel; in 1860 the United States possessed 30,000 miles of track, but in the space of 40 years this multiplied sixfold, until by 1900 there were 180,000 miles of track in the country. In 1860 the United States produced no steel to speak of, but by 1900 mighty steel mills in Pennsylvania and Ohio were producing 11,000,000 tons a year; the United States, in a single bound, as it were, had become the world's foremost steel-producing nation.

Tens of thousands of settlers swarmed out to the West along the new railroad lines, to clear farms and to raise stock. These people needed shoes and clothing, guns, axes, barbed wire to fence their land, steel windmills to suck water out of their wells, steam-powered tractors to haul their farm equipment. This meant that Eastern factories had to build bigger buildings, purchase more machinery and hire more workers in order to produce all these things that were needed.

By 1876, 100 years after the Declaration of Independence had been signed in Philadelphia, the face of America was changing with breathless speed as America turned into a nation of factory workers and city dwellers. Americans were busy inventing all kinds of wonderful new machines and gadgets to do work more quickly than it could be done by hand and to make it easier—things like telegraphs, typewriters and telephones, printing presses, sewing machines, cameras, telescopes and harvesters.

To celebrate the country's 100th birthday, an industrial fair was held in Philadelphia. Here millions of people flocked and paid their 50 cents to wander through five big display halls and to gaze at the mechanical marvels made not only in America but in other industrialized countries as well. There was a Pullman Palace Sleeping Car, the ultimate in traveling luxury; there was the world's biggest steam engine; and there was a cylindrical press that printed 25,000 sheets of paper in a single hours. A lot of people were saddened because a gift that the French government was making in memory of the Revolution wasn't ready to be shipped and so couldn't be on display at Philadelphia; but a portion of this gift was sent over anyway as a promise of what was to come. It was a giant hand holding up a flaming torch. Lots of kids had fun climbing the steps inside the hand. You came out high above the ground onto a circular balcony at the top of the torch and got a fine view of the fair grounds after you had recovered your breath from the climb. It took ten more years before the rest of the statue was finished. Shipped over from France, it was set up on Bedloe's Island in New York harbor to gladden the eyes of European immigrants now arriving by the millions. They called it the Statue of Liberty.

The people who organized all these new marvels of the industrial age were called "captains of industry." Many were hard, driving, unscrupulous men who reaped huge profits.

Four Sacramento storekeepers, for example, were the brains behind the Central Pacific Railroad: Collis Potter Huntington, Leland Stanford, Mark Hopkins and Charles Crocker. These men lined up the engineers who mapped the territory and surveyed the route that the railroad would take. They invested their own fortunes, borrowed money from others and went to Washington to lobby for government help. They set up construction companies that recruited the workers, hauled in the supplies and built the road.

There were many such captains of industry. Andrew Carnegie, who emigrated from Scotland as a boy and grew rich producing steel; John D. Rockefeller, who made millions from the processing of crude oil; Philip Armour and George Swift, small- town butchers who set up mass-production methods in their great Chicago slaughterhouses— these were just a few of the dozens of millionaires and multimillionaires who began to sprout like mushrooms after the Civil War.

Lavish profits drawn from railroads, financial speculation and industrial development made it

The residence of John Jacob Astor III, built on the northwest corner of Fifth Avenue and 33rd Street in New York City. William Waldorf Astor, John Jacob's son, had his father's pile torn down in 1897 before departing, along with his $100,000,000 fortune, for a life of permanent exile in England.

possible for these millionaires to maintain a lifestyle that is only to be compared with the splendors of the pharaohs of Egypt, the magnificence of Louis XIV at Versailles, the opulence of the emperors of China. The American millionaires built palaces and filled them with fine furniture and priceless paintings. They imported Italian gardeners to lay out exotic gardens filled with statues and fountains. They hired flocks of servants to cook their food, to groom their horses and to drive their carriages.

For summer use they built cottages in the cool mountains, on the seashores or by the side of quiet lakes. These "cottages" were on the same splendid scale as were their townhouses. Cornelius Vanderbilt, for example, and his wife, Alice, had a summer cottage at Newport, Rhode Island, that cost $10,000,000. That was an enormous sum for those days, the equivalent of nearly $200,000,000 in modern money. The Breakers, as the cottage was called, had 70 rooms, and the yard was fenced. It was a big fence surrounding a big estate. Just keeping it painted cost $5,000 every year. The billiard room was finished in green polished marble, and water both fresh and salt was piped into the bathrooms.

Two Bessemer converters are shown in operation at a Pittsburgh foundry in 1886. In the Bessemer converter air is blown through molten iron. Carbon residues in the iron combine with oxygen and are given off in a white-hot blast of carbon dioxide. The iron when cooled is left with only fractional carbon impurities; it has become high-grade steel.

In the foreground of the picture an engine pushes two white-hot steel ingots along a track.

Cornelius's sister Alva had an equally fabulous place at Newport; it was an exact copy of an ancient Egyptian temple at Baalbek.

Some of the millionaires were crazy about sailing. They sailed the seas in their pleasure yachts, set up a clubhouse on remote Cumberland Island, off the coast of Georgia, and built a flock of summer cottages there. Waited upon hand and foot by the crowds of servants that they brought with them, the sailors and their wives lived on Cumberland Island for only a few weeks each summer. At the end of the season, all left. The marble halls, high-ceilinged reception rooms and ornamental gardens lay silent and empty. Dustcloths covered the beautiful furniture.

Some of the millionaires had a lot of money left over even after they had built all the palaces they wanted and had bought all the paintings that they could use or store. So they held parties to show their friends how rich and generous they were. Alva Vanderbilt, for example, invited her friends to a fancy dress ball in March 1883 that really was fancy. It cost at least $4,000,000 (in modern money) just for the food, champagne and the band. The ballroom was decorated with orchids and rare flowers that cost more than $1,000,000. Alva also paid for the costumes that her guests wore: This added another $3,000,000 to the bill.

Some of these rich people were troubled by the fact that they enjoyed so much when millions of ordinary people had so little. Andrew Carnegie was of the opinion that fortunes like his were really a trust fund that ought to be spent wisely, so as to benefit the factory workers who had toiled so hard in order to accumulate all this wealth for their employers. Able people like himself, he wrote, had a duty to get rich; the profits they made were the reward, he thought, of giving so much time and talent to benefiting the nation. But Carnegie also thought that the rich had a duty to die poor. How else could they enter the Kingdom of Heaven?

Carnegie and other wealthy people who agreed with him set up special foundations to help them spend their money. They built libraries and filled them with books; they established museums and art galleries to house their statues and paintings; they designed public parks where the workers could take their children on weekends. All this, said Carnegie, was the Christian thing to do. "No more beautiful monument can be left by any man than a park for the city in which he was born or in which he has long lived." Carnegie added that a grateful community would want to name these gifts after the man who made them possible, and so indeed it happened. Many American parks, pleasure grounds, clinics, art galleries, museums, universities and libraries are named in memory of the millionaires who provided them. The library, for example, that Collis Huntington built in California is now world famous, as is the university founded by Leland Stanford at Palo Alto, 15 miles to the south of San Francisco.

When the big factories were built after the Civil War there were no automobiles, subways, or even bicycles. In order to get to their daily work most people, including little children, were obliged to walk. Workers' houses, therefore, huddled around the belching factory chimneys; they were flimsy shelters of wood and brick run up as quickly and cheaply as possible. In many places families were packed into dark, crowded tenements with little space, light, or air; and the streets in between the houses were unpaved and unlit. In these slumtowns many died from diseases like malaria, tuberculosis and smallpox. The children especially suffered: One out of every three or four children in these places did not survive the first year of life. These shacks, as the journalist Jacob Riis wrote in describing the tenements of the Lower East Side in New York, "contained, but did not shelter, the miserable hordes that crowded beneath mouldering, water-rotted roofs, or burrowed among the rats of clammy cellars." When parents died, or there was no more food, children abandoned these "homes" and took to the streets. They lived by their wits, doing odd jobs, blacking boots, begging and sleeping in any sheltered spot they could find, like doorways, stairwells, under the docks.

As America's industrial centers grew larger, so did the cities. By 1914 when World War I broke out, the United States had stopped being a country where most of the people lived and worked on farms: By that time, nearly one-half of the American people were living in large towns. The United States was well on its way to becoming the most highly industrialized nation on earth.

Many of those who streamed into the towns to work in factories and to run machines were native-born Americans who had faced hard times on their farms and were forced to give them up; but many more came from overseas. After 1890 millions of immigrants began to arrive here from eastern European countries like Poland and Russia, as well as from Italy, the Balkans, and Greece. This was in contrast to the immigrants of earlier years, who had come almost entirely from western Europe and Scandinavia. This "new immigration," as it was called, was different from all earlier immigration in terms of the number of people who now arrived on these shores. In the short span of 24 years from 1890 to 1914, 14 million Europeans arrived on American shores; this was almost the same as the entire number of people who had arrived here in the two and one-half centuries before. It was a tidal wave of humanity. In terms both of the numbers who came and the speed with which they moved across the Atlantic, the new immigration was one of the greatest movements of people from one part of the globe to another in the recorded history of man. In some years, like 1907, more than one million people arrived in the course of a single year. The immigrants arrived at various ports, but most came to New York. In 1892 the federal government set up a new reception center, Ellis Island, on a mudflat in New York harbor to handle them. This center was destroyed by fire in 1897, and a new one was built of brick. Ellis Island remains to this day as a memorial to the millions of human beings who passed through it.

Some of the newcomers dreamed of finding themselves a farm out in the open spaces of the West, but almost all of them were very poor indeed; they arrived without money to travel out West or to buy land and tools. Of all the millions who reached Ellis Island between 1892 and 1914, one out of three did not set foot on the American continent—they got no farther than the island of Manhattan. Many others ended up in the mines and steel mills of New York, Ohio, Pennsylvania and Colorado, in the textile and shoe centers of New England, in the packinghouses of Chicago. America's factory and mining towns now became places where many European nationalities mingled, and where almost every European language was spoken.

This shot of a pit boy, who spent his life deep in the mine, was taken by Lewis Hine, celebrated photographer of working children. The boy—he looks 10 or 11, but may in fact be older—stands at the pit head. His work shirt, an adult's castoff, is several sizes too big for him. The child wearing adult clothes does an adult's job. His eyes tell the story.

Lewis Hine traveled the whole country to get pictures like this one. He often developed the negatives, which in those days were made of glass, in the homes of the working people with whom he stayed.

The immigrants were mostly village people from the farmlands of Russia, Poland, Austria, the Balkan countries and Greece. American life at first seemed hard and strange to them, and they were bewildered by its din and dirt and pace. Most stayed, though not a few went back. In Chicago, for example, Greeks working in the mills or running the streetcars saved a few cents a week out of their pay. They worked hard, they saved money, they dreamed of home. When they grew old, they went back to Greece and gave their money to one of their country's ancient monasteries. There they prayed for the world in wooden churches whose walls were painted silver, red and blue, watched the oleander bloom and died in peace.

During these years 1865-1914, it was not unusual for American workers to have to spend 12 hours a day in the factories and steel mills, sometimes more; in some cases the workers didn't even get Sunday off and were made to toil seven days a week. Very often both husband and wife went out to work but still could not make enough money to buy food and clothes and to pay the rent; for this reason parents sent their children into the factories—they needed the few extra dollars that the children brought home. Poverty meant that young people by the hundreds of thousands were sucked into the industrial system.

Many of these young people were not yet in their teens, but they were expected to labor almost as long as a grown person. In 1900, for example, 7,000 children under the age of 16 were employed in glass-making factories alone. They worked a 10-hour shift, sometimes not even by day but throughout the night, when they ought to have been in their beds asleep. That same year, 25,000 boys, some of them not more than nine years of age, were working in the coal mines. Far underground they led the mules that hauled carts loaded with coal, or they sat hour after hour in the cold dark tunnels, opening and closing the doors between different sections of the mine.

Many boys were employed to sift coal as it rolled down a chute, or coal breaker. "Work in the coal breakers," as John Spargo, himself a miner, wrote,

is exceedingly hard and dangerous. Crouched over the chutes, the boys sit hour after hour, picking out the pieces of slate and other refuse from the coal as it rushes past to the washers. From the cramped position they have to assume, most of them become more or less deformed and bentbacked like old men ... The coal is hard, and accidents to the hands, such as cut, broken, or crushed fingers, are common among the boys ... Clouds of dust fill the breakers and are inhaled by

154

Solidarity Forever

To the tune of *John Brown's Body*

1. When the union's inspiration
      through the worker's blood shall run,
   There can be no power greater
      anywhere beneath the sun.
   Yet what force on earth is weaker
      than the feeble strength of one?
   But the union makes us strong.
Chorus:
   Solidarity forever!
   Solidarity forever!
   Solidarity forever!
   For the union makes us strong.

2. They have taken untold millions
      that they never toiled to earn,
   But without our brain and muscle
      not a single wheel could turn.
   We can break their haughty power,
      earn our freedom when we learn
   That the union makes us strong.
Chorus

3. It is we who ploughed the prairie,
      built the cities where they trade,
   Dug the mines and built the workshops,
      endless miles of railroad laid,
   Now we stand outcast and starving
      midst the wonders we have made,
   But the union makes us strong.
Chorus

4. In our hands is placed a power
      greater than their hoarded gold,
   Greater than the might of armies
      magnified a thousand fold
   We can bring to birth a new world
      from the ashes of the old,
   For the union makes us strong.
Chorus

This song was written by Ralph Chaplin in 1915 and set to the tune of "John Brown's Body." It expresses the ideal of the Industrial Workers of the World, founded in 1905: To organize the masses of unskilled and semiskilled workers into a single industrial union regardless of race, creed or color. The lyrics continue to be reproduced until the present time in the AFL-CIO *Songbook*, an official publication of the American labor movement.

the boys, laying the foundations for asthma and miners' consumption.

Little girls were not sent into the mines; they were used in the textile factories to tie up threads when they broke on the spinning wheels, or they worked as "spoolers," to see that the looms were provided with thread for the warp. Both boys and girls, some not more than six or seven years old, were put to work sweeping the factory floors. Marie Van Vorst was one of the first women to write about the way children were treated in the factories. She described two waifs in a South Carolina cotton mill: "She has on one garment, if a tattered sacking dress can be so termed. Her bones are nearly through her skin … Here is a slender little boy … twelve years old, he appears seven … He sweeps the cotton and lint from the mill floors from 6 P.M. to 6 A.M. without a break in the night's routine." After days or nights of work like this, the children were worn out. "They fall asleep at the table," wrote Van Vorst, "on the stairs; they are carried to bed and there laid down as they are, unwashed, undressed; and so lie until the mill summons them with its imperious cry before sunrise."

In order to protect their children and to win shorter working hours and more pay, workers tried to organize labor unions. Unions could put forward demands on behalf of everbody, and could back up these demands with the threat to strike. When the workers went on strike, they threw picket lines around the plant so that other workers could not walk in and take their jobs, and they kept the factory idle until the boss agreed to talk. Then leaders chosen by the workers could sit down with management and discuss their demands.

Organizing unions was dangerous work. Strikes often ended in failure because management just sat on its hands and waited—waited until the workers ran out of food and money and, faced with starvation, came back to work on the employer's terms. Many organizers were fired from the plants in which they worked and *blacklisted*. Their names were placed upon a list and sent around to other employers, which meant that they would have trouble ever finding a factory job again. Even so, many remarkable people during these years served as union organizers. Eugene V. Debs of Indiana organized the American Railway Union, which brought together thousands of unskilled railroad workers into a single national organization. Samuel Gompers, an immigrant from Holland, organized the cigar workers of New York City. "Big Bill" Haywood organized unskilled wage earners from the textile mills of New England to the lumber-woods of the state of Washington into a national organization known as the Industrial Workers of the World. Mary Jones, a fiery Irish woman known to millions of working people as "Mother Jones," began her organizing career in 1891 when she was a widow of 61, rousing the coal miners of West Virginia and leading them in their union struggles.

If it took courage to try and organize a union, it took even more to support a strike and to take part in its activities. Employers called in state militia and police to scatter the pickets and arrest the strikers; some even set up private armies of their own for this purpose. The years 1870 to 1914 are dotted with industrial battlefields on which workers slugged it out with police and troops. At Home-stead, Pennsylvania, in 1892, Andrew Carnegie and his partner Henry Frick broke the steelworkers' union (the Amalgamated Iron Workers of America) by the use of a private army and state militia. In 1894 George Pullman, the Sleeping Car King, broke a strike by workers in his factory town of Pullman, near Chicago, and he smashed Eugene Debs's American Railway Union at the same time. In Ludlow, Colorado, in 1913 state militia slaughtered striking coal miners and their women and children in a fiery onslaught known to history as the Ludlow Massacre. The miners' leader was Louis Tikas, an immigrant from the island of Crete, in the Mediterranean. The miners' employer was the Colorado Fuel and Iron Company, largely owned and controlled by John D. Rockefeller.

By 1900 the United States had four million people working in its factories, 30,000 miles of railroad, huge fiery mills belching forth tons of steel each year, and mammoth textile factories. She had become the world's foremost industrial producer, easily outstripping her nearest rivals, Great Britain and Germany. Now the colossus took steps to seize overseas colonies and to become a world power. In four years of war, from 1898 to 1902, the United States hit the Spanish empire, which at once fell apart, and then picked up the pieces. The new American empire straddled the globe.

The power of Spain had reached its height in 1580, hardly one hundred years after Christopher Columbus had discovered the New World. In that year, when the Portuguese and Spanish crowns were united, Spain was the mistress of vast over-seas possessions: She ruled Central America and the countries of the Caribbean, she held title to all of the South American continent from Venezuela to Tierra del Fuego. From the settlement of Manila, in the Philippine Islands, she exported precious silks to the New World and to Europe.

By the beginning of the 19th century, Spain's vast empire lay in ruins. One by one, the countries of Latin America mounted revolts and established their independence. By 1823 all that remained were mere fragments of a vanished dream of greatness— the islands of Cuba and Puerto Rico in the Carib-bean and the Philippines in the far Pacific. But these fragments yielded rich profits. Cuba, for example, produced no sugar in 1790, but by 1870 its produc-tion of this crop rose to the huge total of 726,000 tons a year. There was no lack of Portuguese and American slave ships to sell slaves to the get-rich-quick planters who, in the first half of the 19th century had flocked to the island. Slavery grew like a cancer in Cuba as half a million African slaves were brought in. By 1898 Cuba was producing 17% of the world's sugar crop; the words *sugar* and *Cuba* became interchangeable terms.

In the years following the end of the American Civil War, the Cuban people entered into fierce

156

struggles not only against slavery but also against Spain's control of their island. The last of these struggles began in 1895, and its objective was total independence from Spain. The Spanish sent in General Valeriano Weyler to put down the revolution. Weyler's method was terror. He stripped the fields and villages of their people and herded men, women and children into strategic hamlets and camps under military guard. When William McKinley was elected president of the United States in 1896, he sent his friend William Calhoun to Cuba to check things out. Calhoun found the country outside the military posts empty. "Every house had been burned," he wrote, "and food destroyed. I did not see a house, man, woman, or child, a horse, mule, or cow, nor even a dog. The country was wrapped in the stillness of death."

American interest in the Cuban struggle was fed by daily stories in the press; Americans showed a deep sympathy for Cuban ideals and for Cuban sufferings. Were these people, they asked themselves, not fighting for freedom against tyrants just as the Americans had themselves fought in 1776? Did not the French people help the Americans then, and should not the Americans help the Cubans now?

A small but powerful group of men close to President McKinley encouraged these generous feelings. Because they wanted war against Spain and the seizure of Spain's colonies, they were called *expansionists*. This group included Theodore Roosevelt, assistant secretary of the Navy; Alfred Mahan, a professor at the Naval War College at Newport; George Dewey, commander of the Navy's Asiatic Squadron; and the Republican leader of the Senate, Henry Cabot Lodge.

In January 1898, there was a riot in Havana. President McKinley, a portly man with a domed forehead who had once been governor of Ohio, sent the battleship *Maine* to Havana on a "friendly" mission—to protect American lives and property in the area, he said. There were indeed Americans living in Cuba. After 1880 Americans had begun to buy Cuban sugar plantations, and more and more Cuban sugar was being exported to markets in the United States.

On February 15 the *Maine* blew up and sank in Havana harbor. Two hundred and fifty American sailors were killed or drowned as a result of the explosion. The American press leaped to the conclusion that the Spanish were responsible for the tragedy. The cry was raised for war against Spain to avenge the national honor.

Spanish and American teams examined the wreck. The Americans said that a mine or torpedo had destroyed the ship; the Spanish said: not so. We don't know for sure, but it is probable that neither side was right. The destruction of the *Maine* was in all likelihood an accident. Ever since battleships had begun to be built in the second half of the 19th century, these steel monsters suffered a very high accident rate. Boilers exploded and so did magazines crammed with dynamite and shells.

As for the Spanish authorities in Cuba, they had no reason at all to blow up the *Maine*. Weak as Spain was, she could ill afford to provoke the anger of the United States. On the contrary, Spain was only too anxious to settle the dispute peaceably and without resort to war. Nonetheless, a wave of anger against Spain spread throughout the United States; the expansionists' clamor for war became louder. Congress declared war against Spain on April 25, 1898. Admiral Dewey sailed from Hong Kong, destroyed the Spanish fleet and seized Manila. Cuba and Puerto Rico fell without a struggle and were subjected to American military occupation. Within a few months, the war was over. In October 1898, by the Treaty of Paris, Spain surrendered to the United States not only Cuba and Puerto Rico but the Philippine Islands as well.

Over the centuries of occupation the Philippine peoples had fought as fiercely as the Cubans for their freedom; they had never accepted Spanish rule. The news that title to their land had passed to the United States was a shock to them. At a meeting in Europe 12,000 miles away, without their knowledge or consent, they had been handed over from one power to another like cattle at an auction. Taking matters into their own hands, the Filipinos launched their own war of independence in February 1899 against the United States, under the leadership of the patriot Emilio Aguinaldo. American troops were soon pouring into the Philippines to quell Filipino resistance.

The thought of the United States sending troops 9,000 miles from home to put down an Asian people's struggle for freedom stirred many Americans to anger. At the end of 1898 leaders like Samuel Gompers, Andrew Carnegie and Carl Schurz formed the Anti-Imperialist League. They traveled around the country, talking to people, trying to explain why the war in the Philippines was wrong and giving out thousands of anti-imperialist leaflets. Their message was a simple one: If the American people permit their government to send soliders overseas to put down other people and grab their land, they would be betraying America's most precious ideals as expressed in the Declaration of Independence.

"The conquest of the Philippines," Carl Schurz told audiences, "was deliberately planned with a cool calculation of profit … This is the spirit of imperialism … I can hardly imagine any kind of government more repellent than a democracy that has ceased to believe in anything, and in which all ambitions are directed towards a selfish use of power."

Soldiers in the field also raised their voices in protest. William R. Fulbright was one of the 70,000 American troops who fought in the Filipino war. "This struggle on the islands," he wrote from Manila in 1901, "has been nothing but a gigantic scheme of robbery and oppression … Graves have been entered and searches have been made for riches; churches and cathedrals have been entered and robbed of their precious ornaments; homes have been pillaged and moneys and jewelry stolen."

Albert Beveridge, a Democratic senator from Indiana, had a different view of the war. Control of the Philippines, he told the Senate in January 1900, would give the United States control of the Pacific Ocean; and, he added, "the power that rules the Pacific is the power that rules the world." As for the Philippine Islands themselves, he pointed out, they possessed rich supplies of minerals and foodstuffs with which to build American fortunes. "No land," he said, "surpasses in fertility the plains and valleys of Luzon … The mineral wealth of this empire of the ocean will one day surprise the world." As for the markets of the Far East that the war would win, said Beveridge, they were bottomless. "Luzon is larger and richer than New York, Pennsylvania, Illinois, or Ohio. Mindanao is larger and richer than all New England, exclusive of Maine. Behold the exhaustless markets they command. It is as if a half dozen of our states were set down between Oceania and the Orient, and those states themselves undeveloped and unspoiled of their primitive wealth and resources."

In 1901 Emilio Aguinaldo was captured, and in 1902 the Filipino fighters laid down their arms. The Philippines became a United States colony. That same year Cuban leaders signed a treaty submitted to them by General Leonard Wood, the military governor of Cuba appointed by the United States. This treaty gave the government in Washington, D.C. the power to direct and control Cuban affairs; Cuba became a dependency, or *protectorate*, of the United States; very soon the bulk of Cuban sugar production fell under American control, and Cuban sugar was shipped to the United States for refining and sale.

The United States thus emerged from the war against Spain as mistress of the Caribbean and as a major Pacific power. America had joined countries like Britain and France, Germany and Japan, that either possessed world empires or were eager to build them.

10

A TIME OF TROUBLES

The United States in War and Peace, 1914–1945

World War I

On August 4, 1914, World War I broke out. At least 11 million human beings lost their lives as a result of this conflict, killed by bullets or shells, dying of starvation or disease. The majority of the war's victims were Europeans, soldiers and civilians of many nations who lived in Europe and who fought there; though, to be sure, fighting also took place on the torrid deserts of Egypt and Arabia and in the frozen solitudes of Siberia.

Why, then, was it called a *world* war? The countries fighting the war were struggling for control of the whole world. Britain, France and Russia, lined up on the same side, were world powers; that is, the lands that they had conquered and the peoples that they ruled were spread across the globe—in Africa, Asia, India, the Near East and the Pacific Ocean. Germany, who fought against them with allies such as Austria-Hungary, Bulgaria and Turkey, was a challenger. Her aim was to win by war the riches and the power that her rivals enjoyed and that she so much desired. World War I was fought in Europe, but the world was the prize. The European powers sucked up the world's riches and drew upon the world's peoples to fuel the furnaces of destruction.

World War I began in the summer of 1914 when three German armies, not far from a million men strong, invaded Belgium, sliced through its peaceful countryside and swept southward into France. The German plan was to knock out the French in one month of fighting, then to throw their entire force of six armies eastward for a second decisive blow against Russia.

The German plan did not go according to schedule. The Belgian people put up a stiff resistance to the invasion. To cow them into submission, the Germans shot hundreds of men and women, burned dozens of villages and destroyed the city of Louvain, with its heritage of medieval manuscripts and works of art. The greater the terror, the more fiercely the Belgians resisted, and they slowed the German advance.

The kaiser's armies finally succeeded in reaching the gates of Paris, where the French rallied and drove them back. The two sides dug in and faced each other: The war settled down to a long stalemate. For hundreds of miles, a double line of trenches threaded its way from the English Channel across northern and eastern France, then southward down the Rhine Valley to the borders of Switzerland. The front-line trenches were only a few hundred yards apart. The space between, pitted with shell holes and barricaded with barbed wire, was called No-Man's-Land.

Since the Germans failed to knock France out as they had planned, they were obliged to fight the Russians at the same time. Thus in addition to the Western Front, an Eastern Front also came into being, stretching all the way from the Baltic to the Black Sea.

For nearly four years the armies of the Western Front—British and French on one side, German on the other—lunged back and forth at each other across No-Man's-Land, trying to break through each other's lines, repeating the same operation again and again. First came the artillery bombardment, so terrible that sometimes it drove men mad; it was then over the top, as the attacking infantry leaped out of the trenches with fixed bayonets and charged across No-Man's-Land, only to face withering fire from the machine guns of the defenders. These machine gunners, as one of them wrote, "fired triumphantly into the mass of men advancing across the grassland ... The effect was devastating ... the enemy could be seen falling literally in hundreds."

Then came a counterattack by the defenders as they tried to take back the strip of soil and the trenches that they had lost. In the end, all was quiet again on the Western Front, an uneasy silence broken by the mutter of distant bombardment, the whine of an occasional shell, the moans of

wounded men. "Five hundred miles of Germans," as an English soldier wrote in one of his poems. "Five hundred miles of French,/And English, Scotch and Irish men,/All fighting for a trench;/And when the trench is taken/And many thousands slain,/The losers, with more slaughter,/Retake the trench again."

Day by day, high explosives and machine guns obliterated heroes and cowards alike. The modern technology of destruction had created a new world, where there was no meaning to life and no meaning to death. In between the hours of combat, existence in the trenches had a special horror of its own. The dugouts in which men lived were tiny, filthy-smelling holes, cold, damp and foul. Torrential rains brought mud through which men might have to wade up to their knees, where wounded men would fall and drown in filth, too weak to pull themselves out.

Käthe Köllwitz witnessed at first hand the miseries that the German people—and others too—endured from 1914 to 1919. Her charcoal drawings from this time rank her with the great European artists, such as Goya and Picasso, who have truly depicted the face of war.

Death Seizes a Child—by Käthe Köllwitz

Corpses were buried where they were found, in shallow graves. Rats came after them in swarms. When one body was disturbed, the rats fled. A soldier described what he saw. "Its helmet rolled off," he remembered; "the man displayed a grimacing face, stripped of flesh; the skull bare, the eyes devoured. A set of false teeth slid down to the rotting jacket, and from the yawning mouth leapt an indescribably foul beast." Such creatures, by the millions, shared the trenches with human beings.

When the war broke out in Europe, many American tourists were caught by surprise and found themselves stranded. Streaming to the railroad stations, they wedged themselves into trains and headed for the ports; they mobbed steamship offices in a frantic scramble to find a ship that could bring them back home. Friends and relatives of such people were often too upset and concerned about the safety of their loved ones abroad to think about much else; but very soon millions of Americans were devouring the pages of the newspapers for battlefield news. Americans of Russian background, of course, sympathized with the Russian side; while people with German ancestors favored the Germans; almost everybody was shocked by stories about the massacre of innocent civilians in Belgium. Some of these stories may have been exaggerated. Many, unfortunately, were not. Nonetheless, most Americans regardless of which side they sympathized with were strongly in favor of neutrality—they believed, that is, that the United States should not become involved in the war.

When the war began, the president of the United States, Woodrow Wilson, seemed to be in full agreement with the feelings of ordinary citizens about the conflict. Wilson, a Democrat, had had a distinguished career as a writer and teacher of history, as president of Princeton University and as governor of New Jersey. Fifty-eight years old, with black hair and pince-nez, he made a speech on August 19, 1914, in which he said that "the United States must be neutral in fact as well as in name."

Neutral means that you don't take sides when two people or countries are in a fight; but, as a matter of fact, many Republican and Democratic leaders were from the very beginning of the war far from neutral. Republicans like Theodore Roosevelt, Admiral George Dewey and Senator Henry Cabot Lodge thought of Germany as America's most dangerous rival; they said so loud and often. Colonel Edward House, Wilson's closest advisor, felt the same way. He warned the president that if the Allies—led by Britain, France and Russia—were defeated in the war, Germany would be the unchallenged ruler of Europe; the United States, he told Wilson, would someday have to face her alone.

On the face of it, Wilson did not agree with House. His policy was "neutrality in fact as well as in name." He appeared to be carrying on the foreign policy that George Washington had proclaimed in 1796, which may be summarized as "friendly rela-

Army recruits in 1917 at camp in Van Cortlandt Park, New York City.

tions with all countries, permanent alliances with none."

But Wilson's acts indicated an attitude that was not neutral at all. In 1914 Great Britain, for example, used her ships and mines to cut off Germany's overseas trade with the United States. Wilson submitted a formal protest but, apart from that, didn't do a thing. American trade with the Allies, on the other hand, increased so quickly that by 1917 the United States was supplying huge amounts of wheat, guns and ammunition for their war effort. In 1915 the Germans threatened to destroy this trade by sinking on sight all merchant ships sailing to Britain. In this situation Wilson took immediate action. He warned the German government that he would take "any steps ... necessary to safeguard American lives and property." In plain words, he warned that if the Germans sank American ships sailing to Britain, they would face war with the United States.

Wilson, evidently, was as early as 1915 committed without compromise to the Allied side in the European conflict.

In the fall of 1916 the war entered upon its third year. Both sides had suffered terribly; but the Germans were closer to defeat. The British blockade of German ports had been a success; with outside supplies cut off, German civilians were on starvation rations and beginning to die of hunger.

The German leaders now resolved to gamble upon one final effort to win. On February 1, 1917, Germany announced that its submarines would attack and sink merchant ships in the seas around Great Britain without warning. They knew well enough that this would bring the United States into the war, for America would not, as Wilson had warned, permit the Allies' lifeline to be cut. Desperation drove the Germans. We will throw our Sunday punch, they told themselves; we will knock out Britain and France before the Yankees have time to train soldiers and send them in.

On March 18 of that year, German submarines sank three American merchant vessels without warning—the *City of Memphis, Illinois*, and *Vigilancia*. That same day news arrived that Nicholas II, Czar of the Russias, had been thrust from his throne. The people of Moscow and Petrograd and the Russian soldiers on the Eastern Front, goaded by hunger and unending bloodshed, had risen and swept away the last of the Romanov Czars who had ruled the country with an iron hand for 300 years. The meaning of this great event was clear to the whole world. Russia would now soon be out of the war; the Germans would no longer have to mass tens of thousands of their best troops on the Eastern Front. They could move all their armies westward for a last-ditch attack upon France and Britain in the spring of 1918. And so, indeed, it came to pass.

Colonel House had warned President Wilson years earlier that this might happen. By the end of March 1917, the possibility of German victory seemed real. On Monday, April 2, Woodrow Wilson called a special session of Congress. It was 8:30 in the evening. All the Washington bigwigs were assembled in the House of Representatives—the judges of the Supreme Court, the lower House, the Senate, the president's family, the members of his cabinet and their wives. Wilson asked Congress to declare war against Germany. "We are glad," said

Great Allied Offense against Germany: Western Front, Summer-Fall 1918

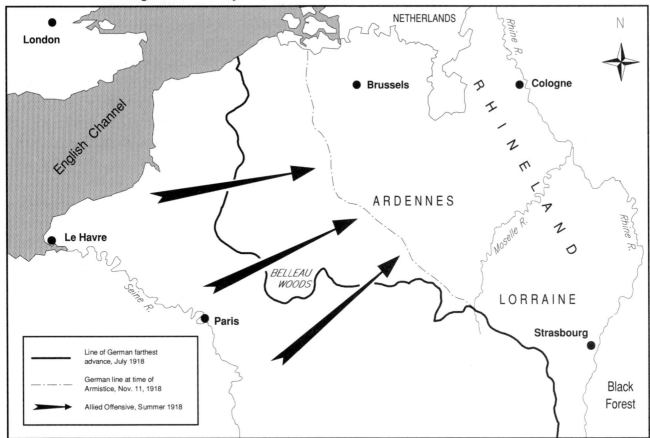

the president, "to fight thus for the ultimate peace of the world ... We shall fight for the things that we have always carried nearest our hearts—for democracy, for the rights and liberties of small nations ... to make the world itself at last free!"

Until the day that Wilson addressed Congress a majority of Americans were still for peace; they did not feel that German threats or the submarine challenge were sufficient reason to plunge the country into war. Now a war fever swept the nation; it was fueled by a propaganda campaign depicting Germans as subhuman monsters, fit only for extermination. All Americans were urged to join a holy crusade to wipe out the "Huns." "If Jesus were alive today," preachers told the people, "He would be in khaki."

On June 5, 1917, 10 million men registered for the draft. Camps sprang up to train and equip soldiers. Workers flocked to the seaports to build ships to transport men, munitions and supplies. Women moved into the factories to fill shell cases and to take the place of men leaving for the front. Blacks quit the fields, both to join the army and to move north to work in the steel factories and munitions plants. People ate less food and planted victory gardens; grain surpluses piled up on the docks for shipment to the Allies.

By 1918 troopships were carrying 50,000 men a month across the Atlantic. They reached the battlefields of France at a critical moment: The long-planned German spring offensive was under way, and the Allied armies were exhausted and at the point of collapse.

Here the Americans played a key role in stiffening the Allied defense and blunting the force of the last German attacks, which were launched on the central part of the front in June and July, with the objective of driving through to Paris. American troops then took part in a series of Allied counteroffensives, which, when autumn came, had thrust the German armies back to the Belgian frontier. By the end of September, with the American 1st Army poised for the final attack upon the German defenses between Verdun and Sedan, the army commander, General John Pershing, had more than one million men in the field.

This American military contribution during the months from June to November 1918 literally turned the tide of battle and ensured that the Allied cause would not go down to defeat. Germany capitulated on November 11.

Early in 1919 Woodrow Wilson went to Paris to help the French and the British prepare a treaty of peace. He believed that it would be shaped in accordance with the Fourteen Points that he had announced to the American people about a year earlier, before the last great battles on the Western Front had begun. Wilson had set forth a dream of disarmament, of an end to colonies everywhere, of a "league of nations" to which all peoples could bring their quarrels, where they could be settled peacefully without the horrors of violence and the murder of millions. His arrival in Paris with Edith, his wife, was greeted with wild delight. "Paris," Mrs. Wilson wrote, "was wild with celebration. Every inch was covered with cheering, shouting humanity. The sidewalks, the buildings, the stately horse-chestnut trees were peopled with men and boys perched like sparrows in their very tops … Flowers rained upon us until we were nearly buried."

The peace treaty was signed on June 28, 1919, in the great Hall of Mirrors at Versailles, palace of the kings of France. As the victors, England and France drove a hard bargain; the treaty that they forced upon the Germans gave to the world little of what Wilson had promised in his Fourteen Points. Germany's colonies were divided up; she lost her battleships, her merchant fleet, her iron and coal mines. The German people had to proclaim that they alone were guilty for starting the war, and they had to agree to pay the victors astronomical money damages, or *reparations*. As for the League of Nations, it figured in the treaty not as an association of all the free peoples of the world but as a club of conquerors. The German republic, set up after the kaiser had fled, was not allowed in; neither was the Union of Soviet Socialist Republics (USSR), which had come into being eight months after Nicholas II had quit his throne in 1917.

Wilson did his best to have the Versailles treaty accepted by the U.S. Senate, but his best was not good enough. The Republican majority would have none of it. Germany has been beaten, the Republicans said, hasn't it? It's time to get back to our own business and to keep from any more unnecessary and costly European entanglements.

This attitude was a terrible blow to Wilson. Early in September he went on a nationwide speaking tour to rouse Americans to the need to support the League. Exhausted by his labors, the president suffered a stroke in Kansas; to the end of his term in March 1921, he lived on in the White House as an invalid. As for the Senate, it never accepted the Versailles treaty. The fine dreams of 1917–1918, the "crusade for freedom" for which Americans had sacrificed so much, lay in ruins.

The collapse of the German empire did not quiet American fears about foreign rivals. In November 1917, Russia's Communist, or Bolshevik, party had seized power under the leadership of Vladimir Lenin and founded a new Russian state, the USSR. The secret of the popularity of Lenin's party was its reform program: food for the starving, land for the landless, peace for everybody. Beyond that, Lenin aimed to rebuild Russia on a socialist basis: This meant that the government would take over factories, farmlands and mines and run them itself. Government ownership and operation of essential services was not entirely a new idea in Russia. For many years the Russian government had run a pony express. It owned the horses and coaches and paid the drivers who carried the mail over thousands of miles of Russian territory.

In this situation, hatred of the Soviet Union took the place of hatred of Germany. Many American radicals (socialists, communists, anarchists) thought the Russian Revolution was great, and they said so. Hundreds of thousands of American workers, too, were out on strike in 1919—shipyard workers, coal miners, steelworkers, yes, even the Boston police were out on strike. They were all asking for higher wages because soaring prices had produced a big rise in the cost of living, so that there was a good enough reason for all these strikes. But it was enough to panic conservatives. The country is full of revolutionaries, they thought, and Russian aliens. They are going to make a revolution here just like in Russia!

Thus began the great Red Scare of 1919–1920. Millions of Americans came to believe, at that time, what their government told them: that the Soviet Union was an enemy, that workers who preached socialism or even went on strike were the agents of a foreign power, that aliens, and especially Russian ones, should be carefully watched and, if necessary, kicked out.

Acting on these beliefs, Wilson's attorney general, Mitchell A. Palmer, organized a series of police raids to seize "subversives." Beginning in November 1919, over 5,000 people were arrested in different parts of the country. Often federal agents knocked upon doors at midnight, arrested people without warrants, roughed them up and held them for days or weeks without hearing or trial. A few hundred aliens were shipped back to Russia, not because they had done anything wrong, but because the government did not like their "dangerous" ideas. The government failed to turn up evidence either that there were very many "Reds" in the country or that these people were doing anything wrong. But its investigation had been carried out with total disregard for the rights of people as they are protected by the Constitution

Unemployed men lining up to register for benefits in 1938, as captured by Dorothea Lange, noted for her photography during the Depression years.

and, in particular, the Bill of Rights. The rhetoric of the holy crusade to save the world for democracy had evaporated into the cold reality of police terror and midnight raids.

After 1920, when prices fell and workers went back to work, Americans began slowly to pick up the threads of peacetime life; they tried to get back to things as they used to be, or, as President Harding put it, "back to normalcy." American industry was now becoming more productive than it had ever been before. Employers were making more money, and workers and professional people were earning higher wages. As factories geared up for the satisfaction of new consumer needs, a flood of time- and labor-saving gadgets hit the market. People began to buy radios, refrigerators, washing machines and toasters; and they began to have their own telephones installed. Going to the movies became the most popular American amusement. Movies in those days were "silent": Subtitles told you what the people on the screen were saying to each other ("Please forsake Mottram and come with me! Everything that I own is at your disposition."), and a gum-chewing piano player sitting below the screen played appropriate music. By 1930, 100 million people were paying their money every week to visit a neighborhood movie palace and to rock with laughter at the antics of Charlie Chaplin, the acrobatics of Harold Lloyd, the song and dance of Eddie Cantor.

There was no bigger event in the 1920s than the arrival of the automobile. Automobiles, it is true, were being made in this country as early as 1900; but before World War I they cost so much that only rich people could afford to buy them. Then Henry Ford, a Michigan engineer, took over the idea of mass production of cars from Ransom Olds, a Detroit manufacturer, introduced the assembly line and began putting his Model Ts together in an hour and a half. Ford sold his cars at prices that almost everybody could afford; by 1926 four million automobiles were rolling off the lines every year, and one million of these came from Ford's Detroit factory alone. By 1929, when the Depression hit, automobile production was America's biggest business, and it had completely changed the American way of life. Gone were the days when a man had to live within walking distance of his job. Suburban development began to take place in huge

A family of father, mother and two sons rides a freight train in the Yakima Valley of the state of Washington in this photograph by Dorothea Lange.

tracts of land surrounding the big cities. Commuting to a suburban home became a way of life not only for the rich, as it had been before the war, but for middle- and working-class America as well.

On Thursday, October 24, 1929, there was a panic on Wall Street. Millions rushed to sell their stocks. In a few hours these titles to a share in the ownership of American industry became worthless. Soon factories all over the country began to lay off workers. The streets became black with hungry and despairing men and women. By 1931, out of a total work force of 50 million, about 15 million had lost their jobs. There was soon no place for these workless and often homeless people to turn, except private charity—church soup kitchens or Salvation Army shelters.

America faced a crisis of total economic collapse. There is no simple explanation for it. Economists and historians are to this day divided in their opinions as to why it occurred.

Town mayors and governors of states were flooded with appeals for help. "I have six little children," wrote a Pennsylvania worker to the governor in 1931. His wife was sick in the hospital, and he faced eviction because there was no money for rent. He asked, "Where am I to go in the cold winter with my children?" Indeed, tens of thousands like this worker lost their homes. They squatted on vacant lots, by riverside swamps and in the public parks; they crammed into abandoned shacks, they pitched tents, they made makeshift shelters from packing crates, corrugated iron sheets and cardboard boxes. Novelist John Dos Passos wrote of Detroit's homeless auto workers that they were "living in shacks and shelters along the waterfront … They have burrowed out rooms in a huge abandoned sandpile. Their stovepipes stick out at the top."

Many young people left home; they had no jobs, and they were only a burden upon their parents. Taking to the rails and the roads, they crisscrossed the country in aimless, endless wandering. Wherever the kids went, they had to move on soon:

This California mural shows farm workers hoeing a field of newly planted corn.

Some towns offered a night's sleep in a city shelter, mission home, even in jail; then you had to move on. Many slept on park benches, begged for bread, scrounged in garbage cans, did odd jobs, picked apples in return for a square meal. Their coats were threadbare, their shoes worn out. They carried tattered suitcases, string-tied bundles, or nothing at all. You saw them, men and boys, waiting at the railroad crossings in shivering clumps for the northbound or the southbound freight.

American farmers, too, were on the move in the early 1930s. In a huge area of the southern high plains droughts and dust storms were the ruin of thousands of small farmers. Losing all they had, they abandoned the land on which they and their mothers and fathers and grandmothers and grandfathers had toiled so hard; they loaded their belongings onto their creaking jalopies and joined the homeless bands trekking across the country. Many other farmers, too, were ruined. As workers lost their jobs and could no longer afford to buy milk and clothing and bread and meat, farm prices fell so low that many farmers could no longer cover their costs and pay their rent. Poor cotton farmers in the deep South, both black and white, were among the hardest hit.

During the Depression years the American people wandered like wastrels in the midst of the abundance that they had themselves created. In these years of the early 1930s, life for millions fell apart and lost its meaning. One famous song told how it was for countless men, women and children: "I've been wandering far and wide,/I come with the wind, I drift with the tide,/And it looks like I'm never going to cease my wandering."

President Herbert Hoover's term of office came to an end in 1932. The mood of the American people was one of despair. Children stayed home from school because they had no clothes to wear; starving men fought each other over garbage. That year the Democratic party chose Franklin D. Roosevelt as its candidate for president. Roosevelt, a distant cousin of Theodore Roosevelt, was a member of a wealthy Hudson Valley family. He started a promising political career when he was elected to the New York State Senate in 1910 and was then made assistant secretary for the Navy in Woodrow Wilson's first administration in 1913. Seven years later, it looked like Roosevelt's public life was at an end when he came down with polio and lost the use of his legs. In 1921 no antipolio vaccine existed. Every other summer, epidemics of the dreaded disease killed dozens of people and crippled hundreds; in the cities you saw crippled children everywhere. With the help of his wife, Eleanor, Roosevelt fought his handicap and made a comeback to public life; in 1928 he was elected governor of New York. Suffering had endowed him with a deep sympathy for ordinary people and the tragedies that too often shadowed their lives.

In his 1932 electoral campaign, Roosevelt promised that if he was elected president he would

Cotton pickers at harvest time.

have the federal government step in to end the depression and create jobs for the jobless. "I pledge myself," he said, "to a new deal for the American people." Roosevelt was elected by a landslide. Nearly 23 million Americans voted for him, as against 16 million for Herbert Hoover; he captured the electoral college votes in all except six states. Roosevelt remained president for 12 years, dying in office in April 1945, at the end of World War II in Europe. The label New Deal refers to his peacetime administration, 1933–1941. It was the sum total of the efforts that he made to end the depression and to put the country back upon the road to recovery.

The most pressing need was jobs. Roosevelt gave jobs to people building hospitals, repairing school buildings, fixing up public playgrounds, and constructing huge dams on the Tennessee River to generate electric power for the countryside. Artists, musicians and writers work with their hands as much as do bricklayers, carpenters and cement workers. Roosevelt gave them jobs, too, so that they might serve the people by writing, teaching, playing music and painting; so that their talents might not rust away unused.

One result was that murals began to blossom in 1935 all over the United States on the walls of public buildings, in high schools, hospitals, zoos,

libraries and post offices. The artists were inspired by a muralist movement in Mexico headed by Diego Rivera and Jose Orozco. Working in teams, they painted doctors, nurses and patients in the battle against disease; children and teachers in the search for knowledge; farmers, workers and miners in their daily toil in the factories, mines, forests and fields; the vision of flight and men and women's struggle to conquer the air. This mural art of the New Deal captured a new American mood: a pride in the American past, a sense of joy in the dignity and power of human beings, a hope for a brighter future.

As the years went by, business began to recover and to hire more workers. In the early New Deal years most American industry was still *open shop*—that is, employers refused to recognize workers' unions and to bargain with them over wages. Some economists now pointed out that this situation had helped to cause the Depression. Since they were not allowed to organize, millions of workers received less than their fair share of the nation's income. Higher income for workers, the economists said, meant higher purchasing power; and that meant more people on the job, working to produce the stuff that workers needed to buy.

Under the influence of this reasoning, in 1935 the Democratic Congress passed one of the New

Deal's most important laws, the Wagner Labor Relations Act. The Wagner Act granted American workers the right to organize unions and to bargain with their employers through "representatives of their own choosing." This sparked a nationwide drive to bring unorganized workers into new industrial unions, like the auto workers', steel workers', and longshoremen's unions. The act spurred a new battle of American workers for the right to organize, for the right to higher standards of living and a better life.

This struggle was the heart and inspiration of the New Deal, giving it human meaning, making it one of the most exciting times in the history of the American people.

* * * *

In 1933 Adolf Hitler seized power in Germany. Half genius, half madman, Hitler applied his talents to rebuilding Germany as a military state and, once, that was achieved, to making a bid for empire. His plan was to conquer first the peoples of Europe, then the peoples of the world.

Hitler was a racist: He taught the Germans that they were *Herrenvolk*, a blonde, blue-eyed master race. As for the other peoples of earth, he said they were inferior stuff, little better than animals, whom the Germans had the right to conquer, kill and enslave.

Millions became only too familiar with Hitler's face, with his hate-filled, screaming voice and mobs roaring approval. People learned about him by watching moviehouse newsreels. One of the big changes by 1932 was that movies had stopped being "silent," and become "talkies," or, as the billboards put it, "100% talking, dancing and singing."

Hitler, too, was consumed with a special hatred for Jewish people wherever they might live, inside Germany or out. Through all his propaganda ran the everlasting theme that the Germans must take special steps to protect the purity of their blood from Jewish "pollution." Many of Hitler's army officers, willing tools in his plan for world con-

quest, sneered in private at his racist ideas, which they called *Quatsch*, "nonsense"; but millions of ordinary German soldiers came to believe what Hitler told them. In obedience to his doctrines, during the years 1938 to 1945 they embarked upon a rampage of conquest in which millions upon millions of innocent people became victims of racist fury.

Adolf Hitler was Germany's supreme warlord. In preparing for World War II, Hitler kept in mind certain lessons from World War I. He knew that Germany was doomed to be defeated if she were forced to split her armies and to fight upon two fronts, east and west. The proper tactic was to isolate your enemies from each other and conquer them one by one. So in 1939 he prepared for the conquest of western Europe by signing a nonaggression pact with Josef Stalin, ruler of the USSR. Hitler and Stalin promised not to attack each other for 10 years. A secret clause of this treaty said that when Hitler invaded Poland, which had a pro-Western government, the two dictators would divide that country between them.

In September 1939, Hitler struck. His tanks, troops and planes swept into Poland and overthrew the Polish government. Poland, as created by the Treaty of Versailles, ceased to exist. Britain and France, who were the *guarantors* of Poland's boundaries, now declared war on Germany. Secure from attack in his rear, Hitler turned his attention to the west. In the spring of 1940, he occupied Denmark and Norway, then massed his armies on the Dutch and Belgian frontiers. Hitler understood that in World War II the tank was going to be a weapon of decisive importance in keeping troops on the move and in preventing the kind of stalemate in the trenches that had produced Germany's earlier defeat. His idea was a lightning strike (*blitz*) against his chosen enemy with hundreds of tanks in the spearhead, followed up by infantry moving however they could—on foot, by bicycle, or in trucks.

In 1940 for the first time Hitler put into practice in a big way his theories of armored or *Panzer* warfare. In May the German tanks broke through the lovely forested hills of the Ardennes, crossed the river Meuse, split and surrounded the Dutch, Belgian, British and French troops who faced them. The attack included a cruel bombardment of the Dutch port of Rotterdam by the German air force; such attacks on civilians were a key part of Hitler's type of warfare—they were a way of telling people "This is what's going to happen to you if you don't quit resisting and cooperate with us." Dirk van der Heide, a 12-year-old Dutch boy, lived through the bombardment. "The ambulances coming and going," he wrote on May 11, "and so many dead people make it hard for me not to cry."

The British forces retreated to the French coast at Dunkirk. There hundreds of civilian craft—rowboats, sailing dinghies, tugs and paddle steamers that in peacetime were used for pleasure trips—cooperated with the Royal Navy to rescue the soldiers and transport them back to England. As for the crews of these vessels, as a journalist described them, "they were bankers and dentists, taxi drivers and yachtsmen, longshoremen, boys, engineers, fishermen and civil servants. Many were poor; they had no coats, but made out with old jerseys and sweaters. They wore cracked rubber boots. They were wet, chilled to the bone, hungry."

In this way 300,000 men were saved from Dunkirk and came back home so that they could fight again on another day. As for the French, they surrendered within weeks: With a speed that stunned the world, Hitler occupied Paris in June. The British, as Prime Minister Winston Churchill promised, would go on fighting; but now a naval blockade of Germany would do little good. Germany was bringing in all the oil and wheat she needed from the Soviet Union. Swedish steel, Norwegian fish and Danish butter were also fueling the German war machine.

The campaign of 1940 marked the true opening of World War II. Far more than World War I this truly was a world war, in the sense that men and women fought and died on almost every ocean and landmass of the globe, with the exception of the western hemisphere.

After the fall of France, Hitler had only two major antagonists left in Europe: Great Britain in the west, Soviet Russia in the east. Selecting the English as his first victims, he launched Operation Sea Lion. The plan was to cross the English Channel with an invading army, just like William the Conqueror had done nearly 900 years before.

The Battle of Britain began in July 1940, when Hitler sent in his air force to rain bombs upon the country and to soften it up for invasion. These savage attacks went on for nine months, inflicting much damage and death. "Not a night passes," wrote Gottfried Leske, a German flyer, "without our setting new fires in the heart of the City of London—not a night when the sky doesn't become blood-red with the glow of flames. London is dying." London was not alone: Cities all over England were being turned into smoking ruins.

The British people, far from losing heart, became only more determined not to give in. The Royal Air Force did not lose control of the skies over Britain, and the pilots in their Spitfire and Hurricane fighters took a heavy toll on the German bombers. "Never," said Prime Minister Winston Churchill, "was so much owed by so many to so few." Without mastery of the British skies Hitler could never hope to launch a successful invasion.

Britain, for the present, had proved too tough for the German dictator to handle. Later for you, he thought. He began, instead, to prepare for the invasion of the Soviet Union, called by the code name Operation Barbarossa. This was to be a five-month *blitz*, starting in the early summer of 1941, to smash the Russian army and to topple the Soviet government before the winter snows set in. Hitler had no doubts about success. One blow of the German fist, he thought, and the Russian state would collapse like an eggshell.

Hitler launched his invasion of the Soviet Union on June 22, 1941. Three German armies moved forward into eastern Europe along a front that stretched 1,500 miles from the Baltic to the Black Sea. The news sent a thrill around the world. Winston Churchill told the House of Commons that England and the Soviet Union were now comrades in arms. Franklin Roosevelt promised aid. Neither man, to tell the truth, thought at the time that Russia would survive the German onslaught for more than three or four months.

At first all went well for Hitler. German tanks and troops moved forward fast and ran rings around the Soviet armies; they captured tanks and big guns by the thousands, prisoners by the millions. Early in October, nearly four months after the invasion had begun, the German armies were approaching the gates of Leningrad and Moscow; the Soviet government, along with thousands of civilians, was fleeing to the east, beyond the Ural Mountains.

Then something happened. Moscow workers went out into the country to dig trenches and antitank ditches; minefields and barbed-wire entanglements filled the forests covering the westward approach to the city. The Moscow subway, at the time the most beautiful transportation system in the world, was taken over by the military to carry troops and supplies. In November winter set in; floods of rain followed, then snow and freezing cold.

The Germans came to a stop within sight of the Kremlin and its gleaming towers. They had no woolen underwear for the winter weather, and no winter overcoats. Heinrich Haape, a medical officer, remembered that on November 13 an icy blast swept the snowbound countryside. One German soldier went out into the cold for a few minutes without his woolen cap. When he came back, both ears were dead white and frozen stiff. Very soon there were 100,000 cases of frostbite in the German army. In a little while the general in command on the Moscow front had to report to Hitler that his troops could not go on. There they sat until the Russians drove them away in the latter part of 1943.

Hitler had been so sure of a summer victory that he not merely forgot about winter clothes for his soldiers, he even told his Japanese allies that he would not be needing their help. The Japanese military, indeed, had little to gain by fighting the Soviet Union. Their central ambition was to make themselves masters of the Far East.

Japanese plans for the building of a huge Pacific Empire were launched when they attacked and occupied Manchuria, a province of China, in 1931; this was followed in 1937 by the invasion of China proper and the military occupation of the eastern part of the country.

With the outbreak of the European war in 1939 the Japanese entered into an alliance with Germany and Italy and stepped up their plans for the conquest of the lands of the western Pacific. The three major European powers with western Pacific empires were no longer in any position to defend their possessions. France and Holland were by the summer of 1940 under German occupation; Great Britain was involved in a life-and-death struggle with Hitler. By July 1941 Japan had occupied all of French Indochina, absorbing it piecemeal; British and Dutch territories in the Malay States and Indonesia were ripe for the taking. The only remaining Western power capable of offering serious resistance was the United States.

Moderates in the Japanese government recoiled from the insane idea of making war upon the United States, but the war party prevailed. The attack, a desperate venture designed to eliminate America as a Pacific power, was masterminded by Japan's brilliant commander, Admiral Isoroko Yamamoto. Early in the morning of December 7, 1941, Japanese planes took off from fleet carriers and bombed the American Pacific base at Pearl Harbor, on Oahu Island in Hawaii. Within two hours, the American Pacific fleet was crippled; close to 2,300 American military personnel lost their lives. On December 8, Congress declared war upon Japan.

Hitler then declared war upon the United States on December 11, probably in accordance with a secret treaty he had made earlier with the Japanese. Thus by the end of 1941 the United States, the

The Allies opened their long-awaited second front in Europe with the invasion of Normandy on June 6, 1944. Here American infantrymen are seen wading ashore at Omaha Beach.

Soviet Union and Great Britain found themselves at war with Germany, Japan and Italy (known as the Berlin-Rome-Tokyo Triangle). This alliance of the Western powers and the Soviet Union brought about, after three more years of bloodshed, the surrender of the Axis powers.

The alliance of the West and the Soviets was called from the very beginning the United Nations. It was composed not only of the Big Five (the United States, Great Britain, France, the Soviet Union and China) but also of many other peoples who had been conquered and enslaved by Germany or Japan. From the start the United Nations was more than a military alliance. It symbolized the goal for the sake of which the war was being fought, a confederation of nation states pledged to live together in peace. Of what use, it was asked, would it be to undergo this frightful struggle if it did not move humankind closer to a peaceful world?

During the wartime years (1942–1945), American industry began to turn out tanks, trucks, guns, planes and all types of military equipment in enormous quantities. Just as in World War I, women and blacks came to work in the factories, millions were taken into the armed forces, joblessness disappeared. Many children grew up in these years with both parents away for a lot of the time— Dad in the army, Mom in the warplant. These "latchkey kids" had the key to the front door on a string around their necks, so that they could let themselves back in when school was over.

The Red Scare was over now. Russians visiting the United States were welcomed as comrades in arms, as friends. Russian soldiers—some of them women—toured the country, talking about the war and asking the Americans to open a second front in Europe.

The year 1942 was the high-water mark of the German and Japanese advance. When spring came, Hitler returned to the attack on the Eastern Front, and his troops penetrated as far as Stalingrad on the Volga, where they fought the Russians in the streets. Hitler now controlled most of Europe, including the Balkans, as well as North Africa. The Japanese ruled much of China, also Indochina and the Philippine Islands. Conquest of many other islands had helped them to turn the Pacific Ocean into a Japanese lake.

But 1942 was also the year when the Allies passed over to the counterattack. In June the American Navy defeated the Japanese at Midway. That same month, a joint British-American invasion force landed in Morocco. General Dwight D. Eisenhower cooperated with Field Marshal Bernard Law Montgomery in an offensive that swept the Germans out of North Africa six months later. On the Eastern Front, the Russians moved over to the attack at Stalingrad on November 19. The German 6th Army found itself trapped between the Volga and the Don within a ring of fire and steel that was drawn tighter each day without pity. "The icy winds," one German soldier wrote, "lashed a million crystals of razor-like snow into our faces." Filthy, frozen, starving and exhausted, the German troops staggered back, and when they could go no farther, thus fell and lay still. Soon shrouds of spotless white covered the tattered remnants of what had once been men. Stalingrad was the

The Peat-Bog Soldiers

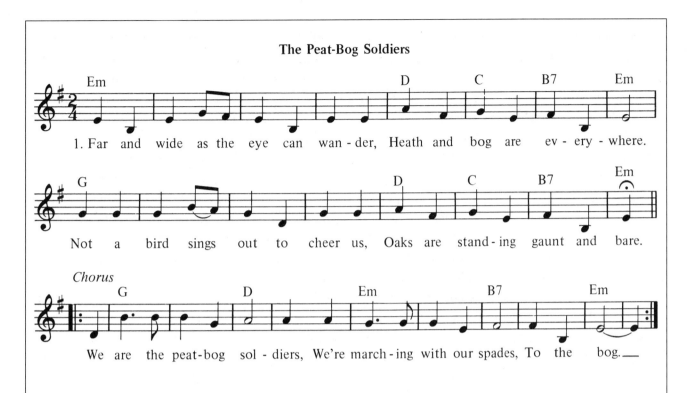

1. Far and wide as the eye can wan-der, Heath and bog are ev-ery-where.

Not a bird sings out to cheer us, Oaks are stand-ing gaunt and bare.

Chorus

We are the peat-bog sol-diers, We're march-ing with our spades, To the bog.__

2. Up and down the guards are pacing,
   No one, no one can go through.
   Flight would mean a sure death facing;
   Guns and barbed wire greet our view.
Chorus

3. But for us there is no complaining,
   Winter will in time be past;
   One day we shall cry rejoicing,
   Homeland dear, you're mine at last.
Chorus:
   Then will the peat-bog soldiers
   March no more with their spades
   To the bog.

1. Wohin auch das Auge blicket
   Moor und Heide ringsherum.
   Vogelsang uns nicht erquicket,
   Eichen stehen kahl und krumm.
Chorus:
   Wir sind die Moorsoldaten
   Und ziehen mit dem Spaten
   Ins Moor.

2. Auf und nieder gehen die Posten,
   Keiner, keiner, kann hindurch.
   Flucht wird nur das Leben kosten,
   Fielfach ist umzäunt die Burg.
Chorus

3. Doch für uns gibt es kein Klagen,
   Ewig kann's nicht Winter sein.
   Einmal werden froh wir sagen,
   "Heimat, du bist wieder mein."
Chorus:
   Dann ziehen die Moorsoldaten
   Nicht mehr mit dem Spaten
   Ins Moor.

"The Peat-Bog Soldiers" was composed in a German concentration camp during the 1930s. Prisoners sang it as they marched to and from their forced labor in the peat-bogs of Hanover. When Hitler and Mussolini invaded Spain in 1936, it became an antifascist battle song. By 1942, "The Peat-Bog Soldiers" was known to millions. No song created during World War II conveys so deeply and so simply the meaning of the struggle against Hitler.

greatest victory of the war on land. When the Germans surrendered there late in January 1943, 90,000 survivors remained of the army of 300,000 men who had gone into battle. Soviet offensives in 1943 and 1944 then carried the Russians westward toward the borders of Germany itself.

On June 6, 1944, the United States and Great Britain invaded lower Normandy, in France, on a broad front that stretched from the Cotentin peninsula to the river Orne (Utah, Omaha, Gold, June and Sword beaches). First came paratroopers, then infantry and an endless stream of trucks, jeeps, tanks and guns. When the bridgehead was secure, the Allied troops moved out, crossed the river Seine and eventually swept the Germans out of France. In less than three months from D-Day (June 6), half a million German soldiers were killed or taken prisoner. Winter found the Allied forces, now two million strong, in Belgium and Luxembourg; in the spring of 1945, the offensive went forward again as, on April 12, the Americans paused briefly to mourn the death of Franklin Roosevelt. On April 25 American and Russian soldiers met at Torgau on the river Elbe. On April 30 Hitler committed suicide in Berlin as the Russians closed in upon the heart of the city. On May 7 the war in Europe was over.

As the Allied forces moved into Germany, they liberated millions of people from Hitler's rule. The path of the advancing soldiers was strewn with flowers.

The Allied armies also freed hundreds of thousands of prisoners of war and slaves seized from almost every country in Europe who were toiling on Germany's farms, in the factories and upon the fortifications. Now for the first time the German concentration camps gave up their secrets.

Very soon after Hitler took power in 1932, Germany became dotted with these camps. They were barbed-wire enclosures where the Nazis and their secret police herded anybody they didn't like or whom they considered as enemies of the regime. Here were to be found Germans who had com-mitted no crime but who, for one reason or another, had become victims of Nazi hatred and revenge—Social Democrats, Communists, Catholics, Protestants, Gypsies and Jews. Black-shirted bullies ran these camps, beating, torturing, starving and murdering the inmates.

When war came in 1939, the camps grew in number and in size. Now not only Germans but also peoples from all the conquered countries of Europe passed through their gates; their victims ran not to the thousands but the millions.

When the Germans retreated before the Allied advance, they took many of the camp prisoners with them, leaving behind evidence that they had no time to destroy—evidence of a crime that ranks among the most terrible in human history.

The camps, and there were dozens of them, were equipped with guards, gas chambers, watchtowers, savage dogs, machine guns, electric fences and crematoria. Here Hitler brought enslaved people and prisoners of war to work and to be killed. Here he sought to carry out one of the central aims of the Nazi wartime program—the extermination of the Jewish people. In these camps it is estimated that he put to death five million Jewish men, women and children, after stripping them of valuables like gold, jewelry, shoes and clothing. R. W. Thompson, correspondent for the *London Times*, described the scene that Allied soldiers witnessed when they broke into death camps like Bergen-Belsen. Death pits were "nearly filled with human bodies staring up to the sky, others with their heads buried in human remains."

* * * *

The end for Japan came three months later. In May American heavy bombers began raining destruction upon Japanese cities from the sky; the American navy was sailing unopposed in Japanese waters. Before May 7, the Japanese generals had been in favor of fighting on to the very end, in the hope that, faced with so determined a will, the Allies would give them easy terms. But when Germany collapsed it became clear that the Japanese would have to face alone the combined weight of the American, British and Soviet forces. The people in the Japanese government who wanted immediate peace discussions were now in a stronger position.

The United States government faced an awesome decision. After five years of work under the direction of General Leslie Groves and physicist Robert Oppenheimer, U.S. engineers and scientists had developed an atom bomb at the cost of $2,000,000,000. Question: Ought this terrible new weapon be used to knock the Japanese out of the war? Leading scientists who had helped make the bomb said no. If we used the bomb, they warned, then other countries would build atom bombs, too, since there was absolutely no "secret" about how to do this. If America used the bomb, they said, it might trigger a new and supremely dangerous arms race. The scientists' report was never given to President Truman by his advisors.

The advice that General Groves and others gave him was: Use the bomb, knock the Japanese out of the war and save the lives of thousands of American soldiers who might otherwise have died in an invasion of Japan.

On August 6 a B-29 bomber, the *Enola Gay*, dropped an atomic bomb on Hiroshima. The city was blotted out in a blinding flash. Nearly 100,000 people died at once. Tens of thousands died months and years later from wounds and radiation sickness. The people at the center of the blast died at once; those hit by the shock wave that spread out for several miles often suffered greatly. As one survivor told it, they "lay writhing on the ground, screaming in agony from the intolerable pain of their burns … Horses, dogs and cattle suffered the same fate as human beings. Every living thing was petrified in an attitude of indescribable suffering."

Japan surrendered on August 14. World War II was over.

11

AMERICANS IN THE NUCLEAR AGE
Human Rights, Superpowers and Peace, 1945–

At the end of April 1945, two weeks after her husband's death, Eleanor Roosevelt went to San Francisco to attend a meeting of the United Nations as an American representative. There she met with people from 50 countries all over the world; they had come together to discuss and to approve a charter, or constitution, for the United Nations. Eleanor Roosevelt was one of the most distinguished people at this important gathering, for she was not only the widow of a great president but a leader in her own right. During the years in the White House she had worked with youth groups and with women's groups; she had championed the civil rights cause when it was not yet at all popular to do so; she had written a column of her own for the newspapers. People around the world viewed her, even more than her husband, as a champion of human rights.

Like the League of Nations before it, the purpose of the United Nations was to help nations work together, to find ways to avoid war and to solve conflicts with each other, not by violence but by peaceful means. These purposes were stated at the beginning of the charter:

To save succeeding generations from the scourge of war, which twice in our lifetime has brought untold sorrow to mankind, and

To reaffirm faith in fundamental human rights … in the equal rights of men and women, and of nations large and small, and

To … live together in peace with one another as good neighbors.

Would the United Nations help to make real the hopes and dreams of mankind for peace, as stated so beautifully in the charter? Or would it, like the League of Nations, end in failure? A big part of the answer to these questions lay with the United States and the Soviet Union. These two countries had come out of the war victorious and as the greatest powers on earth. During the war the two superpowers had worked together as allies; they had set aside the earlier years of hatred and distrust for the sake of a common cause—victory over Germany and Japan. They had followed towards each other what is called today a policy of *détente*, or friendship. *Détente* between 1941 and 1945 had secured the defeat of fascism. Could this *détente* keep on going? Could it keep working, through the United Nations, to help win the battle for world peace? This question is still with us today.

The Cold War

The first answer that the superpowers gave to this question, in the years directly following World War II, from 1946 to 1954, was a loud no. Rivalry and hatred flooded in to take the place of wartime friendship and the comradeship of arms. There were many reasons for the new tensions—what to do with defeated Germany, how to limit nuclear weapons, freedom for Poland and other Eastern European countries now under Russian control. Historians have labeled these years the Cold War—a time of tensions when it seemed that *détente* was no longer possible, that "peace" was only a breathing space in which both sides prepared for inevitable war, using diplomacy, loans and capital equipment to line up the nations of the world upon one side or the other.

As a result of the Cold War and the growing tensions between the superpowers, the globe found itself split into three separate "worlds."

The First, or Free World, consists of the United States and its allies: England, France, Germany, other European countries and also Japan. The Second, or Socialist World, consists of the Soviet Union and its allies in Eastern Europe. As for the Third World, it is the vast expanse of the globe—China, Indonesia, India, Africa, Latin America and the Near East—where teeming millions live in a pre-industrial age and suffer unmentionable poverty and hunger.

Part of the conflict between the U.S. and the USSR was caused by different views about the Third World. How would Third World peoples move into the future? Would they accept the leadership of the Soviet Union or that of the United States? Which of these two countries would dominate the globe and inherit the future?

Two events in 1949 stepped up the tension between the First and the Second Worlds. In September the Soviet Unions set off its first atomic explosion. The news, of course, came as no surprise to American scientists, but it caused a panic among the politicians. We have to keep ahead of the Soviets, they said; we have to keep America strong! That means hydrogen, as well as plutonium bombs, fission as well as fusion. J. Robert Oppenheimer was against this decision; before launching an atomic arms race, he told the government, let us seek an agreement with the Soviet Union to ban these bombs. Oppenheimer was the brilliant physicist who in 1943 had headed the American A-bomb program at Los Alamos, in New Mexico, and who, indeed, was called the father of the atom bomb. When Oppenheimer gave President Truman this advice, he was an official of the United States government—chairman of the General Advisory Committee to the Atomic Energy Commission.

The second event of 1949 that drove the Cold War to a new pitch of intensity was the success of the Communist Revolution in China. From Manchuria in the north to the province of Yunan in the south, the Chinese Communist armies swept all before them. The weak, corrupt government of General Chiang Kai-shek collapsed like a house of cards. By December Chiang, with what was left of his army, had fled to the tiny island of Taiwan, 100 miles out in the Pacific Ocean, off the shores of Fukien.

In 1953, when the first census was taken, there were 700,000,000 people in China; by 1985 that

Senator Joseph McCarthy, chairman of a one-man Senate subcommittee on investigations, is here shown in 1954 with his aides David Schine (on the left) and Roy Cohn.

number would grow to more than 1,000,000,000, or more than one-third of all the human beings on earth. Chinese civilization has had a long and splendid history, but in 1950 China was a Third World country that had barely entered the 20th century and the industrial age. Obviously—or so American leaders assumed—the Chinese people would accept Soviet Russian leadership as they began to create a modern country. There it was—a third of the human race joining with the Second World in a single year! The world, Washington told itself, was indeed turning Red faster than anybody could have dreamed. At this pace the United States might soon find itself like Chiang on Formosa—a tiny First World island in a Second World totalitarian ocean.

In February 1950, in a speech that he gave at Wheeling, West Virginia, Joseph McCarthy seized hold of the Cold War crisis as a way to bootstrap himself to power and to fame. McCarthy was a small-town Wisconsin lawyer. During the war he served for a short time with the Marines in the Pacific, then came back home and was elected as a Republican to the United States Senate in 1946. Who, he asked his audience of women at Wheeling, was to blame for the loss of our atomic secrets and the loss of China? McCarthy's answer was that the U.S. government was honeycombed with spies and saboteurs, Soviet agents who wee carrying out the orders of the Russian enemy. Senator McCarthy held up his hand and waved a piece of paper. "I

179

have here," he said, "a list of Communists in the State Department … still working and making policy."

In the following four years, 1950 to 1953, McCarthy hammered in this theme and made front-page news. Not only, he said, were there spies and saboteurs in the government; they were teaching Red propaganda in the colleges and universities, they were making subversive movies in Hollywood, they were burrowing like lice into the trade unions, they were sabotaging American industry, they controlled T.V. All these enemies of America, said McCarthy, must be investigated, exposed, fired from their jobs, jailed and even deported if the United States was to be "safe."

A few months after McCarthy made his Wheeling speech in 1950, war broke out in Korea when North Korea forces invaded South Korea and President Truman sent U.S. soldiers to help the South Koreans drive the invaders back. The Americans under General Douglas MacArthur advanced almost to the Yalu River, which separates Korea from China. Then the Chinese sent their troops in, and drove MacArthur and his men back to the 38º parallel. At the end of 1950 Americans and Communists were meeting face to face in battle. Joe McCarthy's message about the Red menace seemed literally to be true.

McCarthy's way of dealing with people he said were traitors or subversives was to make accusations that everybody read in the papers the next day in the form of screaming headlines. Starting in 1953, when President Eisenhower came into office, McCarthy had his own Senate investigations subcommittee, which soon became known as the McCarthy Committee. His way of investigating was to order suspects to appear before him and make them answer questions about their beliefs, their friends, their activities. Some suspects answered the questions, some didn't; in most cases it didn't make much difference. Just to be labeled a suspect and to be hauled before the committee was enough: It

ruined a person's good name and often cost him his job.

In the end McCarthy went too far. In his frantic search for new and more sensational exposures, he took on the United States Army itself and charged that it was riddled with nincompoops and traitors. When generals came before the committee in full uniform covered with ribbons and medals, McCarthy yelled at them, told they they were a disgrace to the uniform and they didn't have the brains of a five year old.

The Pentagon soldiers, to be sure, had their moments of panic, but they rallied bravely and counterattacked. One of McCarthy's assistants was David Schine, a young man whom the Army had drafted in the middle of 1953. McCarthy, the Army charged, had moved heaven and earth to make sure that Schine was spared the sweat and toil of being an ordinary foot soldier. McCarthy, they said, demanded that young David be given a job in a Washington office as a special assistant to the secretary of the Army. He had also urged the military to send Schine up to West Point to read the textbooks used in the United States Military Academy and to check them out for subversive propaganda.

The Senate had no choice but to investigate the charges and the countercharges. The Army-McCarthy hearings were televised from April to June 1954. Workers downed their tools, wives quit shampooing the living-room rug, students left their books, businesspeople deserted their offices. Everybody who could sat down to watch. In the whole history of T.V. there was never a show like it. For the first time McCarthy was shown to the public as he really was—a mean, mindless bully, a windbag. Late in 1954 the Senate passed a solemn vote of censure on the investigator. The spell was broken, the game was up. Three years later Joe McCarthy was dead at the age of 49.

The damage that the Cold War did to American life, especially during the years from 1950 to 1954, is almost beyond calculation. First-rate diplomats, administrators and scientists were driven from government service; brilliant thinkers and teachers were hounded from the universities; talented writers, artists and doctors were blacklisted or thrust from their professions; union leaders and workers lost their jobs in factories and trade unions. A cloud of fear, a mood of hysteria and hate, blanketed the country.

Most of these people were purged, not because they were Communists, but because they didn't like the Cold War policies of the Truman and Eisenhower administrations and wanted, in one way or another, to go back to *détente*. The classic example of this is J. Robert Oppenheimer himself. In 1953 Oppenheimer was accused of being an agent of the Soviet Union. In 1954, after a long and secret trial before a government committee, he was formally denounced as a security risk. In the 13 years of life left to him, Oppenheimer was never allowed to serve his government or his country again. Yet this great scientist was also an American patriot. His only crime was the remorse that he felt for building the atom bomb, the conviction that détente between the U.S. and the USSR was necessary for the survival of mankind.

As the 1950s wore on, slowly, very slowly, people began to stop thinking of Russians as their worst enemy. One day in 1956, when President Eisenhower was working in the Oval Room in the White House, he turned to one of his advisors. "Why," he asked, "don't we invite 5,000 Russian students to America and send 5,000 Americans to Russia?" In 1959 Russian Premier Khrushchev visited the United States, ate apple pie on Nebraska farms, hugged children and finally settled down to a quiet visit with Eisenhower at Camp David. During the 1960s and early 1970s, both sides began to work together to bring the atomic arms race under control. "There is no other alternative," as a Russian leader said. "Either we live together or we die together."

The Revival of the Struggle for Civil Rights

Historians have taken the year 1954 to mark the end of the Cold War's first and most dangerous phase. This was the year when millions of people, many of them black, began to take to the streets to fight what *they* now thought of as democracy's number-one enemy: His name was Jim Crow.

Jim Crow is a term that was coined during the Jacksonian era. White minstrels who entertained people on steamboats, at circuses and country fairs were quick to appreciate the extraordinary value for their purposes of the songs and dances of the slaves. But black culture reached a white audience in a perverted form: The minstrels blacked their faces and transformed the slaves from human beings with their own dignity into shuffling, grinning figures of fun and banjo-strumming clowns. This black stereotype received a name: Jim Crow. It was taken from the refrain of a song to which black people dance: "Wheel about 'n turn about and jump Jim Crow.

After the Civil War Jim Crow was pressed into service not as a noun but as an adjective applied to any type of segregation forced upon black people on account of their race, color or previous condition of servitude. Jim Crow laws were state laws that required separate facilities for black people in schools, transportation and other public services, and forbade them to use any other. By the early years of the 20th century Jim Crow, meaning segregation enforced as official policy, reigned supreme throughout the South. There were Jim Crow railroad coaches and Jim Crow schools, even Jim Crow bathing beaches. The message that the Jim Crow laws gave was a clear one. Blacks were assigned Jim Crow facilities because they were deemed inferior people unfit to associate with whites.

During the New Deal years and World War II, the industrial revolution hit the South just as earlier it had hit the North and the Midwest. Machines took

181

the place of people on the cotton farms; millions of farmworkers left the land and looked for jobs in both Northern and Southern cities. At the end of the war, in spite of the fact that millions of them had moved away, blacks still made up more than a quarter of the total Southern population. Life for them was still much the same as it had been since the end of Reconstruction. Black women worked as house servants, black men as farmhands or lumberworkers. When blacks went to town to look for jobs, they were given the leftovers that nobody else wanted, like sweeping floors, cleaning toilets and hauling away garbage.

At the end of World War II Jim Crow laws were still in force, just as they had been for 50 years or more. Black children were not allowed to go to the same schools as white children, much less to sit in the same classrooms; nor could they go to the public libraries and read in the reading rooms alongside whites. Black people young and old were barred from public beaches, restaurants and swimming pools. They could not enjoy movies at the same movie houses as whites, nor even use the same water fountains. When riding on the railroads, blacks were made to sit in separate coaches; they waited in separate waiting rooms, bought their tickets at separate windows and used separate toilets. When using city buses, they were made to sit in the back and even to enter the bus by the back door.

At the end of World War II Jim Crow schools didn't exist just in the South but in other parts of the country, too. Linda Brown, for example, who was born in 1943, went to a Jim Crow elementary school in Topeka, Kansas. Linda and her family lived in a mixed neighborhood near the railroad tracks. When time came for school, colored and white kids left their homes and went off in different directions—the whites to the Sumner school seven blocks away, the blacks and Mexican-Americans to the Monroe school, which was much farther.

One day in 1950, when Linda was seven years old, her father, Oliver, took his daughter to the Sumner school and asked the principal to admit her.

The principal refused. So Mr. Brown, along with other black parents, went to court. Lawyers were provided by the National Association for the Advancement of Colored People (NAACP), which had for years been battling in the courts for fair treatment for black people. The NAACP lawyers asked the federal court in Kansas to tell the city of Topeka to admit Linda to Sumner school. Monroe, the lawyers told the court, wasn't anywhere near as good a school as Sumner. Besides, how could black children grow up properly if they were kicked aside like trash and made to feel that they were some lower form of life and didn't belong?

The federal court in Kansas said no, just like Sumner's principal had. So the NAACP lawyers appealed the decision all the way to Washington, D.C., to the Supreme Court of the United States. Linda's case was called *Oliver Brown (and others) versus Board of Education of Topeka*; it would be known to history as *Brown versus Board*.

At noon on Monday, May 17, 1954, the nine justices of the Supreme Court took their seats in the lofty courtroom with its marble pillars and purple drapes. Chief Justice Earl Warren, a kindly looking gentleman with a shock of white hair, read the court's decision in Linda's case. The Sumner school, he said, must open its doors to *all* the neighborhood children. The state of Kansas and the city of Topeka were defying the Constitution of the United States when they shunted black children off to Monroe just because their skin was dark. Under the law of the United States of America, said Chief Justice Warren, states of the Union must treat all people the same way. Equal treatment of all Americans regardless of their race or color, said Warren, wasn't just somebody's dream; it was the law of the land.

Blacks at once saw that if Jim Crow *schools* were illegal, then Jim Crow *anything* must also be. Many of them now began to think that the time had come for black men, women and children to claim their birthright and to help, in every community across America, to make equal rights a reality for all.

Mrs. Rosa Lee Parks lived in Montgomery, Alabama; she was a tiny, graying lady who never raised her voice. On December 1, 1955, 18 months after the Supreme Court's decision in *Brown versus Board*, Mrs. Parks quit her work at the end of the day in a Montgomery department store, headed for the bus and took a seat at the front of the black section. As more whites boarded the bus, the driver told Mrs. Parks to get up and to give her seat to one of them. Mrs. Parks stayed sitting. "If you don't move," the driver yelled at her, "I'm gonna call the police!" Mrs. Parks shrugged her shoulders. The police came and arrested her.

When they heard what had happened, leaders of the black community acted quickly. They called a meeting, set up the Montgomery Improvement Association (MIA), and vowed not to ride on the city buses until the city and the bus company agreed to let people take their seats on a first-come, first-served, basis. The Reverend Martin Luther King, Jr., was elected chairman of the MIA. King was then 27 years old and a minister of the Dexter Avenue Baptist Church; it was his first job. The Reverend King, with his wife, Coretta, and their first child, two-month-old Yolanda Denise (Yokie), was a new arrival in town. "In our protest," he told the people as they sang, prayed and wept at a mass meeting on Monday, December 5, "our method will be that of persuasion, not force. Once again we must hear the words of Jesus: Love your enemies, bless them that curse you."

The MIA set up a car pool to carry people to and from their jobs. For nearly one year (December 1955 to November 1956), the black people of Montgomery rode to work or walked to work while the city buses rolled along half empty. All over the United States, all over the world, people cheered. Church groups sent station wagons; funds to keep the boycott going poured in from as far away as Japan. In January 1956, a bomb ripped the front of King's house while Coretta and Yokie were inside. The black people swallowed their fury and quietly kept on with the struggle. In February the city

Elizabeth Eckford turns away from the angry mob that bars her from Little Rock Central High on September 2, 1957.

arrested hundreds of boycotters and placed them on trial for breaking an old antiboycott law. Men and women crowded into the courthouse to hear the accused people tell how for years they had suffered at the hands of the city and the bus company. Stella Brooks told how one time her husband boarded a bus and got sucked into an argument with the driver. The driver called the police. They hauled Brooks off the bus, then shot him dead.

In April 1956 the MIA went to federal court, just like Oliver Brown had done, and asked that Montgomery's Jim Crow bus law be struck down. This case, just like *Brown versus Board*, went all the way to the Supreme Court. Late that year, in November 1956, Earl Warren gave his answer: A city cannot make a law to set people apart on its buses just because their skin is a darker shade. Victory for the people of Montgomery! By the beginning of 1957, the buses were again rolling through town filled with passengers; but now blacks were sitting side by side with whites.

By early 1957 school boards in some states had accepted the decision in *Brown versus Board* and begun to admit black children into the "white" schools. But it was also clear that in many parts of

Police drag a demonstrator off to jail during the Birmingham, Alabama, protest movement.

the South there would be resistance. In July 1955 Robert D. Patterson, a diehard segregationist, organized a citizens' council in Indianola, Mississippi, to fight school integration. "There won't be any integration in Mississippi," he said. "Not now. Not next year. Not in a hundred years. Maybe never." Citizens' councils sprang up all over the South. Respectable middle-class whites—bankers, planters and businessmen—flocked to join them. Southern Congressmen added their voices to this movement. In March 1956, one hundred of them issued a statement calling for opposition to *Brown versus Board*.

What this meant soon became clear. In September 1957, the school board of Little Rock, Arkansas, chose nine volunteers to be the first black students to be admitted to Little Rock Central High. Orville Faubus, governor of Arkansas, decided otherwise; there would be no integration in Arkansas, he said, if he could help it. Faubus called up the Arkansas National Guard; guardsmen, armed

with rifles and bayonets, were posted at the school gates. One black student, Elizabeth Eckford, age 15, arrived. She had black curly hair, wore a long white dress, carried a book bag on her left arm. A soldier, gun in hand, barred the way. As Elizabeth turned back, a jeering, howling mob gathered around her. Next day America saw the picture on the front page: Elizabeth Eckford, calmly, quietly and with enormous dignity, walking past the crowd of hate-filled faces. Then she reached a bench at the bus stop; sank down upon it and began to sob. A white woman, whose name we do not know, sat down and put her arms around Elizabeth. "She's scared," said the woman. "She's just a little girl!"

On September 24, President Eisenhower ordered the 101st Airborne Division to Little Rock to enforce the decree of the federal court—that Central High must be integrated, that the black students must be guaranteed their right to go to school. The airborne soldiers pitched their tents on Central High's football field. It was, as Elizabeth Huckaby, Central High's vice-principal, put it, "Little Rock against the United States."

Eight of the "Little Rock Nine" went to Central High for the rest of the school year. A small group of white kids kicked them, slapped them, stole their books, tripped them up in the halls, dumped soup in their laps in the cafeteria. They endured. In the years that followed, hundreds of black students followed the Little Rock Nine and passed through the classrooms of Central High.

Little Rock showed that progress in doing away with Jim Crow was real but also very slow. Starting in February 1960, young black people, most of them students, decided to speed things up by organizing their own movement to end Jim Crow. They began to defy the segregation laws by *sitting in* in drug stores, restaurants, lunch counters, theaters, shopping centers, libraries, art galleries, fair grounds, museums, auditoriums and beaches across the South. *Sitting in* meant that the young people stood or sat in public places where, by state or local law, they were forbidden to be.

The view from the Lincoln Memorial at noon on August 28, 1963, when 250,000 people assembled for the March on Washington. The Washington Monument is seen in the distance.

The message of the sit-in movement was a simple one: "Here we are! We are American citizens, and we have a right to be here. We mean no harm, and we will hurt nobody. If you arrest us, we will gladly go to jail in support of the Supreme Court decision in *Brown versus Board* and the law of the land." The students, too, set up picket lines outside stores that would not serve black customers. These signs said what they wanted in four words: *Jim Crow Must Go!*

Across the South, local police clamped down upon the sit-in movement. By April 1960, they had arrested 2,000 students on charges of "disturbing the peace." In jail the young people linked arms and sang their freedom song: "We shall overcome,/We shall overcome,/We shall overcome some day./Deep in my heart I do believe,/We shall overcome some day."

Easter, 1960. A calm Sunday in spring, with a bright warm sun. Two-hundred young people met together at Shaw University in North Carolina and set up a new student organization to carry on the battle against Jim Crow. It was called the Student Nonviolent Coordinating Committee (SNCC). For the next five years, SNCC took the lead in many parts of the South, both in the struggle against Jim Crow and for the right to vote.

Many of SNCC's members, both black and white, sacrificed much—school, jobs, home, life itself—to carry on SNCC's work in the deep South. Best known of SNCC's leaders were Robert Moses, a high-school teacher with a master's degree in mathematics from Harvard University, and Ella Baker, the granddaughter of North Carolina slaves, who devoted her life to organizing the black struggle for freedom. She was over 60 years old when, in 1960, she joined up with SNCC and became a youth leader.

* * * *

In the spring of 1963, Martin Luther King went to Birmingham, Alabama, to join in a new drive against segregation. Birmingham was the South's

185

In January 1965, Martin Luther King, Jr., launched a campaign in Selma, Alabama, to win the right to register and to vote for the mass of Southern blacks who were, until that time, still disfranchised. A two-month struggle climaxed on March 7 when mounted police rode down marchers at the Edmund Pettus Bridge and clubbed them. Responding on March 15 to the outcry of protest, President Lyndon Johnson asked Congress to pass a voting rights bill. This picture shows part of the line of 25,000 people who walked the last lap of a victory march from Selma to Montgomery, the state capital.

biggest industrial city; it was, as King said, a place where "human rights have been trampled so long that fear and oppression are as thick in its atmosphere as the smog of its factories."

On May 2 the campaign went into high gear. Thousands of young people between the ages of 6 and 16, dressed in their Sunday best and singing freedom songs, marched to the city center to picket the Jim Crow stores. Squads of police blocked the marchers, arrested them and carted them off to a filthy Birmingham jail.

Next day new waves of young marchers thronged Birmingham's downtown streets. The cops began to lash out at the marchers with high-pressure fire hoses, fierce dogs and clubs. This was done not merely in the presence of federal observers but in front of T.V. cameras. America watched in horror and disgust. The black young people did not lift a finger to protect themselves; they cried out in pain, and the sound echoed around the planet. The police, as King put it, were caught "as a fugitive from a penitentiary is often caught—in gigantic circling spotlights ... in a luminous glare revealing the naked truth to the whole world."

The jails were filled to overflowing; and still the marchers came. By May 7 Birmingham's downtown section around its city hall was awash with black people—on the sidewalks, in the streets, in the aisles of the stores. Everywhere there was music in the air: *I'm on my way, and I won't turn back; This little light of mine, I'm gonna let it shine; Ain't gonna let nobody, Lawdy, turn me 'round.*

Birmingham's business community was upset; black customers were buying nothing at their stores and they were losing money. The city politicians now admitted defeat and signed an agreement with the blacks. There would be no more segregation in Birmingham's stores; customers would be treated on a first-come, first-served basis.

This was victory of a sort, but for Martin Luther King it was not enough. It was the year 1963, 100 years since Abraham Lincoln issued the Emancipation Proclamation, which promised freedom to America's slaves. Now, said King, at long last, it was time to go back to Washington, D.C. and demand that the promise be kept. Segregation in all its forms was an ugly relic of slavery days. The black people must support the passage of a new civil rights law that would abolish segregation, not merely in Birmingham, Alabama, but on every inch of American soil, both North and South.

The Reverend King discussed this proposal with his friend Asa Philip Randolph, a Florida-born organizer of black workers and the president of the Brotherhood of Sleeping Car Porters. Randolph lived and worked in Harlem, New York. He made headlines during World War II by demanding that Franklin Roosevelt issue an order banning discrimination against black workers in defense industries, and he warned that he would organize a march on Washington if that order was not speedily forthcoming.

Certainly, said Randolph, there must be freedom from humiliation, insult and discrimination directed against black people. But there was more to it than that. Black people, he said, are blighted at birth. They are born in want and live in hunger. They get only the poorest-paying jobs, and too often they get no jobs at all. They survive by hustling on the streets. We must ask, he said, not only for freedom from discrimination but for freedom from want. The key to that is the right to job training and to a decent job.

Thus out of the Birmingham struggle, the March on Washington for Jobs and Freedom was born. On August 28, 1963, a quarter of a million people, black and white, descended upon Washington by train, bus, automobile and bicycle. Bring salt tablets, they were told, for the weather will be hot; and be sure not to put mayonnaise in your sandwiches.

The people marched down Pennsylvania Avenue and came together in front of the Lincoln Memorial. Rarely if ever before had there been so huge a gathering in the capital. There were many speeches, but Martin Luther King said it best. "I have a dream," he told the cheering, weeping throng, "that one day this nation will rise up and live out the true meaning of its creed … that all men are created equal."

Three months later, in November 1963, President John Kennedy was assassinated in Dallas, Texas, as he rode in an open car in a political parade. Lyndon Johnson succeeded him. The following year Congress passed the Civil Rights Act that President Kennedy had asked for. The act was a memorial to the dead president; it also defined the gains that the civil rights movement had made up until that time at the cost of so great an effort. This 1964 act banned discrimination in "places of public accommodation" whose function is to serve the public in one way or another; it banned discrimination by employers in hiring workers—it authorized the government, for example, to withhold funds from defense contractors found guilty of job discrimination; and it promised federal help, in the form of money and guidance, to communities seeking to desegregate their schools.

The civil rights movement scored a final victory in 1965 with the passage of the Voting Rights Act, which gave blacks the right to register to vote. The results of this law were dramatic: The number of Southern black voters, by 1968, shot up from one to three million.

These were impressive laws, but the bleak conditions of black life did not immediately improve, and the social reforms that Asa Philip Randolph had dreamed of did not come about. One of the reasons for this was that after 1965 President Johnson had turned his attention to waging war in Vietnam.

The Vietnam War

Vietnam is a country in Southeast Asia bordering upon the South China Sea. Until 1940 it was part of the French empire in Indo-China. The Vietnamese considered the French to be invaders and fought against them. Their foremost leader was the Communist Ho Chi Minh, a frail-looking man with a wispy white beard. When the Japanese seized hold of Vietnam in 1940-41, the Vietnamese fought against them, too. The organization that they set up for this purpose was called the Vietnamese Independence League, or Vietminh.

Defeated in World War II, the Japanese quit Vietnam in 1945, and the Vietminh set up their own government in the north with its capital at Hanoi and called it the Democratic Republic of Vietnam (DRV). But the French did not want to give up Vietnam, the jewel of their old empire. In 1945 they, too, set up a government—in the southern part of the country, with its capital at Saigon.

The DRV didn't want the French back. The First Indochina War was fought between the DRV and the French from 1946 to 1954. Vo Nguyen Giap, Ho's top general, called upon everybody—civilians as well as soldiers, women and children as well as men—to help. The people, he said, must lock forces with the enemy "like the hair with the teeth of a comb."

Things went badly for the French, even though the United States sent over two billion dollars worth of supplies between 1950 and 1954; they were forced, in 1954, to surrender their army at the fortress of Dienbienphu. This defeat was to the French what Yorktown had been to the British in 1781—the final blow in a long struggle to hold on to an overseas empire.

The treaty of peace was signed at Geneva that same year. Under the treaty, the DRV was recognized as the government in the north; as for the south, there were to be free elections in 1956 after all the French soldiers had packed up and sailed away. Everybody knew that Ho Chi Minh would win these elections. Then the DRV would run all of Vietnam, north and south alike.

But there was no free elections in the south. In 1955 Ngo Din Diem, a member of the old Vietnamese nobility, set up a government in the south. People in Washington, D.C., led by the secretary of state, John Foster Dulles, wholeheartedly supported Diem and, indeed, made it possible for him to seize power in Vietnam. Diem forgot about the 1956 elections; he arrested Vietnamese patriots who had spent years fighting the French or the Japanese, killing some, throwing hundreds more into jail. Members of the Vietminh fled for their lives to the hills; in 1960, with the support of the North Vietnam government, they set up the National Liberation Front (NLF), called for the overthrow of Diem's dictatorship and stepped up military action against the government. The end came soon. Students demonstrated in the streets of Saigon, while monks burned themselves alive to protest Diem's rule. In November 1963, three weeks before President Kennedy was assassinated in Dallas, South Vietnamese army officers shot Diem to death and put an end to his government.

The new American president, Lyndon Baines Johnson, now made a fateful decision that brought the American people directly into armed conflict in Vietnam. Johnson secured the passage by Congress, on August 4, 1964, of the Gulf of Tonkin Resolution, authorizing him to do "what was necessary in defense of peace in Southeast Asia." This amounted, in an indirect way, to a declaration of war against the DRV. Soon United States troops were pouring in.

President Johnson's Gulf of Tonkin Resolution was the last in a series of steps towards war that had been taken by Johnson's immediate predecessors in the presidential office—that is to say, Truman, Eisenhower, and Kennedy. Truman had provided the French with generous financial aid for their struggle, launched in 1946, to reconquer Vietnam. The Americans weren't particularly interested in seeing France regain her empire, but they dreaded the idea of a Vietnam under Communist government. When the Vietnamese defeated the French and put an end to their war of conquest in 1954, Eisenhower refused to give his assent to the Geneva peace convention; he sought to avoid the recognition of Vietnamese independence by setting up the Diem regime. Kennedy, in his turn, did all that he could to prevent Diem's imminent collapse; he provided the dictator with 16,000 United States military men—"advisors" as they were called—whose mission was to train and equip the South Vietnamese army and thus shore up the South's tottering regime.

Each of these successive presidents—Truman, Eisenhower, Kennedy and Johnson—were trapped, it seems, in a mindset that doomed them, in a succession of fatal, seemingly irreversible steps, to deepen the United States commitment to South Vietnam.

Various explanations have been provided for this situation, which resulted in an unnecessary war that cost, at the very least, 54,000 American lives and that inflicted untold destruction upon the Vietnamese people. One of these explanations is the "domino theory." Third World countries, the theory had it, were faced with a choice of allying with the West or with the Soviets. If any one of these Third World countries was permitted to cave in under Soviet pressure, the rest would follow suit and topple over like a row of dominoes. We, the argument ran, could not afford to lose a single one of these countries. Each must be provided with aid—that is, arms, money, supplies and, if necessary, troops.

The domino theory carried considerable weight in Washington during the Cold War years. In 1949 China and its nearly one billion people had been "lost" when the Chinese Red army made its victorious sweep across China and the Chinese Communist party set up its People's Republic in Peking. Senator Joseph McCarthy exploited the situation to his own advantage; it was all due, he charged, to the treason and incompetence rampant among

Vietnam and Southeast Asia

politicians in Washington. American presidents, not surprisingly, resolved that there must be no more such "losses" during their terms of office. Penetration of Southeast Asia by what they called the "monolithic Communist menace" must be opposed.

So President Johnson took the last, fatal step into war. What he did not understand was that the majority of the Vietnamese people, whether they were Communist or not, were passionately opposed to *any* foreign interference in their country, and to Chinese interference in particular. Here Johnson's advisors withheld from him information that might well have proved crucial to his decisions about war and peace.

Centuries before the French had arrived— Johnson ought to have been informed—the Vietnamese peoples had been carrying on an unending struggle against Chinese military aggression. Readiness to sacrifice everything for independence, indeed, has been an age-old theme of Vietnamese existence. The Vietnamese have fought to the death to defend their independence against *anybody* who threatened it—against

Chinese, Japanese, French, Korean and American intruders alike. "We shall suffer," Ho Chi Minh told an American visitor in the early 1960s, "twenty times the casualties that you will. But you will tire first."

By 1968, when the war reached its height, the number of American soldiers in Vietnam had escalated to half a million. General Giap matched these American troops with reinforcements of his own. As the months passed, resistance to the Americans in the Vietnamese countryside grew greater, not less.

Some of the young American men who were sent to Vietnam for a tour of duty were volunteers; the majority were draftees. A disproportionate number of the enlisted men were African-Americans, drawn from the ranks of the very poor.

Sergeant Bruce Annello, killed in action in 1968, was one member of the American force that had been deployed in Vietnam by that time. When Annello was inducted in 1967, he was 20 years old, a high-school graduate and an employee of the Philadelphia Electric Company. One question was always on his mind as he and his buddies made their endless patrols. "Why are we here?" he asked himself in an entry in his diary made six months before his death. "When will it ever end?"

"Darkness comes," he continued,

and the clouds turn black with threatening rain.... An eerie feeling creeps in your whole being as the beautiful trees of daytime turn into laughing demons from the cold night wind. You lie on the damp ground hungry from the day's march. Eight men and eight individual thoughts of home and how it used to be. One thinking of a quiet sunny morning at a deserted beach. ... Another playing in the backyard with the son he's never seen. And another laughing and loving with his girl, just grooving down the streets.

Later, after a battle, Sergeant Annello wrote that he "admire[d] the spirit of the V.C. [Vietcong: South Vietnamese guerilla fighters]. But who wouldn't have spirit? They have a cause to die for, it's their country. We have nothing to gain."

Back in the United States, people began to realize that they had been sucked into a shooting war without having been told—without, indeed, having been consulted at all. Leaders like Martin Luther King, Jr., began to make speeches against the war. Young people began to burn their draft cards and to sign statements that they would never fight in Vietnam. At colleges all over the country, professors, journalists and students lectured and debated far into the night about why we were in Vietnam and why the Vietnamese were fighting so doggedly against the United States. Peace marches took place; the demonstrators wore long hair, crew cuts, blue jeans, army clothes, flowing dresses, miniskirts; they carried flowers, waved the Stars and Stripes, waved the Vietnam flag. Almost all were young.

Older folk watched with amazement and often anger. Bitter arguments took place at family dinner tables. Parents and children stopped talking to each other, stopped writing, stopped loving. Not since the Civil War had Americans been so bitterly divided.

By 1968 it was clear that a majority of Americans wanted the United States out of Vietnam. Lyndon Johnson, facing a bitter fight for nomination to a second full term by the Democratic Party, stunned the country with the announcement that he would not run. For a while it appeared likely that the Democrats would nominate a candidate committed to ending the war quickly.

The strongest peace candidate to emerge was Senator Robert F. Kennedy, a brother of the slain president. But just as he pulled ahead of Johnson's vice president, Hubert Humphrey, in the nomination campaign, Robert Kennedy too was assassinated. The tragedy took place only a few weeks after the killing of Martin Luther King Jr. at Memphis, Tennessee.

The brutality of an unwanted war and the murder, within five years, of three of the country's youngest and strongest leaders left many Americans numb. The rightness of the American cause, the invincibility of American arms and the freedom of Americans to follow leaders of their own choosing—all were called into question.

Now the presidential election became a contest between hawks: Hubert Humphrey, Democrat, and Richard Milhouse Nixon, Republican. Richard Nixon won the election. The war went on.

The new president sent bombers over North Vietnam in a series of savage raids that killed many civilians but failed to bomb the DRV into submission. Peace accords were signed in January 1973; the last United States troops quit Vietnam two months later. Few people believed that the puppet regime in the south would last very long without the support of American soldiers.

Richard Nixon withdrew American forces just in time to devote his energies to saving himself. In June 1972 five employees of his political campaign committee were caught breaking into Democratic party headquarters in the Watergate apartment complex in Washington, D.C. Months passed. Then, in the spring of 1973 the evidence of a major scandal began to surface. The Watergate break-in was part of a far-reaching secret and illegal operation designed to secure Nixon's reelection in the 1972 presidential campaign. The evidence indicated that Nixon himself bore full responsibility for a concerted effort to suppress the story. The president resigned from office in August 1974 rather than face impeachment by the United States Senate for his deeds.

Watergate cast an ominous light on Nixon's own personal and political ambitions. On June 19, 1972, just two days after the Watergate burglars had been arrested, the Supreme Court of the United States handed down a decision in a case entitled *United States versus United States District Court*. This case involved a number of peace activists whom the administration prosecuted in the eastern Michigan District Court. When the trial opened the prosecution admitted that it had secretly recorded the private conversations of the accused activists. This was an illegal act: It violated the Fourth Amendment to the United States Constitution, which forbids unauthorized invasion of the privacy of American citizens. The District Court judge ordered the government to surrender the tapes, but it refused on the grounds that national security was involved. In such cases, the government argued, the president possessed the "inherent power" to ignore the Fourth Amendment and to proceed any way that he considered proper. When the District Court judge overruled this plea the administration appealed his order all the way up to the Supreme Court.

By a vote of 8-0 the Supreme Court rejected the government's case. No president, it ruled, possesses the "inherent power" to ignore or suspend the Constitution, or any part of it. If the Court had ruled otherwise the president would have advanced a big step in the direction of personal rule unrestrained by the Constitution.

* * * *

On April 30, 1975, the Vietnamese Army took over Saigon and renamed it Ho Chi Minh City. President Gerald Ford refused to recognize the DRV, which now ruled all Vietnam, or to send an ambassador to Hanoi. But Americans as private citizens soon began to visit the country. "It is time," said one of these visitors in 1977, "to make peace with Vietnam, and with ourselves."

EPILOGUE

After Vietnam the United States spent vast wealth to guarantee its supremacy as the world's top military power but fell behind in other measures of strength.

Gerald Ford, and the presidents who followed him, held fast to the cold war views that had brought the country into Vietnam. They continued to treat the Soviet Union as the most serious threat to the freedom of the United States and of the globe. They continued to spend billions of dollars on defense forces, both conventional and nuclear. It was necessary, they said, to fight "brush fire" wars that the Russians had inspired, and to be ready for a showdown with the Russians themselves. Richard Nixon, from retirement, wrote that the opening skirmishes of a long war between the superpowers had already begun in trouble spots across the third world—Africa, Latin America and Asia—where the Soviet Union and the United States contended for influence among desperately poor people. But it was clear that it would take far more than the domino theory to persuade Americans to fight again in a faraway jungle.

If Americans had learned the lesson of Vietnam the Russians, it seemed, had not. In 1979 the Soviet Union tried to occupy Afghanistan—and soon found itself mired in a brutal, senseless and seemingly endless war. Just as, in Vietnam, Moscow had provided weapons for Vietnamese to use against Americans, Washington now provided weapons for Afghans to use against Russians.

During the 1980s the arms buildup went on; the United States government added more to the nation's debts in a single decade than in all the previous 200 years. The military grew stronger; American industry did not. More people had jobs, but economic productivity declined. Inflation sapped the purchasing power of millions. Businesses showed less interest in developing new technology than in financial *coups* and stock market maneuvers.

Other countries moved more quickly than we to develop new technologies and to capture markets. The United States found itself buying more from other countries than it was able to sell to them.

Foreigners, with billions of dollars in American banks, proceeded to buy up whatever American assets took their fancy: Farmlands, historic houses, skyscrapers, businesses, priceless paintings, even offshore islands that were considered ripe for profitable development. They found knowledgeable Americans prepared to advise them, for a price, about which investments they ought to choose.

While the nation armed against communism its cities crumbled; government appeared powerless to control pollution, to curb violent crime and the drug trade, or even to cope with the nation's garbage.

High interest rates and continuing inflation relentlessly pushed up the cost of housing. People who had dreamed of owning their own homes found that they could only afford to rent. Many who could not afford to dream of anything except renting found themselves on the streets.

Young people growing up in an increasingly complex and technical world confronted a public education system distinguished for dullness and mediocrity. The cost of going to college climbed out of sight.

As the 1980s drew to a close, many observers agreed that Americans were not taking care for their own future. It was also clear that the arms race might ruin the world without a shot being fired, simply by using up resources desperately needed to deal with a global crisis of poverty and pollution.

In 1988 the Soviet Union announced in the United Nations that it had had enough, that it didn't matter any more who started the cold war, who was "right" or who was "wrong." The cold war and the arms race had to end.

A series of initiatives by the Soviet Union and eastern European countries began to dismantle the communist party's rigid control of these societies. Electoral processes, independent people's organizations and the free flow of information developed where previously they had been unheard of. Soviet troops marched home from Afganistan.

In the United States many watched and listened. Early in 1989 George Kennan, an important spokesman for the cold war 40 years earlier, told the Senate foreign Relations Committee that the cold war was over. "Whatever reasons," Kennan said, "there may once have been for regarding the Soviet Union primarily as a … military opponent, the time for that sort of thing has clearly passed."

* * * *

If the cold war comes to an end it will spell the beginning of a new era in the history of the United States and of the world; there will be opportunity and challenge to liquidate the wreckage of the twentieth century and its eternal wars, and to use our minds and our resources for the solution of human problems.

From the beginning this nation has struggled to define the meaning of its founding creed: that people possess an inalienable right to life, liberty and the pursuit of happiness.

It has been a long struggle. The American people first insisted that the meaning of the nation's "inalienable right" had to be spelled out in a Bill of Rights. Without this charter they refused to accept the formation of a national government. Half a century later they decided that slavery, finally, had to go. They suffered the carnage of the Civil War to ban it, and to impose upon the national government the obligation to protect the human rights of all citizens without regard to race, creed or color.

The Revolution of 1776 marked the beginning of a movement to define the rights, not just of Americans, but of people everywhere. Two hundred years later this movement is unfolding on a global scale. The outcome is still undecided.

Look back on your history, and be inspired by the bright dream and the bitter sacrifice of the long struggle for freedom. Remember what Tom Paine wrote in *Common Sense*; his words are as valid today as when he penned them more than 200 years ago: "The sun," he said, "never shined on a cause of greater worth … 'Tis not the concern of a day, a year, or an age; posterity are virtually involved in the contest, and will be more or less affected, even to the end of time, by the proceedings now."

SUGGESTIONS FOR FURTHER READING

General

John Hope Franklin. *From Slavery to Freedom: A History of American Negroes*. New York: Alfred A. Knopf, 1963; 2nd edition, revised and enlarged.

T.C. McCluhan, *Touch the Earth: a Self-Portrait of Indian Existence*. New York: Dutton, 1971.

Milton Meltzer and Langston Hughes. *A Pictorial History of Black Americans*. New York: Crown Publishers, 1983, revised; first published, 1956.

National Geographic Society. *The Story of America: A National Geographic Picture Atlas*. Washington, D.C.: The National Geographic Society, 1984.

John Anthony Scott. *The Ballad of America: The History of the United States in Song and Story*. Carbondale: Southern Illinois University Press, 1983; revised second edition.

Chapter 1   Wanderers and Settlers: From Earliest Times to the Coming of the Whites

Hartley Burr Alexander. *The World's Rim: Great Mysteries of the North American Indians*. Lincoln: University of Nebraska Press, 1967; paperback.

William Bradford. *Of Plymouth Plantation 1620–47*, edited by Samuel Eliot Morison. New York: Alfred A. Knopf, 1963.

Peter Farb. *Man's Rise to Civilization: The Cultural Ascent of the Indians of North America*. New York: E.P. Dutton, 1978; revised second edition.

Thor Heyerdahl. *Early Man and the Ocean: A Search for the Beginnings of Navigation and Seaborne Civilizations*. New York: Doubleday, 1979.

Alvin M. Josephy. *The Patriot Chiefs*. New York: Viking Press, 1961.

Stefan Lorant, editor. *The New World: The First Pictures of America*. New York: Duell, Sloan and Pearce, 1946.

Paul Weatherwax. *Indian Corn in Old America*. New York: Macmillan, 1954.

Chapter 2   Wilderness Colonies: Frontier, Farm and City in British America, 1630–1763

Jay Coughtry. *The Notorious Triangle: Rhode Island and the Slave Trade 1700–1807*. Philadelphia: Temple University Press, 1981.

Basil Davidson. *Black Mother: the Years of the African Slave Trade*. Boston: Atlantic, Little, Brown, 1961.

Sarah Kemble Knight. *Journal*. New York: Peter Smith, 1935.

Daniel P. Mannix and Malcolm Cowley. *Black Cargoes: A History of the African Slave Trade*. New York: Viking Press, 1962.

Gottlieb Mittelberg. *Journey to Pennsylvania*, translated by Oscar Handlin and John Clive. Cambridge, Mass.: Belknap Press, 1960.

Edmund S. Morgan. *American Slavery, American Freedom: The Ordeal of Colonial Virginia*. New York: W. W. Norton, 1975.

John Anthony Scott. *Settlers on the Eastern Shore: 1607–1750*. New York: Facts On File, 1990; first published, 1967.

Chapter 3   'Tis Time to Part: The Struggle for Independence, 1763–1783

Donald Barr Chidsey. *Victory at Yorktown*. New York: Crown Publishers, 1962.

John R. Cuneo. *The Battles of Saratoga*. New York: Macmillan, 1967.

Joseph Plumb Martin. *A Narrative of Some of the Adventures, Dangers, and Sufferings of a Revolutionary Soldier*, edited by George Scheer. Boston: Little, Brown, 1962.

Frank Moore. *Diary of the American Revolution*, edited and abridged by John Anthony Scott. New York: Washington Square Press, 1967.

Baroness Frederika Riedesel. *Journal and Correspondence of a Tour of Duty*, translated by Marvin L. Brown Jr. Chapel Hill: University of North Carolina Press, 1965.

John Anthony Scott. *Trumpet of a Prophecy: Revolutionary America, 1763–83*. New York: Alfred A. Knopf, 1969.

Arthur B. Tourtellot. *Lexington and Concord: The Beginning of the War of the American Revolution*. New York: W.W. Norton, 1963.

Willard M. Wallace. *Traitorous Hero: The Life and Fortunes of Benedict Arnold*. New York: Harper, 1954.

Chapter 4   The Early Years of the Republic, 1783–1815

Leland D. Baldwin. *The Whiskey Rebels*. Pittsburgh, Penn.: University of Pittsburgh Press, 1941.

Christopher and James Lincoln Collier. *Decision in Philadelphia: The Constitutional Convention of 1787*. New York: Random House, 1986.

Leonard Falkner. *For Jefferson and Liberty: The United States in War and Peace, 1800–1815*. New York: Alfred A. Knopf, 1972.

James W. Holland. *Andrew Jackson and the Creek War: Victory at the Horseshoe*. University: University of Alabama Press, 1968.

Robert A. Rutland. *George Mason, Reluctant Statesman*. Williamsburg: Colonial Williamsburg, Inc., 1961.

————. *Birth of the Bill of Rights, 1776–91*. New York: Macmillan, 1955.

Thomas P. Slaughter. *The Whiskey Rebellion: Frontier Epilogue to the American Revolution.* New York: Oxford University Press, 1986.

Marion Starkey. *Lacecuffs and Leather Aprons: Popular Struggles in the Federalist Era, 1783–1800.* New York: Alfred A. Knopf, 1972.

J.E. Wright and D.S. Corbett. *Pioneer Life in Western Pennsylvania.* Pittsburgh, Penn.: University of Pittsburgh Press, 1968.

Charter 5   The Age of Andrew Jackson: Building a Continental Kingdom, 1815–1848

Richard Henry Dana. *Two Years Before the Mast.* New York: Pendulum Press, Inc., 1977; first published,1840.

Angie Debo. *And Still the Waters Run: The Betrayal of the Five Civilized Tribes.* Princeton, N.J.: Princeton University Press, 1940.

Harry Sinclair Drago. *Canal Days in America: The History and Romance of Old Towpaths and Waterways.* New York: Bramhall House, 1972.

Ivor B. Hart. *James Watt and the History of Steam Power.* New York: Collier Books, 1961.

Charles Hudson. *The Southeastern Indians.* Knoxville: University of Tennessee Press, 1976.

Hannah Josephson. *The Golden Threads: New England's Mill Girls and Magnates.* New York: Russell and Russell, 1967.

Lucy Larcom. *A New England Girlhood.* New York: Corinth Books, 1961.

Milton Meltzer. *Bound for the Rio Grande: The Mexican Struggle, 1845–50.* New York: Alfred A. Knopf, 1974.

Douglas T. Miller. *Then Was the Future: The North in the Age of Jackson, 1815–50.* New York: Alfred A. Knopf, 1973.

Kerby A. Miller. *Emigrants and Exiles: Ireland and the Irish Exodus to North America.* New York: Oxford University Press, 1985.

Solomon Northup. *Twelve Years a Slave*, edited by Sue Eakin and Joseph Logsdon. Baton Rouge: Louisiana State University Press, 1977.

John Anthony Scott. *Hard Trials on My Way: Slavery and the Struggle Against It, 1800–60.* New York: Alfred A. Knopf, 1974.

Jared Van Wagenen. *The Golden Age of Homespun.* New York: New York State Historical Association, 1953.

Cecil Woodham-Smith. *The Great Hunger: Ireland 1845–1849.* New York: Harper and Row, 1962.

Chapter 6   The Slavery Crisis: War for the Union and the Emancipation of the Slaves, 1848–1865

The Compromise of 1850 and the Antislavery Struggle

Frederick Douglass. *Narrative of the Life of Frederick Douglass, an American Slave*, edited by Benjamin Quarles. Cambridge, Mass.: Belknap Press, 1960.

Frances Anne Kemble. *Journal of a Residence on a Georgian Plantation in 1838–1839*, edited by John Anthony Scott. Athens: University of Georgia Press, 1984.

Julius Lester. *To Be a Slave.* New York: Dial Press, 1968.

Milton Meltzer. *Tongue of Flame: The Life of Lydia Maria Child.* New York: Thomas Y. Crowell, 1965.

Douglas T. Miller. *Frederick Douglass and the Fight for Freedom*. New York: Facts On File, 1988.

John Anthony Scott. *Woman Against Slavery: The Story of Harriet Beecher Stowe*. New York: Thomas Y. Crowell, 1978.

Laurence I. Seidman. *The Fools of '49: The California Gold Rush, 1848–1856*. New York: Alfred A. Knopf, 1976.

Harriet Beecher Stowe. *Uncle Tom's Cabin*. Various paperback editions.

Kansas and the Rise of the Republican Party, 1854–1860

Allan Nevins. *The Ordeal of the Union*, two volumes. New York: Scribner, 1947.

Carl Sandburg, *Abraham Lincoln: The Prairie Years*. New York: Dell, 1959; paperback.

John A. and Robert A. Scott. *John Brown of Harper's Ferry*. New York: Facts On File, 1988.

Civil War and the Emancipation of the Slaves, 1861–1865

Peter Burchard. *One Gallant Rush: the Life of Robert Gould Shaw*. New York: St. Martin's Press, 1965.

Henry Steele Commager. *The Blue and the Gray*. New York: Bobbs-Merrill, 1960.

James McPherson. *Battle Cry of Freedom: The Civil War Era*. New York: Oxford University Press, 1988.

———. *Marching Toward Freedom: The Negro in the Civil War, 1861–1865*. New York: Facts On File, 1990; first published, 1968.

Milton Meltzer. *Thaddeus Stevens and the Fight for Negro Rights*. New York: Thomas Y. Crowell, 1967.

Benjamin Quarles. *The Negro in the Civil War*. Boston: Little, Brown, 1953.

Chapter 7   The South: Revolution and Counterrevolution, 1865–1877

Michael Les Benedict. *The Impeachment and Trial of Andrew Johnson*. New York: W. W. Norton, 1973.

David M. Chalmers. *Hooded Americanism: The History of the Ku Klux Klan*. New York: Franklin Watts, 1981.

W.E. Burghardt DuBois. *The Souls of Black Folk*. New York: Fawcett, 1964; paperback.

Eric Foner. *Reconstruction: America's Unfinished Revolution 1863–1877*. New York: Harper and Row, 1988.

John Hope Franklin. *Reconstruction after the Civil War*. Chicago: University of Chicago Press, 1961.

Leon F. Litwack. *Been in the Storm So Long: The Aftermath of Slavery*. New York: Alfred A. Knopf, 1979.

Carl Schurz. *Report on the Condition of the South*. New York: Arno Press, 1969.

Kenneth M. Stampp. *The Era of Reconstruction, 1865–77*. New York: Alfred A. Knopf, 1965.

Dorothy Sterling. *The Trouble They Seen: Black People Tell the Story of Reconstruction*. New York: Doubleday, 1976.

C. Vann Woodward. *Reunion and Reaction: The Compromise of 1877 and the Era of Reconstruction*. Boston: Little, Brown, 1951.

Chapter 8 The West: Cattlemen and Indian Wars, 1865–1890

Andy Adams. *The Log of a Cowboy: A Narrative of the Old Trail Days.* New York: Doubleday Dolphin, n.d.; paperback. Airmont, 1969; paperback.

J. Frank Dobie. *The Longhorns.* Boston: Little, Brown, 1941.

Bill Gulick. *Snake River Country.* Caldwell, Idaho: Caxton Printers, 1978.

Robert H. Lowie. *Indians of the Plains.* New York: McGraw-Hill, 1954.

Karen Daniels Petersen. *Plains Indian Art from Fort Marion.* Norman: University of Oklahoma Press, 1971.

Mari Sandoz. *Love Song to the Plains.* New York: Ginn and Co., 1931.

Laurence I. Seidman. *Once in the Saddle: The Cowboy's Frontier, 1866–96.* New York: Facts On File, 1990; first published, 1973.

Chapter 9 The American Colossus: Industry, Immigration and Empire, 1865–1914

Dale Fetherling. *Mother Jones the Miners' Angel: A Portrait.* Carbondale: Southern Illinois University Press, 1974.

Tamara K. Hareven and Randolph Langenback. *Amoskeag: Life and Work of an American Factory City.* New York: Pantheon Books, 1978.

Jane Hovde. *Jane Addams.* New York: Facts On File, 1989.

David G. McCullough. *The Johnstown Flood.* London: Hutchinson and Co., 1968.

Milton Meltzer. *Bread and Roses: The Struggle of American Labor, 1865–1915.* New York: Facts On File, 1990; first published, 1967.

———. *The Chinese Americans.* New York: Crowell, 1980.

———. *The Hispanic Americans.* New York: Crowell, 1982.

Ann Novotny. *Strangers at the Door: Ellis Island, Castle Garden, and the Great Migration to America.* New York: Bantam, 1974; paperback, abridged.

Jacob A. Riis. *How the Other Half Lives.* New York: Dover Publications, 1971. With 100 photographs from the Jacob A. Riis Collection.

Upton Sinclair. *The Jungle.* New York: Airmont, 1965; paperback.

John Spargo. *The Bitter Cry of the Children.* New York: Quadrangle Books, 1968.

Joanna L. Stratton. *Pioneer Women: Voices from the Kansas Frontier.* New York: Simon and Schuster, 1981; Touchstone paperback.

John Tebbel. *The Inheritors: A Study of America's Great Fortunes, and What Happened to Them.* London: Gollancz, 1962.

Leon Wolff. *Lockout: The Story of the Homestead Strike of 1892.* London: Longmans, 1965.

Chapter 10 A Time of Troubles: The United States in War and Peace, 1914–1945

Roger Daniels. *Concentration Camps USA: Japanese Americans and World War II.* New York: Holt, Rinehart and Winston, 1971.

John Ellis. *Eye-Deep in Hell: Trench Warfare in World War I.* New York: Pantheon Books, 1976.

J. Wayne Flint. *Dixie's Forgotten People: The South's Poor Whites.* Bloomington: Indiana University Press, 1980; Midland paperback.

Anne Frank. *Diary of a Young Girl*. New York: Pocket Books, Inc., 1981.

Robert Goldston. *The Life and Death of Nazi Germany*. New York: Fawcett Books, 1967.

John Hersey. *Hiroshima*. New York: Alfred A. Knopf, 1946; Bantam paperback, 1948.

Steven Jantzen. *Hooray for Peace, Hurrah for War: The United States during World War I*. New York: Facts On File, 1990; first published, 1971.

Charles Kikuchi. *The Kikuchi Diary: Chronicle from an American Concentration Camp*, edited and with an introduction by John Modell. Urbana: University of Illinois Press, 1973.

Milton Meltzer. *Brother, Can You Spare a Dime: The Great Depression, 1929–33*. New York: Facts On File, 1990; first published, 1969.

———. *Never to Forget: The Jews of the Holocaust*. New York: Harper and Row, 1976.

——— and August Meier. *Time of Trial, Time of Hope: The Negro in America, 1919–41*. New York: Doubleday, 1966.

Carol Ann Pearce. *Amelia Earhart*. New York: Facts On File, 1988.

Erich Maria Remarque. *All Quiet on the Western Front*. Boston: Little, Brown, 1929.

John Steinbeck. *The Grapes of Wrath*. New York: Viking Press, 1945.

A. J. P. Taylor. *The Second World War: An Illustrated History*. New York: Putnam, 1975.

Barbara Tuchman. *The Guns of August*. New York: Macmillan, 1962.

———. *The Zimmermann Telegram*. New York: Viking Press, 1958.

Kurt Vonnegut. *Slaughter House Five*. New York: Delacorte, 1969.

Elie Wiesel. *Night*. New York: Avon, 1969.

J. M. Winter. *The Experience of World War I*. New York: Oxford University Press, 1989

Richard Wright. *Black Boy*. New York: Harper, 1945.

Chapter 11   Americans in the Nuclear Age: Human Rights, Superpowers and Peace, 1945 –

Lerone Bennett Jr. *What Manner of Man: A Biography of Martin Luther King Jr*. Chicago: Johnson Publishing Company, 1976.

Carl Bernstein and Bob Woodward. *All the President's Men*. New York: Warner Books, 1974.

David Caute. *The Great Fear: The Anti-Communist Purge under Truman and Eisenhower*. New York: Simon and Schuster, 1978.

Eldridge Cleaver. *Soul on Ice*. New York: McGraw-Hill, 1968.

Richard M. Fried. *Nightmare in Red: The McCarthy Era in Perspective*. New York: Oxford University Press, 1990.

David Halberstam. *Ho*. New York: Random House, 1971.

Michael Hear. *Dispatches*. New York: Avon, 1978.

Elizabeth Huckaby. *Crisis at Central High. Little Rock 1957–8*. Baton Rouge: Louisiana State University Press, 1980.

Martin Luther King Jr. *Stride Toward Freedom*. New York: Harper and Brothers, 1958.

Arthur Kinoy. *Rights on Trial: The Odyssey of a People's Lawyer*. Cambridge: Harvard University Press, 1983.

Donald Kirk. *Tell It to the Dead: Memories of a War*. Chicago: Nelson Hall, 1975.

Richard Kluger. *Simple Justice: The History of Brown v Board of Education and Black America's Struggle for Equality*. New York: Alfred A. Knopf, 1975; 2 vols.

Richard D. McCarthy. *The Ultimate Folly: War by Pestilence, Asphyxiation, Defoliation*. New York: Alfred A. Knopf, 1969.

Arthur Miller. *Death of a Salesman*. New York: Viking Press, 1949.

Lillie Patterson. *Martin Luther King Jr*. New York: Facts On File, 1989.

Howard Raines, editor. *My Soul Is Rested: Movement Days in the Deep South Remembered*. New York: Putnam, 1977.

Geoffrey Perrett. *A Dream of Greatness: The American People, 1945–1963*. New York: Coward, McCann and Geoghegan, 1979.

Lilly Breslow Rubin. *Worlds of Pain: Life in the Working Class Family*. New York: Basic Books, 1976.

Ellen W. Schrecker. *No Ivory Tower: McCarthyism and the Universities*. New York: Oxford University Press, 1986.

Harvard Sitkoff. *The Struggle for Black Equality, 1954–1980*. New York: Hill and Wang, 1981.

Barry Sussman. *The Great Cover-up: Nixon and the Scandal of Watergate*. New York: New American Library, 1974.

James A. Warren. *Portrait of a Tragedy: America and the Vietnam War*. New York: Lothrop, 1989.

Sheyann Webb and Rachel West Nelson. *Selma, Lord, Selma: Girlhood Memories of the Civil Rights Days*. University: University of Alabama Press, 1980. Recorded by Frank Sikora.

Malcolm X, with the assistance of Alex Haley. *The Autobiography of Malcolm X*. New York: Grove Press, 1966.

Howard Zinn. *SNCC: The New Abolitionists*. Boston: Beacon Press, 1965.

INDEX